The Brazilian

Culture on the Borderlands of the Western World

The Brazilian Puzzle

Culture on the Borderlands

of the

Western World

⊠

edited by David J. Hess and Roberto A. DaMatta

Columbia University Press   New York

Columbia University Press
New York   Chichester, West Sussex

Copyright © 1995 Columbia University Press
All rights reserved

Library of Congress Cataloging-in-Publication Data
The Brazilian puzzle :
culture on the borderlands of the Western World
/ edited by David J. Hess and Roberto DaMatta.
p.   cm
Includes bibliographical references and index.
ISBN 0-231-10114-7(alk. paper)
ISBN 0-231-10115-5 (pbk.)
1. National characteristics, Brazilian.
2. Brazil—Social life and customs.
3. Brazil—Race relations.
4. Popular culture—Brazil.
I. Hess, David J. II. Matta, Roberta da.
F2510.873   1995
305.8'00981—dc20   94-29469
CIP

Printed in the United States of America

c 10 9 8 7 6 5 4 3 2 1

Contents

Acknowledgments

This is a book of collaborative effort. Robert DaMatta introduced David J. Hess to many of the authors in this volume and helped him to pull together a coherent collection of essays. The two anonymous reviewers gave detailed comments and suggestions for revisions and clarifications. Although they may not agree with all our final editorial decisions, they were most helpful. We also wish to thank executive editor Gioia Stevens and the Columbia University Press staff for their support and assistance.

The Brazilian Puzzle

Culture on the Borderlands of the Western World

**MAP OF BRAZIL
AND NEIGHBORING COUNTRIES**

Introduction

In recent years Brazil has received enough international media attention that it is no longer a completely unknown place. Media portrayals point to a diverse and interesting country that is more than the land of Carnival (Mardi Gras), Amazonian jungles, and Rio de Janeiro's beaches. My students, for example, often have much more complex images of Brazil: they think of products that range from oranges and coffee to brand-name shoes and high-tech airplanes, a rapidly growing economy that is renowned for a huge debt and high inflation, a president who was impeached for corruption, Catholics who participate in African religious rituals, abandoned children who live on the streets, movie stars such as Sonia Braga and Xuxa, husbands who believe they have the legal right to kill unfaithful wives, and Amazonian Indian tribes who use camcorders to record visits from Sting. How does one make sense of such puzzling and contradictory images?

Those who know a little more about Brazil are convinced of the importance of understanding this huge South American country. Brazil has one of the world's largest economies and territories, not to mention the second largest population in the Western hemisphere. In addition to sheer size, Brazil is important for being a kind of mirror for the United States and Canada. It is the only other country in the Western hemisphere that has the continental proportions, the regional contrasts, the demographic diversity, and the economic divisions that can be compared to the United States and Canada. As others have pointed out, and as I discuss in the Afterword, Brazil and North America—especially the United States—are like slightly distorted mirror-images of each other.

I would add that in some sense Brazil may also provide North Americans and Europeans with a glimpse of their future. On the one hand, the upper classes are mostly descendants of Europeans, and the language, high culture, and formal institutions are all Western. Brazil is also a Portuguese-speaking Catholic country with a democratic constitution and a capitalist economy. On the other hand, Brazil is something else, something different from the United States, Canada, and the societies of Western Europe. It is a country where Western culture has mixed and mingled with non-Western cultures for centuries, and in this sense it may represent the future for the United States and other countries.

This mixture of Western and non-Western, as well as modern and traditional, is what we are calling the "Brazilian puzzle." It is similar to what Roberto DaMatta has called the "Brazilian dilemma" and to what many Brazilians call the "Brazilian reality." The more one lives in Brazil, the more the Western features of the country appear as a kind of veneer. Catholics also believe in or practice African religions; the political and economic institutions operate through personal relationships as much as general rules; and the music, food, social relations, and—in general—tastes are as deeply shaped by Africa and Native America as by Europe. That, in a sense, is the puzzle: what is this country?

In choosing the title for the book, we wanted to draw attention to this puzzling quality of a country and culture that lies, in a sense, at the borderlands of the Western world. Culturally speaking, Brazil lies at the end of the diaspora of Western civilization, where the Portuguese culture of the Iberian peninsula (already at the fringes of Europe) encountered its non-Western others. (On borderlands and diasporas, see Anzaldua 1987 and the journal *Diaspora*.) Brazil is only a short trip across the Atlantic, both geographically and culturally, from Africa. Furthermore, many Brazilians trace their roots not only to Europe or Africa but also to Native America. "Diversity" is really *not* the best word for describing Brazil and Brazilians; "mixture" is better. Brazil is a nation of the mixing of races (miscegenation), religions (syncretism), and cultures (diasporas, borderlands).

I would therefore answer the "why study Brazil" question by asking another one: is Brazil the future? In the United States and Canada, as well as in other "Western" countries, there has been a great deal of discussion about multiculturalism and the new demographic diversity. The typical North American of the year 2050 will probably look for roots not only in Europe but also in other continents. And it is likely that as countries such as the

United States and Canada become less European in terms of demographics, they will also become less Western culturally. In short, for decades North Americans believed that the rest of the world was becoming like them, but it may now be time for we North Americans to take a second look at ourselves and ask how we are becoming Brazilianized.

A Framework for Studying Brazilian Culture

This book is, to my mind, exciting and new for several reasons. First, it is not a collection of essays on a single topic, such as race relations or economics. Rather, the essays consider a wide variety of aspects of Brazilian society but from a shared, cultural perspective. Second, the authors of the essays represent a mixture of Brazilianists (four, all American) and Brazilians (seven), as well as of men (five) and women (six). That mixture recognizes the tremendous change that has occurred in Brazilian studies during the last few decades. With the huge growth of Brazilian universities that have graduate programs, a new generation of Brazilian researchers has emerged, and the new generation also includes more women. The third reason why this volume is new and exciting—and this is related to the second reason—is that the mixture of researchers in this volume is representative of a turning point that has now been passed: the age of Brazilianists is over. Brazilians are developing their own frameworks for analyzing their own practices and institutions. The new, Brazilian style of analysis draws on European and North American theories but also reworks them. In the process, vectors of influence are now starting to run from Brazil to the United States, as can be seen in some of the essays by Brazilianists in this volume.

In a number of fields, Brazilian intellectuals have developed significant and new analytic frameworks that are no longer just extensions of theories developed in North America or Europe. For example, in economics Brazilians are known for having developed an analysis of political economy that focused on relations of international dependency and underdevelopment (Cardoso 1979, Furtado 1965). In theology, Catholic intellectuals from Brazil have joined with other Latin American clergy to develop the theology of liberation (e.g., Boff 1985). In pedagogy, Paulo Freire (1993) is famous for having developed a theory of educational practice that challenged the conventional, fill-up-the-students-with-knowledge theories. In cultural anthropology and studies of Brazilian national culture, the anthropologist Roberto DaMatta has influenced a number of scholars with his framework for interpreting Brazilian culture in a way that does not take European models for granted.

In Brazil, DaMatta is a well-known public figure who has a column in a major national newspaper and who makes frequent appearances on national television. Outside Brazil, he is less well-known, but with the translation of his work into English (e.g., 1991) he is likely to be better known. I first met Roberto when he agreed to serve as the field adviser for my dissertation project. Since then we have continued our conversations over the years, and I have read almost all of his published work.

As I have studied DaMatta's work, and as I have studied in Brazil or done fieldwork there as an anthropologist, I have come to appreciate the power of his framework as a way to understand the puzzling situations in which I often found myself. Not everyone agrees with his framework and analyses, but I think even those who disagree with him will often admit that he has developed a profound and original critique of Brazilian society, and one that is self-consciously Brazilian. All the essays in this volume develop interpretations of Brazilian culture that are either directly influenced by DaMatta or consistent with his general approach to Brazil. In the process, the reader encounters a creative syncretism of social theories that have been developed in Europe and are being refashioned according to concepts that make more sense in postcolonial societies.

Some Background Theory

In order to understand some of the concepts of DaMatta's anthropology, it may be helpful to step back and look at some of the major theoretical traditions in the social sciences that have been influential for attempts to understand the complexities of Brazilian society and culture. In the nineteenth century, Alexis de Tocqueville and Karl Marx inaugurated ways of thinking about society that the sociologist Robert Nisbet has termed the "two magnetic poles of European sociology" (1968: 94). Whereas Tocqueville focused on what we call today differences in "values," Marx focused on what is often today called "power," particularly in its manifestation via class relations (but to some extent via colonialism, race, and, in Engels, gender). To understand the Brazilian puzzle, it is helpful to begin by looking at what each perspective has to offer.

From a Marxist perspective, Brazil is a product of a particular colonial legacy. That legacy includes a class of wealthy landowners who supported a highly centralized and despotic Portuguese state. In turn the state implanted a "latifundia" or plantation agricultural system in Brazil. The plantations were controlled by patriarchs who exercised a nearly absolute authority over their dominions in a way similar to that of the king over the realm. The Brazilian plantation legacy was radically different from most of Canada and the northern parts of the United States. There, a more egalitarian society arose based first on small-scale or petty bourgeois capitalism: family farms, urban merchants, and small industries as well as a less centralized state with a more open decision-making process. Even in the South of the United States, where there was a plantation economy as in Brazil, there were many small farmers and urban merchants, as well as political, social, and religious structures that put a check on the power of the large landowners. In a word, the Brazilian system still had a foot in medieval feudalism, as to some extent did the American South, whereas the system of the American North and Canada was a product of the modern capitalist societies that were emerging in northern and western Europe after 1600.

Marxist analysis points to the sharp division of classes that is so evident in Latin America, and as a result a large number of Latin American scholars take for granted some version of a Marxist analysis of the political and economic legacy of colonialism. What the Tocquevillian tradition of social theory adds to the Marxist framework is a more comparative and cultural perspective. That perspective involves taking a step from an external mode of sociological analysis to an internal one, that is, to an analysis that shows how members of societies internalize what Tocqueville called "mores" and what are today called the values, categories of meaning, habits, or structures of a culture. For example, upon traveling through the United States, Tocqueville found egalitarian values in all domains of society, from the economy and government to religion, the family, and the arts. He contrasted the more modern, egalitarian values of the United States with the hierarchical values that he saw as the aristocratic legacy of much of Europe. By finding a pattern across a number of cultural domains, he was in effect developing an analysis of national cultures, even though he did not articulate his project in exactly those terms.

Tocqueville's legacy of comparative analysis has influenced a number of twentieth-century thinkers, among them the anthropologists Ruth Benedict (1946) and Louis Dumont (1980). Dumont's comparative studies focused on two key dimensions for comparing values, social structures, and patterns of social relations across societies: hierarchy and equality, and holism and individualism. DaMatta's approach to Brazilian culture departs from these key concepts as developed by Dumont.

Hierarchy and Equality

The concepts of hierarchy and equality are tricky, in part because of the terms' vague usage in everyday language. In modern, democratic societies, we usually think of workplaces as "hierarchical" and the electoral/legal structure as formally "egalitarian." However, in countries such as the United States hierarchy is viewed—and to some extent really is—as a product of a competitive system. Ideally, the competitive system is completely fair for all people, as is suggested by the metaphor of the level playing field. In this sense hierarchy emerges from the equality of a competition in which the teams or players are, in theory, equal. The resulting hierarchical order is "achieved" as a product of fair competition.

Of course, in practice hierarchy is also the result of built-in prejudices that do not allow some people to attain some positions in the society by virtue of their "blood," skin color, gender, religion, sexual orientation, or some other way of distinguishing people that has nothing to do with ability. When Dumont and the essayists in this volume use the word "hierarchy," they refer more to this "ascribed" form, rather than "achieved" hierarchy. In this ascribed form of hierarchy, one's social position is assigned at birth or is limited by one's family position. In the United States, the general ideology is that this type of hierarchy is bad and should not exist. When hierarchy of this sort is acknowledged, it comes with labels such as racism, sexism, agism, and heterosexism. Furthermore, political debate emerges over how to end it or over denials that it exists at all.

Dumont argues that in countries such as traditional India under the caste system, the whole society was set up according to a hierarchical principle by which people were born into a certain position and could not change their lot in life. Unlike in modern societies, the general ideology was that this form of hierarchy is the ideal. In a traditional, hierarchical society laws apply differently to different groups of people. In some societies around the world, and in Western societies in the past, there were actually different legal codes or juridical procedures for different groups of people. Such is also true to some extent in Brazil today (see Roberto Kant de Lima's essay in this volume).

Of course, there are remnants of the ascribed kind of hierarchy even in the most modern of societies, but official, legal (*de jure*) recognition of such hierarchy—such as the old Jim Crow laws of the American South—is considered an affront to the fundamental value of equality. Furthermore, the very fact that sexism, racism, and other forms of customary (*de facto*) discrimination are the source of great contention indicates that the governing principle—equality and achieved hierarchy—is the ideal, rather than ascribed hierarchy. Thus, the distinction between hierarchy and equality is not absolute, with some societies completely egalitarian and others completely hierarchical. There are always instances of hierarchy in even the most egalitarian societies, and vice-versa.

Holism and Individualism

The concepts of holism and individualism are closely related to those of hierarchy and equality. In a hierarchical society everyone occupies a definite position in the whole. The society is often imagined as a kind of huge corporate body with the rulers as the heads, the warriors as the arms, the priests as the heart, and the serfs as the legs (or some other similar mapping of social groups onto body parts). People's identity is rooted in their association with a particular position in society; they are serfs or warriors, or members of this caste or clan. Locally, identity is rooted in one's position in a clan or village—for example, the third brother, the first wife, and so on. DaMatta uses the term "persons" to describe this category of identity, in which one is defined by one's position in a family or in a hierarchically ordered social group.

In contrast, in an individualistic society identity is rooted in one's own life history and choices. According to this logic, social identity and position are a product of which game one enters, how hard one works, how talented one is, and how lucky one is. Social interaction is imagined not as a ordered corporate body but as a great race or competition, with the leaders as the best players. In this sense, people are individuals linked more by the rules of the game, which are assumed to apply equally to all (or universally). Although in an individualistic society people certainly have personalistic loyalties, one's identity as an individual rather than as a person tends to have the upper hand. Likewise, in a personalistic (or what DaMatta calls a "relational") society there are domains of society that operate according to individualistic and egalitarian principles, but in general personal loyalties tend to have the upper hand.

Refashioning Dumont

Dumont is best known for his studies that compare the hierarchical and holistic system of traditional India with the egalitarian and individualistic system of the modern West. DaMatta applied Dumont's framework in a creative way to Brazil, which he argues is somewhere between the two ideal polar extremes. Prior to DaMatta's studies, most research on borderland and "semimodern" cultures operated with a huge conceptual gulf between the modern or modernizing sectors of society and the traditional sectors. Many books examine postcolonial and third world countries by assuming that those societies are modernizing and becoming less traditional. In this way, the modern sector becomes associated with a progressive, Westernized, urban elite, and the traditional sector is associated with non-Western, rural, or poor sectors of the society.

DaMatta has changed the terms of the debate by rejecting a model of "two Brazils," in which a traditional culture located in the lower classes of the cities and in the rural hinterlands is opposed to a modern Brazil in the upper classes and the big cities. Instead, DaMatta shows how in societies like Brazil Dumont's distinctions can be applied simultaneously throughout the society. In other words, societies like Brazil are not divided into social classes, groups, or sectors that can be labelled either modern or traditional, Western or non-Western, egalitarian or hierarchical, individualistic or holistic, and so on. Instead of working with an "either-or" model, DaMatta opts for a "both-and" model. In other words, DaMatta argues that both tendencies are present in any number of social groups, institutions, and practices. To understand how he achieves this more dynamic analysis of cultural conflict, it is necessary to look at his analysis of social action and practices.

Rituals and Social Dramas

To accomplish the deconstruction of the classic oppositions of "West and the rest," modern and traditional, DaMatta turns to the work of another influential thinker in contemporary anthropology, Victor Turner (e.g., 1974). Turner was best known for studies of social action as "social dramas." Instead of focusing on institutions or beliefs from a utilitarian or functionalist perspective, Turner looked at historical events, rituals, or social practices as meaningful action. Turner's detailed case studies provided a model for many anthropologists who wished to interpret the complexities of what social action means to the people who engage in it.

By focusing on a number of case studies, DaMatta shows how both hierarchical/personalistic and egalitarian/individualistic codes operate simultaneously. (Generally, scholars tend to use the term "personalism" for the particular kind of holism evident in Latin American societies.) In a number of case studies—Carnival balls, popular religious ceremonies, and soccer games, to name a few—DaMatta demonstrates the power of seeing Brazil as an interstitial culture with a double-edged ethic. To understand DaMatta's method, it might be helpful to follow his analysis of one case of a social drama involving this two-way intersection. Probably the most well-known case study appeared in his book *Carnivals, Rogues, and Heroes*, where he studied in detail a ritual of reversal known as "Do you know who you're talking to?" Based on interview data, DaMatta found that Brazilians consider the little ritual unpleasant and authoritarian, for it is generally used in anonymous, individualistic situations by people who wish to establish their position of authority and importance. As a result, the ritual is generally used by powerful people, or by those who are attached to the powerful through family, friendship, or work-related ties.

Consider one example of where the question might appear in Brazil: someone has parked a car illegally and is stopped by a police officer, who asks the person to move the car (DaMatta 1991: 160–161). In both Brazil and the United States, the situation is one of the most egalitarian and individualistic available. One is in the domain of laws and traffic regulations, and unless one is either very famous or in a small town the relationship between the officer and the traffic law offender is likely to be anonymous. In theory, doctors, workers, movie stars, the unemployed, young, and old are all expected to obey the same traffic rules. No one is above the law, and the law applies equally to everyone. In this sense, there are no major differences between Brazil and other Western countries such as the United States.

However, DaMatta argues that in Brazil people often successfully subvert the universalistic order of the legal system and the marketplace. For example, in this situation of a parking violation a well-connected Brazilian might ask the police officer: "Do you know who you're talking to? I'm a friend of so-and-so, who is a friend of so-and-so, who is your boss." DaMatta notes that the outcome of such a situation might be that the traffic offender would walk away angrily, and a few days later the police officer might actually be obliged to apologize. In other words, the parking offender occupies a social position above that of the police officer and has the personal connections to interfere in the police force. The result is that in Brazil the "Do you know who you're talking to?" operates as a ritual of inversion that transforms an egalitarian, individualistic situation into a hierarchical, personalistic one. The situation is hierarchical because, implicitly, there are now two legal systems, one for the well-connected and another for the rest.

Americans (and other people from "modern," Western countries) who read this summary of DaMatta's analysis might say, "Well, that is all very interesting, but it could happen in the United States just as easily." In a way, they are right. One could imagine the chauffeur of a mafia don, a big-time politician, or a well-connected fat cat using the same line. Privilege certainly exists in the United States, and even if the officer proceeded to hand out a ticket, a rich person might be able to get out of it later via connections at city hall. More generally, it has long been recognized that the icon of blind justice is far from a reality in the United States. For example, African Americans have frequently pointed to a double standard in the American legal system. On this point, see Roberto Kant de Lima's essay in this volume and my comments in the afterword.

Notwithstanding these similarities, there are a number of ways in which the use and meaning of "Do you know who you're talking to?" are different in the two countries. First, there is the question of frequency and scope. DaMatta finds that the ritual is used in a wide range of situations in Brazil, and from his examples it seems that the ritual is used both more frequently and by a wider range of people than in the United States. Second, in the United States it is more likely that the officer would respond to the question by laughing at it as ridiculous or by handing out a more serious citation for threatening a police officer. As DaMatta noted, Americans are likely to respond to "Do you know you're talking to?" situations with "Who do you think you are?" questions. (I also find it difficult to imagine an American police officer having to apologize to someone for legally giving them a ticket for a traffic violation.) Finally, even if one were to use successfully the "Do you know who you're talking to?" in this situation in the United States, it would be generally perceived as corruption. In Brazil, there is a greater tendency to shrug one's shoulders and say simply that the system works that way.

Through this very brief summary of a case study, one can see how DaMatta's analytical framework differs from the older approaches that looked at the dynamics of modernization in terms of two sectors of society. DaMatta looks at rituals and social dramas—from big national parties such as Carnival (Mardi Gras) to the interactions of everyday life—to show how Brazilians are constantly negotiating between a modern, egalitarian code and a traditional one. In some situations, modern practices predominate. However, as DaMatta shows, even in situations where one would expect modern, egalitarian practices to be firmly in place, such as procedures for traffic violations, one finds instead that hierarchical and personalistic practices often "encompass" modern ones.

Encompassment

By focusing on case studies, DaMatta puts the statics of Dumontian comparative analysis into a dynamic framework that elucidates everyday life in Brazil through a case study method. In the process, he overturns the self-assured, ethnocentric complacency of many Westerners who would think that the rest of the world will slowly become like the modern West. To accomplish his own theoretical ritual of inversion, DaMatta adopts the idea of "encompassment" from Dumont and applies it in a new way.

For Dumont, "encompassment" referred to the way in which one social group or idea includes its opposite at a higher level. He explicitly connected the idea of encompassment to hierarchy when he argued that hierarchy "is not, essentially, a chain of superimposed commands, nor even a chain of beings of decreasing dignity, but a relation that can succinctly be called the 'encompassing of the contrary'" (1980: 239). In other words, Dumont is interested in hierarchy in terms of its cultural meaning. The classic example is the case of Adam and Eve, which is an opposition at one level: the contrast between the "man" and "woman" as two halves of a species. However, as Dumont points out, at another level Western ideology constructs that opposition as a hierarchy in the story that Eve was created from Adam's rib: she is a "wo-man." In this sense, the woman is "encompassed" by the male; or, to use the term of the philosopher Jacques Derrida (1974), she is viewed as "supplementary" to the encompassing term, the male. Most Western languages—including English and Portuguese—continue that linguistic hierarchy through usages of "man" as the generic term that refers to the species as a whole, including both men and women. Hierarchy, of course, is not considered good in societies or among segments of a society with egalitarian values, and hence language and other systems of meaning become sites where people challenge hierarchical symbolism and work for egalitarian symbolism, such as gender-fair language (as is used in this book).

Because traditional, patriarchic forms of gendered language are familiar to so many people, they are an easy way to describe hierarchy. However, gender is less useful as an example for getting across the ways in which encompassment is a recursive or nested process. One might, for example, find ways in which linguistic usage puts into play a gendered hierarchy within the categories of men and women (such as the use, in some settings, of "men" as an encompassing term for "men" and "boys"). Perhaps a better example involves the symbolism of traditional leadership. The "crown" stands for the king (who at another level is part of a pair, king plus crown), just as the king stands for the court (that includes a king and the court), and the court for the kingdom (that includes the court) in a chain of hierarchical oppositions.

DaMatta's use of the term encompassment focuses on the relationship between the modern, egalitarian, and individualistic cultural forms versus the traditional, hierarchical, and personalistic ones. In a sense, he took the conventional relationship of encompassment and turned it on its head. Whereas many scholars had previously assumed that traditional elements of societies such as Brazil were giving way before the inevitable developments of modernity, DaMatta showed how the nonmodern ethic of Brazilian culture was actually, in many cases, encompassing its more modern alternative. Such was the case in the ritual of "Do you know who you're talking to?" In analyses of this type, he puts into question facile evolutionary models that assume Brazil will someday be just a tropical version of the United States, Canada, or Britain.

Mediating Terms

As part of his argument that Brazil is an intermediary society, neither modern nor traditional, but emphatically both, DaMatta also developed an analysis of intermediary terms or symbols that dramatize the Brazilian situation. In Protestant cultures there was usually a clear division between categories, with one of those categories usually marked as superior. In contrast, in Brazil there was a tendency to move toward a middle ground of mediation and ambiguity. Those mediating terms became sites for the conflict of values and the encompassment of the modern by the traditional.

For example, in religion the Protestants got rid of purgatory and the saints in the churches. That historical event was part of the overall modernization of Protestant culture that moved it toward a clear, either-or system. In contrast, in Brazilian Catholicism purgatory and the saints not only remain, but flourish within a densely populated spirit world sanctioned by popular religion. That world includes not only the Catholic saints but also African nature spirits (*orixás*), slave and native spirits, Asian sages, famous dead white European men, and other beings that mediate between earth and heaven.

Purgatory and the mediating spirits, both of which are retained in Brazilian religion, provide a way out of the strict, either-or system of Protestant cultures. They provide, on the spiritual level, a sense of flexibility and an ability to bend rules that is characteristic of everyday life in Brazil.

Likewise, in the economic and political domain the sharp injustices of Brazil's authoritarian and hierarchical system are blunted by the existence of a number of mediating institutions. Those institutions include the godfather or patron-client tie, extended kin networks, nepotism, professional palm-greasers, the *jeitinho* (jay-chee'-nyoo, the art of bending rules described in the first chapter), and all sorts of other social practices that would appear "corrupt" in North America and Western Europe. In another area, race relations, the sharp dichotomies of North America's black/white polarization are muted in Brazil by the celebration of the mulatto(a), the mestizo(a), and other forms of racial mixing, as well as by the mixture of Catholic and African religious practices. Even in the area of gender, where Brazil's patriarchy has sanctioned both violence against women and the keeping of mistresses, women carve out alternative bases for power from their huge family and friendship networks as well as from their role as mediums (channelers) in the spirit mediumship religions.

In short, personal relationships (including those with the spirits) form the flip-side of official hierarchies (church, state, race, gender). Personalism is more than a cultural system that gives people a social address in a hierarchical society; it is also a resource that people can use to get around the official rules of the hierarchical society. Of course, personalism does not work the same way for everyone. The networks of the weak are usually smaller and less influential, whereas the networks of those at the top of the hierarchies are usually much larger and more influential. As a result, although personalism can be used as a resource to subvert hierarchy, as an overall system it ends up reproducing the general hierarchical order.

House, Street, and Other World

Perhaps the most well-known of DaMatta's studies of mediation is his discussion of street, home, and other world (1985). For DaMatta, those spaces are less physical or geographical places than symbols of moral universes. The space of the home is identified with the hierarchical and personalistic moral world, whereas that of the street is egalitarian and individualistic. Of course, in Brazil the two worlds of home and street interact considerably. In the "Do you know who you're talking to?" example, the world of the home is brought into that of the street, in effect turning the street into the home. When a motorist asks the police officer that question, in effect the motorist is transforming the moral space from that of egalitarianism and individualism to that of hierarchy and personalism.

Furthermore, DaMatta argues that the two worlds are mediated symbolically by a third space: the other world. The other world is the symbol of a space in which both moral systems come together. In the other world there is the universal, unshakable equality of all people who stand as individuals before God and are judged on their individual merits. (In a sense, the position one gains in the other world is the outcome of a competitive race.) Yet, at the same time the unshakable judgment of the other world is softened by such intermediary forces as spirits, saints, or the Virgin Mary, who are able to intercede in the hierarchy on one's behalf. In a sense, then, what DaMatta looks for is the dynamism of the other-world throughout Brazilian society.

It may be worth pointing out that the house/street dimension is also polarized in terms of race, class, age, and gender. As DaMatta notes in his book *The House and the Street*, the street is a male domain, just as the house is a female domain. (The distinction is a familiar one not only in Brazil, but in many other cultures.) As a social space, the home—and institutions modeled on the home, such as the church and the workplace—are places where relations among family members and servants institute the familiar hierarchies of race, class, age, and gender. Servants in middle class households are generally people of color, and the father/husband is the titular head of the household. The street is a different sort of place where these hierarchies are suspended: poor may rob the rich, women may flirt with men, the young may deviate from their parents' rules, and people of color may disobey the whites. In short, the street is the location of inversions (including that great ritual of inversions, Carnival). As Martha Carvalho notes in her essay in this volume, the street is also a place where a woman (even a black woman servant) may walk freely, no longer encaged in the house, and watch the men (even wealthy, white men) who are paralyzed because their work requires them to remain in one place.

The street is therefore both a place of excitement and danger. Although the street is a place where the egalitarian and individualistic principles of the marketplace or legal system are in operation, the idea of the "street" in Brazil is a far cry from the idea of the "public" in traditional English-speaking cultures. In English-speaking North America, the relationship between house and street is configured more as a relationship between private and public domains, or spaces that symbolize the relationship between individual rights (home) and community responsibilities (the street). In Brazil, that dimension exists, but it is overlaid with the conflict between personal obligations (home) and personal freedom and individual anonymity (the street). Of course, in Anglophone North America there is also a Brazilian dimension to our streets, but that dimension becomes easier to see and articulate after having examined its elaboration in Brazil.

Brazil and the United States

In DaMatta's work and in many of the essays in this volume, the United States and to a lesser extent other wealthy, Western countries appear as touchstones against which an analysis of Brazil is made. One very interesting aspect of this book is to discover how Brazilians portray the United States. Most of the Brazilian authors in this volume have lived in the United States and are quite sophisticated about the contradictions and complexities of American society. However, in these essays they tend to use the United States as a kind of literary device, and as a result they tend to focus on the modern aspects of American culture. As anyone who has lived in both countries knows, there is a dramatic difference in institutions and values between Brazil and the United States; however, there are also large areas of overlap. It would take another volume, one focused on the United States, to bring out the depth of that overlap. However, because the topic is likely to be of some interest to readers, I will discuss some aspects of the complexities in the afterword to this volume.

On a personal note, I can say that the more I have learned about Brazil, the more I have come to appreciate the ways in which North American society is hierarchical and personalistic. I am not referring merely to obvious areas of hierarchy such as the problems of racism and sexism that continue to go unresolved or the preferential treatment often afforded to the very rich. I am also referring to the ways in which members of the middle class utilize personal contacts to maneuver through professional worlds. Likewise, I am thinking about the ways in which friendships, romantic relationships, and marriage preferences remain patterned along lines that often reproduce longstanding patterns of ascribed hierarchy. Certainly, there are some signs that the United States and other modern, Western countries are becoming less hierarchical, particularly via the new policies of multiculturalism, harassment, and affirmative action in many institutions. However, at the same time the gulf between rich and poor in the United States has grown wider during the last decades, and the large numbers of Latin American and other immigrants bring with them many of the practices and values that DaMatta has described for Brazil. In this sense, then, I think it is instructive to watch, listen, and learn from Brazil. In some ways, and let us hope it is not just through government debt and high crime, Brazil may represent the future for the Western world.

Questions of Methodology in the Study of National Societies

Changing Concepts of Culture and National Society

Since about 1980, the concept of culture in the social sciences has undergone a dramatic transition. Most readers of this volume will have some familiarity with the culture concept as it is used by anthropologists. To review, "culture" in this sense refers to the basic patterns, structures, or values—whatever term with which one is most comfortable—that cut across a wide variety of domains of a society: not only the arts, ritual, and literature, but also the economic and political institutions, the family, race and gender relations, and all sorts of aspects of face-to-face social relations. To interpret culture in this more general sense, anthropologists assume a comparative perspective. Their training involves reading about the widest variety of the world's cultures, and often their fieldwork involves living in a radically different society.

In the past, anthropologists tended to go away to remote villages of peasants or indigenous peoples. Since the middle of the century anthropologists have in increasing numbers studied national societies—countries such as Brazil, the United States, Canada, Germany, India, and Japan. In many cases, anthropologists still do fieldwork in a relatively small community within the national society, such as a hospital, neighborhood, factory, or school. Among the reasons for anthropologists' increasing interest in national societies, perhaps the most obvious is the historical fact that small-scale, indigenous, and peasant societies are disappearing as they face assimilation, the destruction of their lands and way of life, and in many cases genocidal incursions from national societies and multinational organizations (as has occurred in the Amazon). Furthermore, increasing limitations on funding and access to indigenous peoples, as well as the danger of working in areas marked by terrorism and violence, have made it necessary for greater numbers of anthropologists to stay at home or to do fieldwork in cities and towns. Even those anthropologists who still do traditional village fieldwork often find that the communities are far from isolated. The most remote communities are now frequently connected to the rest of the world via roads, airplanes, radios, bulldozers, miners, ranchers, and so on.

Partly as a result of those changing circumstances, and partly as a result of theoretical developments in the academy, anthropologists have changed their traditional culture concept in several ways. We now tend to focus on relations between the community and the larger world, or on the ways in which different groups within a society have different viewpoints and values. In short, rather than thinking of culture as an isolated and integrated whole, we tend to think of it as situated—connected to other cultures—and contested—subject to debate among various member groups. As a result, many of the essays in this volume focus on the divisions and diversity of Brazilian society, and they also situate Brazilian institutions and practices in comparative or transnational settings.

Just as the culture concept has been changing in recent years, so has thinking about national societies. The anthropological study of national societies as it is understood today should be carefully distinguished from the questionable legacy of the "national character" studies of the 1930s and 1940s (see Lindesmith and Strauss 1950, Varenne 1984). Those studies tended to develop a psychological portrait of a people as a whole that missed all the internal differences. That research tradition also tended to explain cultural integration through a single institution such as childhood socialization patterns. Anthropologists today are less willing to privilege any given aspect of a society as an independent variable that can explain or in some sense determine the other domains of a society. We have also come to recognize that the concept of a "national society"—such as Brazil—is only one level of analysis that we *construct* for specific analytical purposes. Larger levels may also be constructed—such as Latin American culture—just as more restricted levels are also available: the cultures of cities or neighborhoods, ethnic groups and classes, professional and religious groups, genders, regions, and so on. In other words, we work today in a world where we recognize the contingent and constructed nature of categories that we nevertheless find analytically, and even practically, useful.

Furthermore, we are now living in a world in which the very idea of a national society is made complex by crosscurrents of various sorts. Multinational corporations, international organizations, and other transnational actors are only one, highly visible aspect of a world that some have called "postnational." Europe, once the bastion of the stable nation-state, now seems to be moving toward fragmentation in the east and unification in the west. Furthermore, in other parts of the world free trade zones similar to the European Economic Community have been emerging. In addition to NAFTA, an example of those zones is Mercosur, a block of the South American trading partners that in the early 1990s included Brazil, Argentina, Uruguay, and Paraguay. Another form of postnationality comes from the huge population movements in the wake of political and economic dislocations. As a result, diasporas of immigrant communities that crosscut national boundaries have become increasingly common in many large cities throughout the world. Furthermore, some societies have fallen into such utter chaos that it has become possible to speak of a failure of the nation-state to take hold in some parts of the world.

Notwithstanding all the challenges to national societies and cultures, national identity and ethnic identity have become a topic of increasing concern, in part because of the increased contact of peoples across cultural borders of various sorts. Given the increased mixing of cultures that occurs in immigrant communities and international organizations, the so-called postmodern or postnational condition may frequently involve a mingling of cultures identified as relatively traditional and relatively modern. In other words, the mixture of traditional and modern, which is so characteristic of Brazilian culture, is also likely to characterize many other cultural encounters in an increasingly international world.

Methods for Studying National Societies

How, then, does one study something as complex as national culture, particularly when both national identity and national borders are contested and transgressed with increasing frequency? I admit to having no simple answer to this very difficult question. However, I can point to some of the solutions found by the authors in this volume. Consider first the traditional anthropological method of fieldwork, by which I refer to the combination of participant-observation, informal interviews, and the cultivation of relationships with insiders whom we call "informants." In classical anthropological fieldwork, one learns the language, lives in a community for at least a year, observes action, participates in activities, and develops relations with insiders who become one's teachers. During that time, the anthropologist writes up fieldnotes every day based on observations and conversations. Over time, the fieldworker pieces together the various domains of a local culture—material, economic, political, social, religious, etc.—and how they hang together. Some of the essays in the volume are based on methods that approximate classical anthropological fieldwork. Perhaps the closest to this model are the essays by Leni Silverstein, Cynthia Sarti, and Rosane Prado. Although Prado and Sarti are both Brazilians and did not have to learn Portuguese, they still had to learn the local concepts and lingo of the town and neighborhood where they did fieldwork. All three essays are instructive for the study of national societies because although they focus on a specific city, town, or neighborhood, they reveal perceptions of and divisions in the larger national society. In this sense, they use the local as a lens through which they can begin to understand the national. Thus, when the focus is on culture, microsocial studies can also say a good deal about the macrosocial or national level.

Other essays rely more exclusively on the informal or unstructured interview, which is still suited for an analysis of cultural meaning. For example, Lívia Barbosa used that method in her work on the *jeitinho*, that is, the tradition of "bending rules," and I also used unstructured interviews in my study of the Brazilian religious system. The method seems to work especially well when one is studying not a local community but perceptions of national organizations or practices. Another example of informal methods is Conrad Kottak's use of his autobiographical experience with his children in swim meets. His personal reflection (sometimes called a "fieldwork account") shows how sometimes the greatest insights occur when one is not even intending to be gathering data.

What may be of most methodological interest to the study national societies from a cultural perspective is how the essays combine fieldwork, interviews, and life experience with textual or media sources. Although, as DaMatta (1991) and Kant de Lima (1992) have discussed, Brazilians in general tend to have a strong preference for oral communication, there is also a rich source of cultural insight available in the form of written texts, television and movies, or popular songs. If in tribal societies oral myths are the royal road to the elementary forms of culture, then in contemporary societies electronic and printed texts are the royal road to national and transnational cultures. Sources of this sort vary widely in the essays. Among them, Maria Claudia Coelho uses newspaper accounts, Martha Carvalho relies on musical lyrics, Roberto Kant de Lima works on legal documents, Roberto

DaMatta works with novels among other texts, and I draw on the texts of popular religion and parapsychology. In short, this collection of essays suggests that studies of the culture of national societies are likely to adopt a pluralistic and opportunistic approach that mixes fieldwork, interviews, personal experience, and textual interpretation. Thus, the classical method of anthropology—fieldwork—and that of cultural studies—the analysis of texts and documents—are likely to come together in interesting and new ways.

In addition to methods in the sense of techniques of data-gathering, there is another aspect of methodology that deserves to be mentioned. Most of the essays in this volume make use of a comparative perspective. Some, such as the essays by Roberto DaMatta, Jeffrey Jarrad, Conrad Kottak, and Roberto Kant de Lima, provide detailed and explicit comparisons based on observations in Brazil and other countries. Others utilize a comparative perspective as a general background. In either case, a comparative perspective is crucial for understanding what is specific about Brazilian national culture. That perspective is also, as I shall argue in the next section, a literary device that is used as a way of positing an alternative future for Brazil.

Positions

Related to the question of methods is the more complicated issue that is sometimes referred to as a "meta" level or reflexive level of political positions. In other words, in the humanities and social sciences it is no longer possible to write about culture and society as if they were objective "things" apart from the observers. The old metaphor of a biological organism, with social scientists as the biologists, no longer seems appropriate. (Or perhaps the metaphor needs to be updated, for biologists are now actively intervening in biological and evolutionary processes.) In today's world researchers tend to see themselves as part of the ongoing *dialogue* that constructs the societies they write about, even if our role at times appears to be limited to whispers in the storm. Most of the authors in this volume write from a deep sense of concern about the directions that Brazilian society has taken in recent years. We have all—Brazilians and foreigners alike—felt a deep frustration with the political and economic crises of the country and with the travails of crime and everyday life. Thus, several of the essays collected here are rooted in a critical perspective that hopes to see the eventual emergence of a transformed country with a higher level of social justice. Visions of the nature of this transformation vary from one author to another, but all believe that anthropology and associated disciplines can contribute to understanding the failures and potentials of a reconstructed Brazil.

There is a longstanding tradition, both in everyday life and in the academy, in which Brazilians turn to the United States as their point of comparison and basis for critique. For many Brazilians, the United States is an example of a New World society that turned out well (*deu certo*), whereas Brazil is a failure. Brazilians look at their huge continental country and ask why they do not have the political stability, civil liberties, and economic success of their apparently similar sibling to the north. At the same time, many Brazilians who have lived in the United States ask why Americans do not have the personal warmth and the relatively relaxed ethnic relations that Brazilians have. Conversely, many Americans who have lived in Brazil return to the United States frustrated at the almost obsessive individualism and relative coldness of their countrypeople. Americans may also return to the United States with a sense that they have seen in modern Brazil a possible future for the United States: a nation marked by a continuous economic crises, sharp polarization of classes, uncontrollable street crime and urban violence, and political instability. Thus, Brazil and the United States can serve as lenses through which people from each country can reflect on their own and each other's cultures.

Although the perspective of the essays is rooted in the cultural, comparative tradition of the social sciences, that perspective should be seen as complementary to and not an alternative to that of political economy. I do not doubt the importance of the analysis of class domination and international finance as a way of understanding the Brazilian crisis. However, even if the Brazilian government were able to resolve its ongoing economic crisis, Brazilians would still have to confront the "cultural crisis" that is part of their daily struggle of life on the streets. Corruption and political instability are not just a product of a colonial legacy or neocolonial economics; they are also products of a continued reproduction of practices, values, and institutions in the informal institutions of everyday life. The essays in this volume address this other crisis of Brazilian society, as it is lived in everyday life. It is in the vicissitudes of everyday Brazilian life that one uncovers the systematic conflict that makes it possible to understand the dialectic between the political events of the headlines and the hierarchy and personalism of the informal side of Brazilian society.

By focusing on questions of hierarchy and personalism, it may be possible to identify the stumbling blocks to democracy and democratization in

Brazil. As Roberto Kant de Lima notes in his essay, a cultural approach can help extend discussions of democracy from the official sphere of constitutions, law-making, and economic policy to informal and more hidden institutions. In general, anthropology and cultural studies can contribute to the democracy debate by showing how democracy is not simply a question of economic modernization or a new constitution, clean elections, and civil rights. The essays in this volume point to the complexity of building a democratic society in Brazil. To be meaningful and lasting, that process will involve not only writing a new constitution and electing honest officials, but also probing and questioning the diverse institutions of everyday life: the bureaucracy, police and judicial practices, sports, voluntary organizations, gender, family, neighborhood relationships, the *jeitinho*, music, and religion.

Overview

I have divided the book into four sections: Brazilian Styles of Social Relations; Race, Class, and Gender in a Changing Culture; Ideologies and Cultures on an International Stage; and Brazilian Society: Macrostructures in Comparative Perspective. Each section has its own brief introductory essay. The order of the sections was chosen to provide readers first with a sense of what everyday life is like in Brazil, and how hierarchy and personalism work in everyday social relations. The next two sections are set up to explore the ways in which national society is both contested and situated (or not isolated). Regarding the way it is contested, the essays on race, class, and gender show how those divisions mark differing constructions of Brazilian society. Likewise, the essays on ideologies and cultures on an international stage show how national culture and identity are constructed in a global world. The last section consists of the most general, comparative, and difficult essays. Some readers may wish to begin there, especially those who wish to sample Roberto DaMatta's work immediately. However, I have put that section last because for many readers the essays will be easier after having first read the other authors.

Brazilian Styles of Social Relations

The first section includes three essays on hierarchy and personalism in local-level social relations. The essays also serve to flesh out the theoretical framework discussed above. Thus, Lívia Barbosa's discussion of the *jeitinho* shows how this national institution operates to mediate the complicated cultural contradictions of Brazilian society. The phrase *dar um jeitinho* does not translate easily into English, but roughly it has the meaning of "bending the rules" or "figuring out a way" around authoritarian institutions and bureaucratic roadblocks. First popularized by Roberto DaMatta, his student Lívia Barbosa now takes a detailed look at the different forms and meanings of the *jeitinho*. In addition to providing an anatomy of the contexts and uses of this all-important Brazilian institution, Barbosa adds to the theoretical discussions of DaMatta and Dumont by introducing a Brazilian form of equality that is linked to the *jeitinho*. She also shows how the ambiguity of the *jeitinho* makes it a highly appropriate symbol for Brazilians' discussions of national identity.

Conrad Kottak draws on his and his sons' personal experiences in competitive swimming meets in Brazil and the United States. Kottak asks why Brazilians do not excel in the Olympic Games to the extent that Americans, Germans, and some other nationalities do. Avoiding a facile explanation based on Brazil's relative poverty, Kottak shows how the comparative organization of competitive swimming in the United States and Brazil is consistent with the values of the two countries. In an exposition that weaves carefully back and forth between ethnographic detail and analytical explication, he shows how competitive swimming in Brazil is *Brazilian*.

Rosane Prado shows how the framework of personalism and hierarchy can be applied internally to understand the regional and local differences of Brazilian culture. She compares life in the small town with that in the big cities, where life is more individualistic. In the small town where Prado did her fieldwork, the tension between personalism and hierarchy on one side and individualism and equality on the other side is tipped toward the former. In a sense, then, life in small-town Brazil magnifies and exaggerates the condition of life in Brazil, what Prado calls the heaven and hell of personalism. It might be seen as exemplifying the dilemma of all Brazilians, who long for the freedom of big cities and foreign countries, but simultaneously are reluctant to give up the security that their personal ties afford.

Race, Class, and Gender in a Changing Society

The second section shows how this very traditional domain of cultural studies looks in a Brazilian context. Maria Claudia Coelho examines as myth and ritual the media reporting and national scandal that developed around two cases of murder and rape, one from the 1950s and the other from the 1980s. She shows that although there are many similarities between the two cases, they also reveal that cultural values and notions of gender have changed dramatically across the generations. Cynthia Sarti also examines changing cultural patterns through a study of the poor of urban São Paulo. She focuses on questions related to modernization and its impact on the traditional social structures such as the neighbor relationship and the patriarchal family. She reveals a complex set of social hierarchies at work among the urban poor, a group that is often considered to be amorphous and monolithic. She also considers how the patriarchal family structure is both modified and conserved when women become the heads of households. Her critique and analysis of the patriarchal family extends the cultural analysis of hierarchy and personalism to gender relations within the lower classes.

In "The Celebration of Our Lord of the Good End: The Washing of the Steps of Nosso Senhor do Bomfim," Leni Silverstein discusses the well-known and complex relationship between the African religions of Bahia and the Roman Catholic church. The famous ritual of washing the steps of the Catholic church Our Lord of the Good End is often seen as an example of the relatively benign coexistence of the European and African races and religions in Bahia. However, Silverstein questions the ideology of "syncretism" and shows instead how the recent tourist and state appropriations of the African religions continue the older cultural hierarchy that keeps Catholicism as the dominant religion.

Ideologies and Cultures on an International Stage

The third section focuses on the cultural meaning of ideology in a context of various international cultural currents: music, an international organization (Alcoholics Anonymous), and international religious and scientific thought. Martha Carvalho's essay "Tupi or Not Tupi MPB: Popular Music and Identity in Brazil" provides a complex analysis of the interwoven history of Brazilian society and music. She shows how the tradition of "anthropophagy" or cannibalism has marked Brazilian music and art from the time of the first encounters between the Tupinambá and the colonial missionaries through popular Brazilian music today. Carvalho also shows how one of the constants of Brazilian music over time is the "cannibalism" of foreign musical styles and elements, generally viewed as more prestigious than whatever is considered to be merely "Brazilian." In this way, she considers local versus foreign musics in terms of hierarchical relationships. (On eating, encompassment, and hierarchy, see DaMatta 1986.)

My own essay discusses religions that have originated elsewhere—Catholicism, Pentecostalism, and Spiritism—as part of a system that includes an indigenous Brazilian religion, Umbanda. I draw on interviews with and writings by representatives of those four groups to show how each constructs the entire religious system in a way that, to use the Dumontian term, "encompasses" the worldviews of the others. I also show how the strategies of encompassment vary in ways that are associated with the position of the religion in the broader social structure, and in the process I am able to broach the question of how an analysis of hierarchy might be articulated with one concerned with questions of power or hegemony.

Jeffrey Jarrad's essay on "The Brazilianization of Alcoholics Anonymous" is of special interest because Alcoholics Anonymous is a product of North American Protestantism. This historical fact raises an interesting question: what happens when such a cultural-bound discourse and practice diffuses to Brazil, the world's largest Catholic country? As Martha Carvalho also shows in her essay on "cannibalism" (*antropofagia*) in Brazilian music, Brazilians have adapted Alcoholics Anonymous to make it better fit with their own cultural style. Jarrad shows this "Brazilianization" through a finely detailed study that uses an American group as a point of comparison for his discussion of a Brazilian AA group.

Brazilian Society: Macrostructures in Comparative Perspective

The fourth section includes two essays that grapple with Brazilian national culture and society as a whole and in comparative perspective. Roberto Kant de Lima's profound comparative essay points to the complexities of a legal system that combines modern, liberal institutions with those that are rooted historically in the hierarchical truth-finding practices of the colonial church and state judiciaries. Perhaps more than any other essay in this volume, Kant's work points to the ways in which the comparative perspective of anthropology can help Brazilians think through the enormous problem of modernization and reform in the political and legal system, but he also turns his comparative analysis back to the United States to reveal complexities in that judicial system as well.

The final essay is by Roberto DaMatta. This essay is written as a critique of foreigners, especially North Americans and Europeans, who have written about Brazil as a society that does not make sense: the "Brazilian puzzle" as the Brazilian mess. In a sense, DaMatta provides a solution to the Brazilian puzzle. He sees it as an artifact of the narrow dichotomies that North Americans and Europeans use when describing Brazil. Because Brazil does not fit into the neat categories of modern or nonmodern, Western or non-Western, foreign scholars tend to write off Brazil as a place of chaos and things that are out of place. DaMatta provides a corrective to this intellectual legacy by showing the logic of the apparently illogical country. In the process, he also argues for an independent intellectual tradition, one created and led by Brazilians. This alternative tradition would analyze Brazil on its own terms without thoughtlessly applying inappropriate and ethnocentric analytical categories.

The essays in this volume as a group show how a number of Brazilian and American scholars are already coming up with their own frameworks that are more rooted in the "Brazilian reality." Although some of the essays in this volume might be called "DaMattian," there is also considerable room for individual variation and independence. Yet, the essays all share a comparative, cultural perspective that brings out the hierarchical and personalistic structures of Brazilian society. The essays also describe Brazil on its own terms rather than through models of "Westernization" or "Americanization."

With this volume, I have worked to bring some of the results of this alternative Brazilian tradition to American readers. Many of these scholars have not published before in English, and it is indeed a pleasure to bring them to American readers. In the pages that follow, not only will the reader encounter a new side to Brazil as a national society, but the reader will find a Brazilian way of looking at Brazilian culture.

References

Anzaldua, Gloria
   1987 *Borderlands/La Frontera*. San Francisco: Aunt Lute Books.
Benedict, Ruth
   1946 *The Chrysanthemum and the Sword*. Boston: Houghton Mifflin.
Boff, Leonardo
   1985 *Church, Charism, and Power*. New York: Crossroads.
Cardoso, Fernando Henrique
   1979 *Dependency and Development in Latin America*. Berkeley: University of California Press.

DaMatta, Roberto
1985 *A Casa e a Rua: Espaço, Cidadania, Mulher, e Morte no Brasil*. So Paulo: Brasiliense.
1986 *O Que Faz brasil, Brasil?* Rio de Janeiro: Rocco.
1991 *Carnivals, Rogues, and Heroes*. Notre Dame, Ind.: Notre Dame University Press.
Derrida, Jacques
1974 *Of Grammatology*. Baltimore: Johns Hopkins University Press.
Dumont, Louis
1980 *Homo Hierarchicus*. Chicago: University of Chicago Press.
Freire, Paulo
1993 *Pedagogy of the Oppressed*. New York: Continuum.
Furtado, Celso
1965 *The Economic Growth of Brazil*. Berkeley: University of California Press.
Kant de Lima, Roberto
1992 "The Anthropology of the Academy: When We Are the Indians." In David Hess and Linda Layne, eds., *Knowledge and Society*. Vol. 9, *The Anthropology of Science and Technology*. Greenwich, Conn.: JAI Press. (Translation of *A Antropologia da Academia: Quando os Indios Somos Nós*. Niterói: UFF; Petrópolis: Vozes.)
Lindesmith, A. R. and Anselm Strauss
1950 "A Critique of Culture-Personality Writings." *American Sociological Review* 15: 587–600.
Nisbet, Robert
1968 "Tocqueville, Alexis de." In David Sills (ed.), *International Encyclopedia of the Social Sciences*. Vol. 16. New York: Macmillan and Free Press.
Turner, Victor
1974 *Dramas, Fields, and Metaphors*. Ithaca: Cornell University Press.
Varenne, Hervé
1984 "Collective Representation in American Anthropological Conversation: Individual and Culture." *Current Anthropology* 25(3): 281–299.

One

Brazilian Styles

of

Social Relations

⊠

By "social relations" I refer to the informal, face-to-face side of society that involves people in action. In contrast, the term "social structure" includes class, race, gender, and other large structural aspects of a society. For a personalistic society such as Brazil, social relations are a good place to start. Barbosa's essay on the *jeitinho* is also a good starting point because the *jeitinho* is a national institution dedicated to personalism. Barbosa carefully explains her methodology, which is to explore the cultural meaning of the *jeitinho* rather than to explain it sociologically. She argues that Brazilians see the *jeitinho* as universal and democratic because everyone can have recourse to it. Unlike the "Do you know who you're talking to?" the *jeitinho* is not a resource of the powerful or connected who wish to impose hierarchy on the situation. Rather, the *jeitinho* is more a resource of the unconnected that encourages people to see themselves as all equal. Barbosa refers to this equality as human or biological, that is, the kind of equality to which we can all appeal as people who sometimes get stuck in bad situations and need help.

The paradox of the jeitinho, however, is that it is generally used in formal situations, such as getting help from a bureaucrat, and it involves bending rules. In this sense, the jeitinho implies subverting rules that are meant to be applied fairly and equally to everyone, and it can be a corrupting force on those institutions that are, at least on paper, modern, universal, and egalitarian. However, the reality in Brazil is that nothing is as it is on paper, and formal institutions tend to be the place where services are dealt out based on access and privilege. Thus, the institutions that in North America and Western Europe are often scenes of fairly egalitarian and universal treatment—such as waiting in line to get a driver's license—may in Brazil turn out to be places where exactly the opposite occurs. In this situation, the jeitinho can be an equalizing and humanizing institution, even as it contributes to the reproduction of hierarchy and personalism.

Kottak's essay explores another side of the complex nature of Brazilian social relations. One would expect that competitive swimming meets would be a premier site for a modern style of social relations. After all, individuals meet together to compete in a race, and the rules are applied fairly and equally for all. One cannot imagine a more perfect image of a level playing field than a still swimming pool before a race. However, Kottak also shows that Brazilian attitudes toward time enter into the area of competitive swimming to make for some important cultural differences between Brazil and the United States. In short, Brazilian swimmers pay less attention to clock time than do their American counterparts, and instead they pay more attention to who wins. In the United States, winning is important, but swimmers also keep track of their time. As a result, they are racing not only against other people but also against themselves. American swimmers live in a world of continual improvement, a prospect that resonates well with a Protestant culture that emphasizes self-betterment. In Brazil, racing is more relational: one is racing against the other people in the meet, not against oneself. Swimmers therefore do not walk away from meets with a sense of accomplishment against their own best times; everything is contingent on the relational status of winning or losing.

The attitude toward time in the Brazilian swim meets is characteristic of Brazilian and Latin American attitudes toward time in general. It is worth flagging this issue because it will reappear in some of the other essays. Brazil is generally known as "polychronic," that is, a culture in which people sometimes juggle more than one thing at a time, and time is subordinate to personal relationships. As Jarrad describes for the Alcoholics Anonymous meetings in Brazil and as others have noticed in a number of contexts, meetings are often delayed until the right people arrive, and they end when the leaders have said what they want to say. The idea of holding a meeting from, say, 7:15 to 8:30, and beginning and ending on time, is almost unheard of in Brazil. That pattern is more a product of a "monochronic" culture such as the United States, in which social relationships are subordinated to time. In Brazil, time is subordinated to the social; the clock waits for people instead of people waiting for the clock (see Hall and Hall 1987, 1990; Kant de Lima 1992). Thus, clock time is another example of a modern institution that is reshaped in Brazilian culture.

Kottak's essay is also valuable because he demystifies some popular ideas about social difference and sports performances. For example, the poor performance of athletes from countries such as Brazil in international competitions such as the Olympics is usually attributed to poverty. Kottak argues that cultural factors also intervene. For example, Brazilian swimmers do not get as many chances to compete for reasons that include fewer meets, fewer races per meet, and more stringent cutoff times. Furthermore, Kottak notes that in the case of the 1984 Olympics the Brazilian Olympic Committee did not send any women because none had passed the arbitrarily established cutoff times. Another misconception that Kottak debunks is the biological argument that people sometimes give for why some races and ethnic groups are better in some sports. Kottak shows that in Brazil the poor children, including many people of color, have greater access to swim clubs, and as a result their participation in swimming as a sport is much greater than in the United States.

Prado's essay rounds out this section on social relations by pointing to some of the ways in which personalism and individualism vary within Brazilian society. She notes that in the small town of Cunha, São Paulo, where she did fieldwork, the dialectic of personalism and individualism is tilted much more toward the former than in big cities. People in Cunha look toward the larger town of Guará, and beyond it to the big cities of Rio and São Paulo, as more individualistic places. Likewise, local-level politics tends to be guided very much by personal networks and loyalties, but state and higher-level politics are less influenced by personalism. Finally, she notes that the people of Cunha look to the past as a time when there were more festivals and a greater sense of community, both of which suggest that personalism and hierarchy may be changing over time (or at least that people think they are changing).

Thus, in a number of ways, Prado points to how analytic categories such as personalism need to be qualified by rural/urban differences and time period. She points to the geographical diversity of Brazilian society, and she shows a method for analyzing that diversity. Rather than sending out a survey to everyone or interpreting texts that are published nationally, Prado shows the power of doing fieldwork in a small town. From there, she can show how people in the community understand differences of space, social level, and time as part of their way of life. For those readers who have some experience living in small towns, it may be interesting to think through the similarities and differences between their experience and that of the people of Cunha.

References

Hall, Edward T. and Mildred Reed Hall
    1987 *Hidden Differences*. Garden City, N.Y.: Doubleday/Anchor.
    1990 *Understanding Cultural Differences*. Yarmouth, Maine: Intercultural Press.
Kant de Lima, Roberto
    1992 "The Anthropology of the Academy: When We Are the Indians." In David Hess and Linda Layne (eds.), *Knowledge and Society*. Vol. 9, *The Anthropology of Science and Technology*. Greenwich, Conn.: JAI Press. (Translation of *A Antropologia da Academia: Quando os Indios Somos Nós*. Niterói: UFF; Petrópolis: Vozes.)

Chapter One

The Brazilian Jeitinho:
An Exercise in National Identity

⊠

Lívia Neves de H. Barbosa

This paper analyzes from two different perspectives a typical Brazilian institution or social mechanism called the *jeitinho* (jay-tchee'-nyoo). The first perspective treats this "institutional bypass" as a ritual or social drama in the sense proposed by Roberto DaMatta (1991). Within this theoretical framework, a ritual is a displacement mechanism which brings into play a society's fundamental values. The second perspective uses this typical Brazilian social drama as a vehicle for a general inquiry into Brazilian national identity.

I begin the essay with a definition of *jeitinho* for an English-speaking audience, indicating its different uses. This is followed by a brief review of the relevant literature and methods of research. In the following sections, I analyze the meaning that this social mechanism has for Brazilian society, and I discuss the *jeitinho* in terms of the theoretical frameworks of Dumont (1977, 1978, 1980) and DaMatta (1987, 1991). In the final section I analyze why this social drama was chosen as an element of our national identity and what values it dramatizes when it is used for defining Brazil as a nation and its people.

Definitions and Theoretical Background

Anyone who wants to understand Brazilian society will eventually learn the meaning of the terms *jeitinho* and *jeitinho brasileiro*. In order to perceive and understand the subtlety of our social system, this knowledge will prove to be

This article is based on research that is presented in more detail in my book *O Jeitinho Brasileiro* (1992).

indispensable. Although very similar, the two expressions refer to and are used in different situations in our everyday life. The *jeitinho* is predominantly linked to a specific way of asking for things in the context of a social drama, and *jeitinho brasileiro* always refers to a way of defining Brazil as a nation and Brazilians as a people.

There is no precise translation in English for this idiomatic Brazilian expression. It can be defined, in a very broad sense, as a fast, efficient, and last-minute way of accomplishing a goal by breaking a universalistic rule and using instead one's informal social or personal resources. "The land of the *jeitinho*" or "*jeitinho brasileiro*" (Brazilian *jeitinho*) is a way of identifying Brazil by using as the main reference point this particular mechanism for by-passing rules and getting things done. However, it is also worth noting that both expressions, *jeitinho* and *jeitinho brasileiro*, are used in formal and technical settings as well as in the informal side of Brazilian society. Furthermore, the two expressions can be used to emphasize either positive or negative aspects of the Brazilian social system, depending on one's point of view.

There is no possible English translation for the expression *dar um jeitinho*. "To pull a string" or "to cut through the red tape" are the most similar idiomatic expressions that I can find. However, neither expression implies breaking rules or using personal resources. Thus, in order to clarify more the meaning of the expression *jeitinho*, I will give some examples:

A young man goes to a government agency to request some documents. The clerk explains that he will only be able to get the documents after five days. The young man explains to the clerk that he needs the papers very badly in order to get a job, and then he asks if the clerk could not "give a *jeitinho*." The clerk tells him that he will talk to the boss and see what he can do. After a few minutes, the clerk comes back and tells the young man to come back the next day to get the papers.

A young woman gets lost in an unfamiliar neighborhood. She asks for advice from a firefighter whom she meets in the street. The man explains to her how to get where she wants to go. He tells her to turn left and then "give a *jeitinho*" by taking the second left turn and going the wrong way down a one-way street. He explains that this will make things easier for her and that everybody does it anyway.

It is important to notice two points in these examples. First, the *jeitinho* can be asked for and it can be given. Second, the arguments and the values involved in both examples are of the same ideological nature. These points will be developed in more detail in the course of the essay.

Although widely used and practiced, this important informal Brazilian institution has not aroused much interest among social scientists. A broad literature search yielded only five texts about the topic written between 1940 and 1979, ranging from social essays to humorous comments about this "Brazilian way of doing things" (see Abreu 1982, Campos 1966, Ramos 1966, Rosen 1971, Torres 1973). This almost total absence of studies of the *jeitinho* can be explained, at least in part, by the lack of theoretical importance that has been attributed to the study of everyday life in general. Brazilian historical and social studies have tended to focus on macro social processes such as race relations at the beginning of the century or economic and political structures from the 1950s to the present.

However different in styles, the existing works on the *jeitinho* have points in common regarding some basic interpretations of it. First, almost all the texts try to establish links between the *jeitinho* and some distant and vague aspects of the Brazilian process of colonization, such as the humanistic and general educational legacy of the Jesuits or the Catholic dogmatism of the Portuguese authoritarian tradition. Seen as part of our colonial history, the *jeitinho* is then conceived of as a Portuguese legacy. Consequently, it is seen as something that has always been a part of Brazilian society. Another common ground in these studies is their explicitly evolutionary perspective. They see the *jeitinho* as a survival of old structures, an underdeveloped trace from the past that will wither away with economic and technical growth. A third common point is the exclusive emphasis that the studies place on the structural and functional aspects of the *jeitinho*, without reference to its symbolic meaning. All the authors interpret the *jeitinho* as a flexible mechanism that allows adjustments to the perverted social and economic conditions of Brazilian society. At the same time, they also see it as conveying costs and benefits to everyone. Finally, all the authors consider the *jeitinho* as a typical Brazilian institution.

Although rich and suggestive, the conclusions reached by most of the authors fail to address fundamental issues. Why and how, for instance, did the *jeitinho* become transformed from an ordinary social drama to a central element in the social construction of our national identity? If the *jeitinho* is a mechanism that is used to soothe perverted social and economic conditions, why it is used in situations where these perversions are not present? Why, we might also ask, is the *jeitinho* more present today in the media and daily speech than ever before, after two decades of intensive growth and considerable modernization in our society?

I would argue that the answers to all those questions depend on the adoption of a different methodological approach. Instead of giving priority to the structural setting of the *jeitinho* or its functional aspects, our attention should also be focused on the analysis of its symbolic meaning. The key question would then become: which values does the *jeitinho* put into play? What guides its use in the Brazilian social context? What does it mean as a ritual? What does it mean when it is used as part of narratives of national identity?

Investigating the *jeitinho*'s symbolic meaning implies, at first, distinguishing it as a social fact from other social mechanisms that are similar to it. It is possible to delineate similar mechanisms in other societies in which friendship, empathy, idiosyncratic characteristics, and personal relationships are activated to intervene or solve certain social dramas that are not unique to Brazilian society. Bourdieu (1963), for example, identifies a similar social institution known as the "chtara" among the working class of Algeria (see also MacFarlane 1978). However, what is peculiar about the *jeitinho* is the recognition of the social mechanism as a native category that clearly identifies the spaces and processes that are situated between favor and corruption, and between what is socially desirable and what actually happens in practice. The fact that most if not all societies have similar mechanisms of social adjustment does not imply that they recognize the mechanisms in an explicit way. For this to happen, it is necessary to attribute a value or symbolic weight to these practices.

Approached from this point of view, it is possible to analyze the question of the Brazilian character of the *jeitinho*. Brazilians might say, "You can find the *jeitinho* all over the world," or "No other country has this special way of dealing with things," but both perspectives are inaccurate because they share an essentialist interpretation of the *jeitinho*. These expressions confer on the *jeitinho* an essence, and they reveal a tendency to see other countries through indigenously Brazilian categories. Thus, there *is* a uniquely Brazilian aspect to the *jeitinho*, but it is not as a social practice. Rather, it is as a uniquely recognized institution and value configuration.

Thus, it is important to recognize that the *jeitinho* and *jeitinho brasileiro*, although intimately linked, are not the same. When the terms are used they refer to different values and aspects of Brazilian social life. As a social drama, the *jeitinho* is a privileged moment of our social reality in which we express our most fundamental values. On the other hand, the *jeitinho brasileiro* is an element that is considered to be paradigmatic in certain definitions of national identity; it is a specific way of speaking about our country and our national identity.

An Anthropological Interpretation of the Jeitinho

In order to explore the meaning of the *jeitinho* in the terms suggested above, I developed an ethnographic study of the social institution and its ideology. The research relied on questionnaires and interviews, as well as an analysis of written sources (newspapers, television, popular music, and fiction). More than 150 informants—representing a wide variety of people in terms of class, income, education, age, religion, and geographic origin—were interviewed.

Rather than develop a quantitative or statistical analysis of the data, I drew on the interpretive methods of cultural anthropology to develop an analysis of the *jeitinho* as a social institution and ideology. The analysis operated on three different levels. First, I mapped out the occurrences of the *jeitinho* in our society with the goal of developing an understanding of its particular social grammar. In other words, I developed a map of which situations, social characters, and domains of society were appropriate markers for the use of the *jeitinho*. At the second level, I analyzed the different symbolic representations that are attached to the social drama. At the third level, I compared the *jeitinho* with another important Brazilian social drama, the ritual known as "Do you know who you're talking to?" (DaMatta 1991).

Regarding the first level of analysis, several factors emerged as consistent preconditions for the successful deployment of the *jeitinho*. The factors centered on the general understanding of the *jeitinho* as having a universally democratic character. According to most people, the *jeitinho* is well-known and used by all persons, regardless of their economic and social position. As one of my informants noted, "Everybody uses it, from the clerk to the president." Yet, regardless of social status, there were consistent "rules" that everyone has to follow if they are to "get" or "receive" a *jeitinho*. For example, the majority of the informants consider that the way in which a person asks for the *jeitinho* to be fundamental to a successful outcome. The manner must be sympathetic, kind, and egalitarian, and never arrogant or authoritarian, because the strength of the social mechanism derives directly from the values on which it is based. In order to be successful, the request has to be done in a situation pervaded by an ethos of moral equivalency between the parties involved. The popular philosophy behind the process is the notion of life's variability: "Today someone else is in trouble, but tomorrow it could be me."

Although my informants explained that the *jeitinho* is available to everyone, they also felt that status, money, and personal relations were important assets for getting a positive response to the request for a *jeitinho*. Yet, the influence of these assets depends on the way they are manipulated. To use the social assets in an aggressive and coercive manner—that is, by trying to establish some type of social hierarchy—is the easiest way to make everything go down the drain. A rich person who behaves as people imagine a rich person will behave has a big chance of getting "no" for an answer. Status and money are very important social assets, but only insofar as they are used in a way that indicates their unworthiness for the person who is requesting the *jeitinho*.

It is also very important to emphasize that Brazilians distinguish the *jeitinho* from related social practices such as corruption or favor. In fact, the *jeitinho* seems to occupy a midpoint between the two. The *jeitinho* differs from corruption because it does not necessarily entail any kind of monetary gain or influence peddling. Unlike corruption, the *jeitinho* involves a way of talking with the other person, a special ethos, and a sense of special relationships. Likewise, the favor generates a sense of direct reciprocity and a hierarchical difference between givers and takers. The person who receives a favor is in debt to the person who gives it, and it is understood that the receiver will reciprocate as soon as the opportunity arrives. In contrast, the *jeitinho* seems to ignite a diffuse sense of reciprocity, and it implies no hierarchy between givers and takes. Another fundamental distinction, according to the persons interviewed, is that the favor is a more restricted social category, because we do not request favors from everybody.

The second level of analysis, the investigation of symbolic representations attached to the *jeitinho*, involved an analysis of the opposing ways that people perceive and interpret the social mechanism. In general, people tend to view the *jeitinho* either positively or negatively, and often the two interpretations overlap or are not mutually exclusive. The same person can make use of one or the other interpretation of the *jeitinho* according to the social framework or background against which it is considered. When the emphasis is on the sphere of personal relations in Brazilian society, people tend to see it as a healthy, human, and positive institution. From this perspective, the *jeitinho* is a flexible way of dealing with the surprises of daily life, a way of humanizing the rules that takes into account the moral equality and social inequalities of persons in the society. However, when the perspective shifts from personal relations to the level of politics and economics, the *jeitinho* emerges as the result of the vicious and perverse Brazilian social structure. Yet, both the positive and the negative perspectives share a framework that locates the *jeitinho* in the context of a conflict between human equality and the inequalities of society.

The third level of the ethnographic analysis focused more on the semantics of the *jeitinho*. This analysis was accomplished through a comparison with another well-known Brazilian social drama or institution known as "Do you know who you're talking to?" As DaMatta (1991) has discussed, this ritual is used by powerful or well-connected people who wish to pull rank on others of inferior social status who are simply following the rules. For example, when stopped by a police officer, a rich person might say how s/he has connections high up in the local government or police department, and ask, "Do you know who you're talking to?" The police officer, afraid of repercussions, may then decide not to issue the ticket.

I compared the grammar of the two mechanisms—when, how, and with whom they are used—and the system of social representations that are attached to them. As a result, it was possible to identify very important similarities and differences. From the perspective of our value system, the "Do you know who you're talking to?" is based on a hierarchical world view, whereas the *jeitinho* presents a doubly ideological character.

To begin, the *jeitinho* uses a way of talking and a set of values that emphasizes equality. It does not use authority and power, it is accessible to everyone within the society, and the positive outcome of a request for a *jeitinho* does not depend in any necessary way on one's social assets. In short, the *jeitinho* works as a equalizing ritual. Yet, at another level, the *jeitinho* is similar to "Do you know" in that both transform a situation of the individual (and universalistic values) into a situation of the person (and particularistic values). Both illustrate a social drama where the people involved refuse to abide by a universal and impersonal rule that requires them to perform a specific role, that of the citizen. Both are devices that imply the change from a universalistic role to a particularistic one, which is seen as more desirable and considered encompassing in that situation.

However, there are also some important differences between the two social mechanisms. "Do you know" erects a barrier to the adoption of more modern values, where the individual (in Dumont's sense, 1980) is the normative subject of all institutions in Western society. In contrast, the duplicity of the *jeitinho* suggests a complex relationship between the hierarchical and individualistic world view. In a sense, the *jeitinho* reconciles the principle of equality with the personalistic approach conceived and expected within the framework of hierarchical values. It does that by displacing one set of values from one social setting to another where new meanings are attributed to it. From this perspective, the *jeitinho* is not a shadow from the past, but a social mechanism borne out of the impact of modernizing values on traditional ones.

My hypothesis is that this social drama acquired its actual meaning as a consequence of a peculiar historical process. The "modernization" process that Brazilian society has undergone and the set of values attached to it have gone through a different process of reading at the symbolic level. More emphasis was placed on the notion of equality than on freedom. The individual, as a social creation, was related, predominantly, to a moral whole instead of to a social one, as has happened in other societies, such as the United States. In order to develop these ideas in more detail, I will turn to the work of the anthropologist Louis Dumont on hierarchical and modern societies.

The Jeitinho and Brazilian Notions of Equality

Dumont (1980) distinguishes between two broad types of societies, modern and traditional. The first has as its main characteristic the notion of the individual as a social creation around whom the whole social universe is built. The individual's basic attributes are the values of freedom and equality. In contrast, in traditional societies such as rural India, the basic principle is the notion of hierarchy. The ideas of complementarity and difference are the basis of the entire social order. Society is pervaded by a holistic perspective.

Dumont also distinguishes between the empirical or *natural* individual, a member of the human species, and the individual as a value—a typical and recent creation of Western society. This second conception of the individual and the basic role it assumes within Western society are, according to Dumont, a product of a peculiar and recent historical development. Western society is the only one to be built around the individual as a value. In contrast, traditional societies are based on the notion of totality. The social universe is conceived as a whole and functions like one. In the first type, the individual's personal life is the final end of the whole system, and the social universe is the means to reaching the end. In the second type, society is at the center of the system, and the individual's personal life is the means to maintain it.

Linked to each of these societies, there are two basic social actors, entirely different from each other: the individual and the person (persona). The social universe of the first type is made up of universalizing and impersonal rules, of voluntary political association and friendship. There are no spheres of mediation between it and the totality. Although the person is implicit in Dumont's work, the typical social actor of traditional societies was developed fully by DaMatta (1991). The entire set of mediating contacts with social reality are made through different types of spheres (clan, lineage, family, etc.). There is no free political association and the whole system is based on a relational worldview. Whereas the individual is defined by performance, the person is defined by a social network. According also to DaMatta (1991), in addition to the two broad types of society defined by Dumont we could include a third: the semitraditional. Its main characteristic is the combination, within its social universe, of these two types of ideology and social characters. DaMatta considers Brazilian society to be an example of this third type. He also argues that it is characterized by a social dilemma that is expressed through the tension between the individual and the person.

In Brazil, the universal and impersonal perspective of the law is the encompassing value in certain spheres, mainly at the representational level. In daily life, however, it is displaced by the logic of personal relations. The individual, as a social creation, and its main attributes—freedom and equality—are always competing with the person and its relational worldview. This means that a higher value is attributed to social relations than to the individuals who participate in them. This last aspect is fundamental. Modernity attributes intrinsic value to all elements of a system, despite their relations to each other. However, the attribution of intrinsic value to all individuals, independently of their social relations, as would be the case within a strictly modern framework, is very difficult in Brazil. Performance is always bypassed or combined with a person's "social capital." This makes our social universe idiosyncratic. When we analyze it more closely, we perceive the existence of a series of informal institutions that accommodate the tension among the social actors. The *jeitinho* can be seen as one of them.

I would therefore like to suggest another perspective in this theoretical discussion. It is my view that the individualistic ideology, as analyzed by Dumont (1980), of which the best example is the United States, is only one possible expression. Different historical developments could have resulted in different and indigenous readings of this same set of values. Freedom, equality, and the individual as a social creation could be interpreted in different ways and be related to other types of wholes. Even the pattern of relationship among them could have undergone changes. Brazilian society could be, in my interpretation, one of these instances.

It is beyond doubt that the individual as a social category is well-established as the central actor of the Brazilian symbolic system and social institutions. It is around the citizen that the public, political, and legal systems are built. The individual is also the central figure in middle-class political statements and in intellectual circles, and it is the key character of our economic institutions. Furthermore, in all these instances the only whole which restricts the actions of the individual is society, conceived of as a nation. Its universal rules are the most clear expressions of the idea of equality among citizens.

However, at other levels of our social system the individual, as the narrative subject of our institutions, is replaced by the person, which is the central reference point of each situation and is located in reference to the moral whole of society. In this context, legal equality cedes its place to moral equality, which is defined in the context of another order that encompasses even society. Brazilians therefore think of themselves as equal not because a legal order defines them as such, but because a more encompassing system defines them as morally equal in terms of their common biological membership in the human species. Phrases such as "Rich or poor, everybody is the same," "My blood is as red as his," and "After death everybody ends up in the same place—beneath the earth" all express the idea that the shared biological and physical constitution provides us with a modicum of equality.

This notion of equality appears more as a fact than as a right. Furthermore, it is the double nature of equality in Brazil—as a fact and as a right—that makes it possible for people to transgress or circle around the universal and egalitarian rules. In other words, they rely on a principle of equality—but a substantive, biological one rather than a modern, legal one—to justify the *jeitinho* as a social drama. The *jeitinho* transforms one form of equality into another. Everybody has the right of equal treatment by government agencies. However, individuals in a hurry who expose their personal drama to one of our public servants can move to the front of the line. This is not viewed as unfair favoritism because everybody can understand the personal drama of the person who has a special problem, and also because everybody supposes that they can be in a similar situation someday.

Ironically, the Brazilian ideology of a radical, substantive equality does not allow any kind of hierarchizing based on merit or other universalistic criteria, as in more fully modern societies. In the end, the Brazilian ideology of equality nullifies what it was intended to value: the individual.

The Jeitinho Brasileiro and National Identity

National identity is a particular type of social identity that refers to a specific country or national society. It is a terminal identity in Epstein's sense (1978), because it encompasses a whole series of specific identities (ethnic, regional, occupational, gender, etc.). However, this does not mean that national identity is the most important identity that a person can build or develop. It is just one type of identity, among a great number of possible choices, that a person can manipulate. It shows up in specific moments, when the country (in our case, Brazil) is put into question. That is why the process involved in constructing national identity is always linked to aspects such as nationalism, citizenship, and so on. It is through national identity that we define ourselves as citizens and the country we belong to, in the face of similar geographical and political units. In this specific moment, all other social identities are encompassed by the national identity.

National identity is not always a positive identity, as, for example, in the case where Brazilians get emotionally excited as they root for their country in the World Cup matches. On the contrary, national identity can be negative, as when Brazilians frequently state that they are ashamed of being part of Brazil. A perfect example of this is when the *jeitinho brasileiro* is used to define us as a backward country with respect to the First World (as in the phrase, "This country has no solutions") or as a "real banana republic." In instances such as those, Brazilian society is homogenized from a negative perspective.

Another important aspect of national identity (similar to ethnic and gender identity) is that it characterizes what people *are* rather than what they *do*, as in the case of occupational identities such as blue collar or white collar. From this perspective, Schneider's (1968) concept of the desocialization of the ethnic group can be applied to national identity as well. The national status is entirely devoid of any specific social content. No one needs to learn a specific and elaborate role in order to be a Brazilian. In this sense, the differentiating signs of identity are devoid of elaborate social distinctions, which allow them to function freely in the social system, and simultaneously to maintain a symbolically distinctive social identity.

In a similar way, the *jeitinho brasileiro* is a way of defining *brasilidade* ("Brazilianness"). When we classify certain types of action or behavior as the *jeitinho*, or when we define Brazil as the land of the *jeitinho*, we are dissolving internal diversity—be it ethnic, gender, or occupational—and we are adopting instead a homogenizing category that defines millions of people. At the same time, we bring together a great variety of geographical, political, and sociocultural units, with innumerable distinctions, under a single rubric that locates us on a broad international scene of nation-states.

As a symbol of national identity, the *jeitinho brasileiro* focuses an entire way of perceiving Brazil and Brazilians. It also emphasizes the side of Brazilian society that privileges the *human* and *natural* aspects of social reality over the legal, political, and institutional ones. Thus, the *jeitinho brasileiro* expresses the cordial, conciliatory, happy, warm, and human spirit of a country that is young, tropical, sensual, beautiful, and full of possibilities. Those aspects are used for comparison with the Anglo-Saxons, mainly Americans, who are seen in just the opposite terms as cold, inflexible, and unemotional. In this context, our historical heritage is manipulated in a very positive way. Our racial mix, our climate, and the Portuguese manner of linking with other ethnic groups are seen as some of the possible causes for this way of being. In this sense, the *jeitinho brasileiro* promotes a positive sense of national identity.

In contrast, when the lens for seeing the *jeitinho brasileiro* is the performance of our economic, political, and legal institutions—especially in contrast with those of the developed countries—then the sense of national identity is highly negative. From this perspective, Brazilian society deviates greatly from the premises on which it is based, especially in regard to the main social actor—the individual or citizen. The *jeitinho brasileiro* then comes to represent all that must be ended in order for Brazil to become a truly modern society. Thus, when we condemn the *jeitinho brasileiro*, we call for the prevalence of impersonal and universal principles. What better exemplifies the tone of this negative identity than the famous phrase about Brazil attributed to the late French President Charles DeGaulle: "Ce n'est pas un pays sérieux" ("This is not a serious country"). The phrase is frequently used and plays a paradigmatic role in our negative self-attributions.

Why are we not a serious country? We are not reliable because we admit that friendship can have more value than the rule of law; because personal relations, once established, have precedence over any other criteria; because Brazilian citizens have several close relatives who do not allow them to reign absolute in their social universe. In summary we are not serious because the parameters of the individualistic ideology are bypassed at every moment in our social practice. Our relational worldview changes the public domain into the private and attributes legitimacy to what in other circumstances would be considered spurious. However, from the native's point of view, the structural force of our personal relations is not perceived as a fact to be taken in account in our perception and analysis of our society. It is seen more as a *feeling* residing outside the realm of dominant analytical models, which focus almost exclusively on our institutional structure.

In the context of this negative national identity, our historical heritage is seen in a very pessimistic tone. Our Portuguese roots speak for themselves. We descend from a country that was always seen as incompetent and inept in the conduct of its business and in our colonization. At the same time the Anglo-Saxon world is perceived exactly as the social universe we would like to be, in institutional terms. Unhappily, we are not like the Anglo-Saxons.

It seems clear to me, therefore, why the *jeitinho brasileiro* has come to play a role in the social construction of Brazilian national identity. Synthesizing our multiple and contradictory nature, it promotes, depending on how we use it, a positive or negative encompassment, without imposing exclusive and definitive choices. It is a symbol of our institutional disorientation, incompetence, and inefficiency as much as it is a symbol of our cordiality, street smarts, and conciliatory character. It reasserts our eternal marriage with a relational and traditional worldview and our equally unending affair with an individualistic and modern ideology.

References

Abreu, Clovis
    1982 "O Jeitinho Brasileiro como um Recurso de Poder." *Revista de Administração Pública*. Rio de Janeiro: Fundação Getúlio Vargas.
Barbosa, Lívia Neves de H.
    1992 *O Jeitinho Brasileiro, ou a Arte de Ser Mais Igual que os Outros*. Rio de Janeiro: Editora Campus.
Bourdieu, Pierre
    1963 *Travail e travaileurs en Algerie*. Paris: La Maye, Mouton.
Campos, Roberto de Oliveira
    1966 "A Sociologia do Jeito." In *A Técnica e o Riso*. Rio de Janeiro: Edições Apec.
DaMatta, Roberto
    1987 *A Casa e a Rua*. Rio de Janeiro: Guanabara.
    1991 *Carnivals, Rogues, and Heros: Toward a Sociology of the Brazilian Dilemma*. Notre Dame: University of Notre Dame Press.

Dumont, Louis

1977 *From Mandeville to Marx*. Chicago: University of Chicago Press.

1978 "La Conception modern du individu." In *Esprit: changer la culture et la politique*. Paris (14).

1980 *Homo Hierarchicus*. Chicago: University of Chicago Press.

Epstein, Arnold L.

1978 *Ethos and Identity: Three Studies in Ethnicity*. London: Tavistock and Aldine Publishing Co.

MacFarlane, Alan

1978 *The Origins of English Individualism*. Oxford: Basil Blackwell.

Ramos, Alberto Guerreiro

1966 *Administração e Estratégia do Desenvolvimento: Elementos de uma Sociologia Especial da Administração*. Rio de Janeiro: Fundação Getúlio Vargas.

Rosen, K. S.

1971 "Brazil's Institutional Bypass of the Formal Legal System and its Developmental Implications." *The American Journal of Comparative Law* 19: 516–49.

Schneider, David

1968 *American Kinship: A Cultural Account*. Englewood Cliffs, N.J.: Prentice Hall.

Torres, João Camilo de Oliveira

1973 *Interpretação da Realidade Brasileira*. Rio de Janeiro: José Olympio Editora.

Chapter Two

Swimming in
Cross-Cultural Currents

⊠

Conrad Phillip Kottak

Why do athletes from some countries excel at particular sports? Why do certain nations pile up dozens of Olympic medals while others win only a handful or none at all? It is not simply a matter of being rich or poor, developed or underdeveloped. Cultural values and social conditions also play a role in international success. The United States and Brazil, giants of the Western Hemisphere, with populations of 235 million and 135 million, respectively, offer a good contrast in Olympic success. Both are countries of almost continental proportions; both have people of ethnically diverse backgrounds, with roots in Europe, Africa, Asia, and Native America. Each is the major economic power of its continent. However, in the 1984 Summer Olympics, the United States won 174 medals, while Brazil managed only eight. The contrast was particularly noticeable in swimming, where the United States won 34 medals and Brazil one.

From early August 1983 to late August 1984, I was in Rio de Janeiro to set up a research project on the impact of nationwide commercial television on traditional Brazilian culture. Among other aspects of the project, I was interested in television sports coverage, but I also had a personal connection with swimming because my son is a competitive swimmer. During those thirteen months, I noticed many striking contrasts between Brazilian and American swimming. Since most successful international swimmers begin their training in childhood, a closer look at the cultural values affecting children's swimming may help us understand some of the reasons that the United States excels at that sport and Brazil does not.

The most obvious contrasts between competitive swimming in the

United States and Brazil have to do with different cultural attitudes toward time, which is valued more highly and calculated more carefully in the United States. Many Brazilians find the American obsession with time to be the outstanding contrast between the two cultures. Brazilians do not make appointments for such punctual times as 1:45 or 2:15, and they react suspiciously to the precision offered by digital watches. As they point out, delays are common in traffic-jammed cities such as Rio de Janeiro; no one arrives, or is expected to arrive, on time.

I have been following children's competitive swimming since my son, an age-group swimmer in the USS (United States Swimming, formerly AAU) program, was seven. (Age-group refers to the organization of most events by age-based categories: eight and under, nine–ten, eleven–twelve, thirteen–fourteen, and fifteen–sixteen. Age groups in the United States don't have ages similar to those of everyone else. In the tribal vocabulary, instead of being six or seven, one is "eight and under"; my son just turned "thirteen–fourteen.") During a period of six years, I have attended dozens of swimming practices and meets. I have discussed swimming with other parents and coaches, have chaired the swim committee of a local club, and have helped out at swimming meets. USS swim meets, which take place throughout the winter and summer, lead to state and national championships.

A swimmer's objective in a given meet is not just to win but to better his or her time. One's time for any event is always the fastest time yet achieved in that event. At a given meet, swimmers may participate in all events in which they have made certain cutoff times announced at the beginning of the season. There are A meets for swimmers who have achieved A cutoff times, B meets for those whose times are slower, and C events for the slowest. One's time for any event can only get better, never worse.

Within the swimmer's world, time is paramount. Even winners are disappointed if they do not better their times, since a new time means progress compared with other swimmers and a step toward state and national championships—and toward that final goal, Olympic gold and a new world record. I have watched small children sob on discovering that a win did not better their time. On the adult level, a gold-medal-winning American backstroker in the 1984 Summer Olympics reacted similarly when he won the finals without beating his own previously set world record.

Conversation among swimmers could be mistaken for chitchat at a convention of time and motion study experts, so frequent are the references to hundredths of a second. Kids who have not yet studied long division routinely reel off "19.16s" (nineteen and sixteen-hundredths seconds) and "35.97s." The most common question among American swimmers is probably, "What's your time for the 50 free?" Swimmers not only know their own times but also those of their teammates and their fiercest rivals.

It is easy to find out a swimmer's times. Just buy a mimeographed program at a meet. This program lists, by numbered event, the name of each swimmer and his or her time for each event. In this way, an American swimmer's times become public knowledge. Parents consult the program as they watch each event, comparing previous best times with those achieved that day. As they monitor their own child's performance, parents also comment favorably to other moms and dads whose children have done well. Parents sit in silent embarrassment or make audible excuses when their children do not match or better their former best times.

American children are motivated to keep on swimming because they know that even if they do not achieve a new time in one event that day, they might better their time in another. Because they are allowed to swim in as many events as they have A times (for an A meet) or B times (for a B meet), most swimmers usually have something to be happy about when they get home.

An American swimming meet closely mirrors the larger society in that most people have good and bad moments, strong and weak performances, and despite disappointments, generally find rewards. Swimming is a particularly appropriate sport for a competitive, achievement-oriented society in which lines of social class are not clearly and rigidly drawn. Status within the American swimmer's world is like the form of social organization that anthropologists call the chiefdom, common a century ago in the Polynesian islands. In the chiefdom, slight gradations in prestige and power, rather than demarcated social classes, meant that everyone had a distinctive social status, just a bit higher or lower than anyone else's. A swimmer's unique status is the end result of a complex scoring process that takes into account a series of constantly changing times in different events. Like a Polynesian, every swimmer has a social status slightly different from everyone else's.

Time, then, is the basis of social status in American swimming. Public recognition of excellent times is, in itself, a potent reward. The more tangible prizes—medals and ribbons—go to only a small number of finalists (normally six, eight, or twelve), but everyone has a best time.

Since precious commodities usually have guardians, the swimmer's world has guardians of time (for example, parents armed with the most modern stopwatches). Even when electronic timing pads are used, each lane always has two human timers. There are also finish judges to determine finish order in close races and, for important meets, winning-lane timers. At the end of each heat, times are written on cards, which are used to determine and list finish order, official times, and winners. The results of each race are posted one by one in the halls of the building (usually a high school) where the meet usually takes place. By consulting these sheets, parents can compare their children's times with previous bests and with those of other swimmers. In this way the adult members of the society monitor whether their young are keeping up with their peers and whether they are bettering themselves in terms of the values emphasized in American culture, including individual achievement and hard work.

Swimmer's times—these public, precious symbols of achievement—are tended, guarded, enshrined in print, and transmitted from local to state to national levels, where they are used to establish rankings. The most important source of information about times and national rankings is the monthly magazine *Swimming World*. *Swimming World* also publishes results of meets held throughout the country, and sells a popular T-shirt proclaiming "I made it in *Swimming World*," an achievement that confers considerable prestige among fellow swimmers. The particularly American character of the swimmer's world just described emerges crystal clear when we consider the same sport in Brazil.

Before enrolling my son in a competitive swim program in Rio de Janeiro in 1983, I accepted the above procedure as part of swimming per se—not as an illustration of distinctive American cultural values. Even though I am accustomed to comparing American institutions and behavior with those of other cultures, I had not thought much about how swim programs might be run differently elsewhere or what the meets might tell me about different values and traditions. But striking differences between Brazilian and American swimming were soon apparent. First, Brazilian swim teams are associated with private, money-making professional clubs, such as the Fluminense Football (soccer) Club, for which my son swam. Most of the soccer clubs that battle for city, state, and national championships have divisions of amateur sports, which manage swimming, gymnastics, and other competitive programs for children.

The clubs are commercial organizations, rather than the high school, college, age-group, and sports-club teams that dominate competitive swimming in the United States. It was as though my son were swimming for the

Detroit Tigers. One of the tasks of the vice-president for amateur sports of a Brazilian club is to find rich sponsors, businesses or individuals, national or foreign, for the swim team. The soccer rivalry between such teams as Fluminense, Flamengo, and Vasco spills over into amateur sports. In Rio de Janeiro, swimmers and gymnasts play their own small parts in an ongoing battle for sports supremacy, and the system is similar in other Brazilian cities.

Daily practices are held in the Olympic-sized pools of the different clubs, and the competition is stiffer in a city of eight million than in the Detroit metropolitan area. Many Brazilian national champion age-group swimmers live in Rio, and their times (at least through the early teens) are comparable to those of top American swimmers. Cutoffs are much more stringent, however, and there are fewer meets—which means that swimmers lack opportunities to better their times and to gain experience.

Compared with the United States, Brazilian meets are badly organized. In the United States, meets are planned a year in advance; in Brazil, coaches often do not know until a day or two before the meet where it will be held, and sites are frequently changed at the last minute—for example, from a convenient pool a few blocks away to a suburb requiring an hour's drive. Cariocas (residents of Rio de Janeiro) are accustomed to associating with family and friends, but not with such strangers as the parents of their children's colleagues. There is no tradition of car pooling, and swimmers frequently miss meets because of last-minute changes. For American swimmers, to miss a meet is practically unheard of; mild illnesses or relatives' birthday parties are not acceptable excuses for letting down one's teammates. If one is scheduled to swim a relay, to miss a meet is considered especially unfair to other team members.

American swim meets almost always have relays—freestyle and medley (backstroke, breast stroke, butterfly, and freestyle, or crawl). Brazilian meets, however, rarely include relays; only one of the half dozen meets I attended in Rio had them. Perhaps relays are almost always a part of American meets because they embody key American values so well. The free relay is based on pure speed; it is the fastest of the races because everyone swims the fastest stroke, the crawl, normally called "the free."

The medley relays test speed through specialization; each of four specialized swimmers tries for a best time to bring his or her team in first. It shows specialized individuals working rapidly together, like an efficient industrial or managerial team. Making the relay through a best time is a valued achievement. In relays, the win is more important than in individual events.

Since relay members can change from week to week, swimmers have a less accurate recollection of relay times than personal ones. In these events, swimming celebrates certain American values: winning organization, competition through speed, efficiency, and specialization with other, similar groups. These values have spread out from the American economy to the larger society and are well represented in competitive swimming. In Brazil, the absence of relays helps focus attention on the individual win.

Even more noteworthy, however, than capricious meet planning and the absence of relays is the treatment of time in Brazilian swimming. In the United States, times are recorded electronically, as well as by people with stopwatches, and are publicly posted. In Brazil, however, times are not published in the mimeographed meet program. The swimmers' names and club affiliations are listed for each event, but their times are not. At first I supposed that, as in the United States, names were listed in an order established by prior best times and that the fastest swimmers swam in the last heat. After observing the results of several races in different meets, I learned this was not the case. Swimmers in the first or second heat were as likely to win as those in the last one.

Since times are not listed, parents and swimmers can concentrate only on who wins, not on who betters former times, which means that, rather than several possible winners, each event has only one. Public recognition of improvement—a key reward and powerful reason to keep on swimming—is missing. Nor are times publicly posted after each race. They are announced by loudspeaker after finish order is determined, beginning with the slowest swimmer and laboriously moving up to the winner—sometimes through twenty or thirty names. In this way parents and swimmers are reminded, not that many swimmers have improved, but that there are twenty times as many losers as winners.

Another feature of the Brazilian meet illustrates different cultural values about time. Where were the many guardians of time? I saw no attentive parents with stopwatches; there were no frantic winning-lane timers. Each lane had a single timer—even when the electronic pads were not working. And, since timers often chatted as swimmers raced home, times were occasionally lost, an unheard-of occurrence in USS swimming. Times are not gathered, tended, and cherished as in the United States. This is one of the many symbolic statements in the swimmer's world of the different values attached to time in the cultures of the two Western giants.

Brazilian coaches do keep track of their swimmers' times, which they use to determine who will swim what events in the next meet. But in contrast to USS swimming, in which kids are normally entered in all races for which they have made cutoff times, in Brazil they are limited to three of four races. This further reduces their opportunities for meet experience.

Why are there so few opportunities to swim competitively in Brazil? One reason is the absence of public school, particularly high school, athletic programs. Another is the reduced level of parental involvement in organizing and running meets, compared with that in the United States. There are simply too few volunteers to provide the needed chances to compete, particularly in a city of eight million where thousands of young people train as swimmers.

The pattern of stiff cutoffs and restricted competition is persistent and has unfortunate consequences for Brazil in international competition. For example, the Brazilian Olympic Committee did not send female swimmers to Los Angeles in 1984 because none had made arbitrarily established cutoffs. This excluded a South American record holder, while swimmers with no better times were attending the Olympics as representatives of other South American countries. The attitude was that only swimmers who had made the cutoffs had any chance to place in Los Angeles. No one imagined that the power of Olympic excitement might spur swimmers to extraordinary efforts. During television coverage of the 1984 South American Championships, held in Rio, I was aghast to hear commentators downgrade chances that any Brazilian other than Ricardo Prado might win a medal. More than once I heard this comment about a new champion: "He doesn't have a chance to win at Los Angeles because his time isn't good enough"—as though it could never get better.

American coverage, in contrast, dotes on unexpected results, showing adherence to an American sports credo: "It's not over till it's over." In Brazil, the credo seems to be "It's over before it's begun."

Winning, of course, is an important American cultural value, and this is particularly true for college and professional team sports like football, basketball, and baseball. Football coaches are fond of making such comments as "Winning isn't a good thing; it's the only thing" and "Show me a good loser and I'll show you a loser." For sports such as running and swimming, however, in which the focus is on the individual, American culture also recognizes and admires moral victories, personal bests, comeback athletes, and special Olympics, and commends those who run good races without finishing first. In amateur sports, personal improvement can be as important as winning.

Americans have been told so many times that their culture overemphasizes winning that they may find it hard to believe that Brazilians seem to value winning even more. Prior to the 1984 Summer Olympics, swimmer Ricardo Prado (instead of the eventual Brazilian gold medalist, Joaquim Cruz) was touted by the media as Brazil's most likely gold medal winner (he was a silver medalist). Prado had won 200- and 400-meter individual medley (IM) events in the 1983 Pan American Games and, until 1984, held the world record for the 400 IM. Commenting on his massive press coverage, Prado observed that only winning athletes were noticed in Brazil—only number ones, never number twos. He blasted the press for formerly neglecting his achievements and those of other Brazilian swimmers who were not, or not yet, world record holders.

Perhaps Brazilians value winning so much because it is so rare. In USS swimming, the focus on times means there are always multiple winners. This may be the key to the relationship of swimming to cultural values. In American society, where poverty is less pervasive, resources more abundant, social classes less marked, opportunities for achievement more numerous, and individual social mobility easier than in Brazil, there can be multiple winners. Brazilian society is more stratified; a much smaller middle class and elite group makes up at most thirty percent of the population. Brazilian swimming echoes lessons from the larger society: victories are scarce and reserved for the few.

But there is another dimension to the relationship between competitive swimming and society. Even in the United States the opportunity to swim competitively is limited, generally to people of the middle class and above. To swim seriously in America requires money, time, and parental involvement. American children begin swimming competitively for sports clubs or country clubs, which have membership fees. Success in summer swimming may then lead them to join Y or USS programs, for winter competition. The United States is an automobile-oriented culture. Cars and parents' time are necessary to drive to practices and meets. During Michigan winters, in order to arrive at distant meets for 8:00 a.m. warmups, my son and I have sometimes spent the night in a motel. Swimmers' parents have money to spend on gas, food, lodging, and club memberships. Children whose parents can afford to belong to clubs are more likely to get interested in swimming in the first place.

In Brazil the situation is somewhat different. Public transportation is better in Brazilian cities than in most parts of the United States. There is less residential segregation of rich and poor, black and white. Given the dense urban populations and that the major soccer clubs—and therefore their swimming pools—are located right in the city, poor kids, including black children, can work out as swimteam members almost as easily as children from middle-class families. As a result, in contrast to the United States, where it is rare to see a black swimmer at a USS meet or in a state championship, swimmers with dark skins and fast times are present at virtually any Carioca swimming meet.

Some Americans think that black and whites excel in particular sports because of biological and physiological differences, but Brazil, which has proportionately as many blacks as the United States, demonstrates that sports abilities reflect culture rather than biology. When blacks have opportunities to do well in swimming, soccer, or tennis, they are physically capable of doing as well as whites. In schools, parks, and city playgrounds in the United States, blacks have access to baseball diamonds, basketball courts, football fields, and tracks. However, because of restricted economic opportunities, black families have traditionally lacked the resources to invest in hockey or ski equipment or join clubs with tennis courts and swimming pools. But as Brazilian swimming demonstrates, when these opportunities are available, blacks do well.

Here then is a different way in which the swimmer's world provides a microcosm of the surrounding culture. Despite the emphasis in the United States on the possibility of rising through hard work and individual achievements, in swimming, as in society, success is easiest for those who are better off to begin with.

What can we conclude about the different cultural models for competitive swimming? Perhaps the more relaxed approach to swimming encountered in Brazil reflects a culture in which there is less emphasis on time, measurement, comparison, and achievement. Brazilians may even experience fewer stresses and be happier because they live in a less competitive, less achievement-oriented society. Whatever the case, one thing is eminently clear: the United States is a better training ground than Brazil for international competitive swimming. As we know from years of Olympic games and a glance at today's world records, the countries that do best at swimming are the United States, Germany, and the former Soviet Union. State support of Russian and German swimmers is a powerful incentive for talented young people in those countries. Other nations that do well in international competition—Australia, Canada, Great Britain, the Netherlands—are more like the United States than Brazil in their cultural background and current socioeconomic conditions.

Despite pride in country, Brazilian swimmers know that it was not accidental that the South American giant could manage only one medal while its North American counterpart was winning thirty-four. Recognizing this, most of the Brazilian men who swam in the 1984 Olympics, including silver-medalist Ricardo Prado, are now training in the United States.

Acknowledgment

"Swimming in Cross-Cultural Currents" originally appeared as an article in *Natural History* (May 1985), copyright 1985 American Museum of Natural History, and is reprinted here with permission.

Endnote

Because *Natural History* addresses a general readership, the article was written not to include references. Country names such as Germany and the USSR have been updated. Readers interested in the author's work or the question of sports in Brazilian society might wish to consult the following references.

References

DaMatta, Roberto
    1988 "Hierarchy and Equality in Anthropology and World Sport." In Sin-pyo Kang, John MacAloon, and Roberto DaMatta (eds.), *The Olympics and Cultural Exchange*. Korea: The Institute for Ethnological Studies, Hanyang University.
DaMatta, Roberto (ed.)
    1982 *Universo de Futebol*. Rio de Janeiro: Edições Pinokotheke.
Kottak, Conrad P.
    1990 *Prime-Time Society: An Anthropological Analysis of Television and Culture*. Belmont: Wadsworth.
    1992 *Assault on Paradise: Social Change in a Brazilian Fishing Village*. 2d ed. New York: McGraw-Hill.
Levine, Robert
    1980 "Sport and Society: The Case of Brazilian Futebol." *Luzo-Brazilian Review* 17 (2).
Rodrigues, Mário Filho
    1964 *O Negro no Futebol Brasileiro*. Rio de Janeiro: Civilização Brasileira.

Chapter Three

Small Town, Brazil:
Heaven and Hell of Personalism

⊠

Rosane Prado

Much of the anthropological research on Brazilian national society, excluding the studies of peasant societies, is based on life in the big cities in the tradition that is known as "urban anthropology." It is therefore important to make sure that the emerging anthropology of national societies does not remain restricted to urban anthropology, and instead that it takes into account important differences that may exist between life in big cities and in small towns. This essay draws on fieldwork in one small town in southeastern Brazil—Cunha, São Paulo—to develop and expand the cultural interpretation of Brazilian national society. Briefly, I will show how in this small town, the cultural tension between individualism and personalism of the larger cities in Brazil becomes tilted toward personalism to such an extent that it is difficult to speak of individualism at all.

Background

This essay is drawn from my master's thesis (Prado 1987) that was based on fourteen months of fieldwork in Cunha from January 1985 to February 1986, and again in July and August of 1986. Cunha was chosen as a research site in part because it had already been studied twice before, first in the 1940s by Emilio Willems (1961) and again in the 1960s by Robert Shirley (1971). Thus, there was a rich background of historical and ethnographic research available for baseline comparisons. My fieldwork in Cunha, supported by a research project on the impact of television in rural Brazil, focused on the reaction of local women to the female characters that appear on the prime-time television "soap operas" (*novelas*) that have earned for Brazilian television an international reputation.[1] During 1991 I was also engaged in doctoral research that involves similar fieldwork in a small town in the Midwest of the United States.[2]

The name "Cunha" refers to both a county and a town located in a rural part of the state of São Paulo on a plane in the Paraiba River Valley. Cunhenses distinguish between the outlying rural areas—the *roça*—and the town itself—the *cidade*. At the center of town is the town square (*praça*), which is surrounded by the business district and the residences of the local elite, and in the outlying areas and countryside are the various neighborhoods (*bairros*), each with its own reputation. Monjolo, for example, is associated with "wild" and "tough" people; Capivara is the more backwards area where the "hicks" live; and Jericó is associated with the Methodists and the "tight wads." All these distinctions—*roça* and *cidade*, *praça* and the various *bairros*—collapse as "Cunha" when the town is mentioned in the context of other neighboring towns and villages. Cunha is located about halfway (thirty miles each way) between two other towns that are important points of reference: Guarantinguetá, on the Dutra highway, which links the cities of Rio de Janeiro and São Paulo; and Parati, on the coastal highway, which connects Rio with the port city of Santos, São Paulo.

Cunha was founded in the mid-seventeenth century as an overnight stopping point on the "Old Road," which ran between the port at Parati and the towns of Guarantinguetá and Lorena, from which the road—an important transportation route for merchandise throughout two centuries—extended on to the interior of the present-day state of Minas Gerais. Cunha emerged and developed around the production of food and other items for the travelers of the Old Road, and the town has historically occupied a rather peripheral position with respect to other towns in the area.

Even in 1985, when I studied Cunha, the town—which had 5,973 inhabitants in the urban area and 14,899 in the rural part—was still economically based on agriculture and ranching, both oriented toward local consumption and markets in the state of São Paulo.[3] Although Cunha has a good climate with a potential for tourism, the town has not developed its tourist industry very successfully. It does have businesses, a hospital, and a medical clinic, but they are not deemed sufficient for the local population, which frequently goes to Guarantinguetá, Lorena, or other towns in the Paraíba Valley. Thus, Cunha remains in the same peripheral position that it had when others studied it in the past (Cunha 1944; Willems 1961; Shirley 1971).

Living in Cunha

Given the small size of Cunha, it is not surprising that most people know each other, a condition which makes it markedly different from larger cities, where anonymity prevails. The small-town flavor of Cunha is, for Cunhenses, a mixed blessing: on the one hand, they like their town "because everyone knows everyone else," but on the other hand, they complain about it "because everyone interferes with everyone else's lives." As can been seen, those are two sides to the same coin: the fact that the majority of people know each other or recognize each other, and the fact that in Cunha everyone always knows who is whom or "who one is talking to," a condition that would be impossible in a large city. This is what Cunhenses like most about their town, and always what they complain about most: the level of personalism in their relationships.

In effect, in a town like Cunha one cannot be anonymous. It is not possible to be an "individual"—a citizen among others, without identification, in an impersonal and equal situation, with the absence of privileges and discriminations. One is always a "person," identified and positioned in various ways: the son or daughter of someone or the relative of someone, from the countryside or the town, and belonging to a family, group, or social position. In terms of the framework of Louis Dumont (1980), Cunha's social world is a predominantly holistic universe—with the preponderance of the totality (society) over the parts (each social actor), in the sense that everyone is identified by his or her position, which is complementary to other positions in the whole. In turn those positions are formed from segments that complement each other and that provide an identity and prescribe the rules for their components. In this type of society, a person's place is determined by belonging to a segment—the family, caste, kinship group, neighborhood, professional category, etc.—that in turn connects the person with the totality.

Dumont shows how the notion of the "individual"—autonomous, an equal among others, with the rights of choice, feelings, and particular emotions, and very close to the notion of citizenship—is a product of the modern West, where it predominates. In turn the "individual" can be distinguished from the "person," which is linked to the whole society, is defined in a complementary relationship to the other positions, and is determined by its position in the whole. The "person" is associated more with holistic and traditional societies, as in the case of tribal societies, or India, where one's relationship to a clan or caste determines one's way of life at all levels.

Roberto DaMatta develops this framework and shows how these two notions can coexist in the same society, although with one of them predominating. In his work, particularly *Carnivals, Rogues, and Heroes* (1991), *A Casa e a Rua* (1985), and the article "The Quest for Citizenship in a Relational Universe" (1987), DaMatta demonstrates how these two notions coexist in Brazilian society as two codes: one modern and egalitarian, according to which we are "individuals," that is, autonomous beings, equals before the law and the state; and the other traditional and hierarchical, according to which we are "persons" or relational beings, with prerogatives given by the place we occupy in certain segments of the society. Thus, as DaMatta describes it, we oscillate from the condition of "individual" to "person" depending on the context. Likewise, the universe of the "street" in Brazil is very much the universe of "individuals," just as that of the "house" is the place of "persons."

The essay that follows employs this theory, which makes it possible to think through the case of life in a small town such as Cunha. In a big city, we are "individuals"—when we are on the street, anonymous people in the masses, or citizens, with the conditions of equality in the exercise of rights and obligations—or we are "persons"—when we are at home, when we are identified and recognized by our relations and positions in specific contexts, and thereby able to curry favors or suffer discrimination. However, in the small town, the tendency is for us to be "persons" all the time, always recognized and localized. Thus, it is not simply Maria, but instead Maria, the daughter of so-and-so, of such-and-such family (prestigious or not), of such a neighborhood, poor or rich, teacher, married to so-and-so, of such-and-such family, who works there and is the friend of so-and-so and the neighbor of . . . in short, the *person* Maria. Thus, the case of Cunha is considerably different from that of a big city, where there is the possibility of being simply the citizen Maria Doe.

According to the anthropologists Gilberto Velho and Luiz Antônio Machado, in the big cities there is always the possibility of being "relatively anonymous" as a result of the "highly differentiated nature of the organization of production in the big cities of the industrial society" and of "the possibility of playing different roles in socially distinct domains that do not coincide and, to some extent, are impervious to one another" (1977: 80). The situation is different in small towns, they argue, where despite the differentiation of roles, everyone knows everyone else. Such is the case in Cunha, where one finds what the anthropologist Max Gluckman has called "multiplex relations," in which "a man plays most of his roles, as several kinds of productive worker, as consumer, as teacher and pupil, as a worshiper, in closer association with the people whom he calls father and son and brother, wife and sister." (1962: 27). It is where, as we have already seen, "everyone knows everyone else" and it is impossible to be anonymous. As DaMatta notes, the expression "Do you know who you're talking to?" which is used to unmask situations and social positions, has no place in a small town: "In a small community no one will use this ritual form in order to escape anonymity in such an environment. The same is true of tribal groups where the position in one's family, or the fact of having a certain set of proper names or belonging to a lineage, is enough to define a person as having certain social prerogatives" (1991: 170).

In fact, in Cunha one can only ask "Do you know who you're talking to?" of a stranger who has recently arrived; they are the only people who can fail to be recognized or related, and not to have a place in the local hierarchy. Such a place, however, will be sought for the stranger and assigned after only a short stay in the town. Quickly everyone knows, or invents, who the strangers are and where they came from, and thus they pass from being "individuals" to "persons." If, as DaMatta writes, the universe of the house is the typical space of "persons"—where everyone has their own position and assigned roles are complementary to the others, within a hierarchy and according to a code of relations to a specific ethic—I would say that the small town is, from a certain point of view, a "big house." If the opposition between house and street is neither static nor absolute, both in the physical and moral sense (1985: 47), I would say that in the small town the house—with its code—spills out into the street. In Cunha, personal relations rule; it is a world of "persons," where almost everyone passes through the domain of personalism. This essay will examine the role of personalism in Cunha by selecting three important domains: social relations and naming, the economic and political-juridical areas, and notions of space and time.

Social Relations and Naming

To begin with names and naming, everything suggests personal ties. Beyond one's surname, it is common for children to be called by the first name or nickname of either of the parents: Zé do Emílio (the son of Emílio), Antônio Liziário (the son of Eliziário), Luiz do Antônio Liziário (here extended to the grandchild), Vilma da Dona Palmira (daughter), Regina

"Foguinho" (the daughter of Mr. Foguinho), and Duardo "Barba" and Cida "Barba" (the sons of João "Barba"). As is evident, such a system of naming can cut across generations as well as marriages, such that a woman may marry but may still be called by the name that connects her to her father. One can refer to a woman and her children as a group designated by the name of the husband/father. Frequently, no one knows the official or complete names of people, and instead people are known only by their first name or nickname. The identifications made by personal ties and nicknames are illustrated, for example, in the announcement of a death from the loudspeaker of the main church: "We announce the death of Dona Maria do Carmo, the grandmother of the wife of Zé Paes"; or "We announce the death of Antônio Geraldo da Silva, or Pachá." If they did not announce the family tie or nickname, it is possible that people would not know who had died.

In the same way, commercial establishments, estates, and political parties are not designated by their official names but instead by the names of their owners or leaders. Thus, "o Laércio" is not just "Senhor Laércio" but also Laércio's hardware store, which no one refers to as the hardware store and much less as "Lorena's Hardware," which is its name. Thus, one buys bread in "Wardinha," cuts hair at "Dina," buys clothes at "o Jorge" and "o Antônio Mauro," and snacks at "o Zé Veloso." In turn, these commercial establishments are frequently run by several members of the same family, and it is common to see the children of the owners as waiters or clerks. Only rarely do people refer to the names written on the doors of the local shops and stores; they would say instead "o João Coelho," "o Rubinho," or "o Zininho." Likewise, for bars and restaurants they will say: "Ana is closed," "João Newton is out of beer," "Zé Sardinha has rum," "Tonico has beer," "Let's go to Didi Amato," and "There in Dona Lena." The level of personalization is even greater when one considers that these owner-names are actually there attending their clients. Thus, when one hears that "Caiado has beer," the phrase can mean both the bar and the person; in other words, the person encompasses the property: "Ana without Ana is hopeless," someone might say; and "Cash your check in João Coelho" has the same meaning as "Cash your check with João Coelho."

"At Dino" means at the Imperial Hotel, which belongs to Senhor Dino. "At the Gaúcho" means at the restaurant called "Bub's" that originally belonged to a gaúcho (a person from the state of Rio Grande do Sul). "O

Osmar" can mean the ranch (or waterfall found there) or Senhor Osmar Felipe, the exmayor of the city. Some neighborhoods in the countryside are also designated by the names of original or present-day owners: Sertão dos Marianos, Sertão dos Chaves, Barra do Bié. The "party of Zelão" or the "party of Osmar"—the two mayors who traded office for seventeen years— were also referred to in that way, even to the extent that some do not know the official name of the political party.

In such a way "everyone knows everyone" in Cunha, so that when one walks down the street, one is constantly confronted with greetings, and if one is in a hurry, one must try to avoid all the little stops for conversation. Whenever one enters into a store, bar, or restaurant, it appears to be some-one's living room: greetings, a "hello" here, a "how are you" there, a lit-tle conversation there. On the bus, at the post office, in the banks, stores, hairdressers, grocers, market, in the lobby of the hospital, it is always the same. On Saturday night, the bars and restaurants all appear to be party rooms: the people go from table to table, pausing here and there, and the overall impression is a generalized conversation. When one goes to visit a patient in the hospital, one absolutely must visit other acquaintances encountered there: relatives and friends of the patients walk down the hall-ways, exchange news and information, make mutual visits, and wish each other the best.

Recognition is, therefore, basic to this system—recognition in the sense of knowing who is whom. Along with recognition comes trust, in the sense that everyone is identified, or rapidly identifiable, by their relation-ship to someone else. Practically no one uses identification documents in Cunha, not even for driving; it is not necessary because everyone knows who everyone else is. In situations when one is waited upon in a public agency, both parties recognize the person on the other side of the counter. Thus, it is not a mail clerk who is waiting on a customer, but instead it is "o Seu Filinto" or "o Dirceu," and the customer is "o Seu Virgílio," "o João Veloso," or "the daughter of Dona Cida," and both clerk and cus-tomer talk and ask how things are going as the mail is being stamped. I.D. is only presented when the situation demands it and the clerk, for exam-ple, being "an outsider," does not "recognize" the client. But if by chance the customer did not bring the I.D.—as is most likely the case—the situ-ation can be resolved easily: someone nearby who knows the customer "testifies" to his or her identity: "It's OK. I can confirm that she is Mrs. So-and-so."

Economic and Political-Juridical Relationships

As DaMatta states regarding the exercise of citizenship in Brazil, "Brazilian social institutions are always subject to two types of pressure. One of them is the universalist pressure, which comes from bureaucratic norms and laws that define the existence of the agency on a public service. The other is determined by the webs of personal relations to which all are subjected and by the social resources which these networks mobilize and distribute" (1987: 318–19). Thus, when dealing with one of these agencies, our tendency in general as Brazilians is to find someone we know inside them who can guide us and facilitate the process, and thus we are happy when we find "an acquaintance or relative on the inside." This enables us to cut through the line, the waiting, the normal condition of the citizen—the "individual"—and instead to receive a special treatment due to our relationships and therefore to obtain a special condition—that of the "person." In a small town like Cunha, familiarity (= relationships) among people is so generalized—relatives, friends, godparents, and acquaintances are all over—that things function almost all the time based on personal relationships, on favors, considerateness, and trust (*confiança*).

Likewise, credit, in the financial sense of the word, is exercised in a peculiar form in the town, more in this sense of trustworthiness and consideration. Credit does not exclude the records of negotiation such as contracts, bills, and checks, but there is a great deal of toleration and flexibility, so much so that it appears that familiarity among the contracting persons—in fact what validates the contract—predominates over the contract in its legal, written form. Regarding contractual clauses, terms of payment and rent are altered through an understanding among the interested parties: as they say, "Things tend to work out." It is easy to cash a check on the weekend in a shop or store in the town, and likewise one can cash a predated check, which is, in fact, a loan based on trust. Another similar institution in the stores of the town and countryside is the "account" (*caderno*), in which the owner of the store notes down purchases made by the customers, who only have to say "put it on my account" and who pay at the end of the month or, sometimes, whenever they can. Likewise, children are "picked up to bring up" without major problems or even adoption agency bureaucracies: "The mother had him there in the clinic, but she didn't want him, so we picked him up. We've already registered it all"; or "A little girl was born there yesterday. The mother couldn't keep her, so we went to get her."

In Cunha, the confrontation that DaMatta refers to for Brazilian society—"between the public world with its universal laws and contracts, and the private universe of the family, of godparents, relatives, and friends" (1987: 320)—is tilted much more to the second side. A good example of the weight of personal relationships involves the adjustment of prices that occurred during the first semester of 1986 as a result of the "Cruzado Plan."[4] When I returned to Cunha on a visit, I heard the priest ask, "How many have the table to use to watch over the prices?" Very few people raised their hands, and he said that it was a duty and a right, which everyone should fulfill, to make sure that everyone was obeying the wage and price freeze. "But," the priest added, "you're lucky because, in our community, the business people are honest and they themselves have posted the table of prices in their own establishments."[5]

However, there were cases in which some proprietors disobeyed the price freeze, and people confessed to me that they "didn't have the guts" to report the owner "because we knew each other." Although there were some cases of proprietors who were reported and punished, those cases were relatively rare, and, as far as I could tell, only people who "didn't know" the proprietors "had the guts" to report them. Likewise, when the town market was reopened, a delicate situation emerged: because it was a small space, all of the booths were visible at the same time, and as a result the owner of a booth could see when the customer was buying from someone else (a different situation from when one buys from separate grocers); and various people mentioned to me their discomfort at having to buy from one person and not another—since "everyone knew everyone." Even I, once I became part of the local life, felt this same discomfort, and, like everyone else, I discovered the solution: buy one thing here, another there, one day here, another there. In other words, in Cunha it is difficult to deal with purely legal, impersonal, and practical situations at the level of, again in DaMatta's terms, "a form of universal citizenship, built on modern roles which are tied into the operation of a bureaucracy and a market," in contrast with "other forms of citizenship" in Brazil (1987: 321). These other forms, which "stem from the intimate relational world of the *casa* (household)," are especially evident in a small town such as Cunha (321). It is true that in Cunha there are the laws of the market economy, a judicial system, and party politics, but they are crosscut and undercut by the webs of personal relationships.

In his monograph about Cunha, Robert Shirley (1971) follows and develops the discussion by Emilio Willems (1961) to argue that until 1932 Cunha was characterized by patrimonialism and *coronelismo*, with a few elite, property-owning families dominating the area through their clientelist politics. With the failure of the 1932 Revolution, this elite lost power in São Paulo, and the "clan oligarchy" was substituted by "a functional oligarchy" that was "related less by kinship than by the members' professional ability to complement each other's work in an increasingly complex social environment" (Shirley 1971: 82). Shirley emphasizes this change and particularly its effect on the legal system in Cunha, with the passage of power from local hands to those of the state bureaucracy—which, in the terms being used here, marked the beginning of a passage from a traditional, personalistic, and hierarchical system to a more modern, individualistic, and egalitarian one. In Shirley's terms, the transition involved "the difference between the society where the real power lies with the local leaders—personal law—and a society where power lies with an enforcement agency—metropolitan law" (Shirley 1971: 184). He mentions various cases in which this new situation is evident: the increase in judicial activity at all levels, the legalization and commercialization of land, and the distancing of the judge and the district attorney from the local mafias (*panelinhas*). He admits, however, that although clientelist politics were declining, they were not extinct. Although state and national loyalties and politicians were emerging at the expense of the local chiefs, and although political independence was increasing "with the improved education, communication, and economic independence of the voters," Shirley also notes that "there has always been a *very small* group in the town who vote for ideological reasons" (1971: 109 and 107, emphasis added).

It is true, therefore, that the judicial and party systems exist in Cunha, but I would argue that they work under the counterpressure of a system of personal relationships. Thus, justice is there, eventually complaints are reported to the police, investigations are undertaken, arrests are made, and cases go to trial; but in this process, as I observed it, the *way of doing it* (or, at times, of not doing it) reveals how personal relationships permeate the whole process. Frequently, I heard references to the fact that the police overlooked the misdemeanors of some people. To understand how this works, consider the following example that illustrates the point.

On one occasion I witnessed the embarrassment of a victim who was almost run over. Although the guilty driver did not even stop, the victim did not want to face the consequences of reporting the incident to the police, and I ended up facing much the same dilemma. The victim had a slight wound and needed to get help, but because it was Saturday night and the drugstores were all closed, she had to go to the hospital. However, going to the hospital would mean that the woman would automatically have to report the incident, and thus she refused to get any help. "No," she said, "it's not necessary. If I go there, I'll have to file a complaint." "Then do it!" one of her friends said, thinking about the careless attitude of the driver. "Go there and say it was X. You have to tell, so why don't you?" "Just because of the family? So what? Go to the hospital and report it. This guy is a menace. He has to be stopped." I, who had witnessed the whole scene and knew the woman, entered into the group—in which everyone knew each other—and insisted that she go to the hospital, and she was finally convinced and accepted my ride. As a result, I was able to stay with her, and I also ended up getting involved as a witness to the event.

The details of this incident illustrate the clash between, on the one side, the law to be fulfilled and the punishment to be inflicted, and, on the other side, the counterpressure of personal relationships that shaped the mutual recognition that was so typical of this small town. For me, the whole incident happened so quickly that I only saw the car, and I didn't see who was driving it or how many people were in it (which was my luck, I later thought, because I was also free from "having to report" someone personally). I still had not managed to associate cars with their owners, but for the people from Cunha, even in a scene that happened so quickly—and it was exactly the high speed, completely inappropriate for the area around the town square, that caused the accident—it was possible to know who was involved. But at the same time that these people told the woman to "go to the hospital and report it," none of them volunteered to go with her and to serve as a witness. They said to her and *to me*: "Go there, and tell them it was X—you can't let this go by!" In turn, I responded, "But I didn't see who was driving and I don't know the guy," and I really didn't know (thank God, I thought to myself). They answered, "It's So-and-so, of So-and-so," thus giving a name that was linked to the name of the father, whom I did know, along with his mother and brothers. Despite all this complaining and the emphatic nature of their discourse, they would not think of going themselves and doing what they proposed that I and the victim do.

Why did they want me to go? In principle, I was an outsider (not enough, as I was already seeing), and perhaps this meant that I would not be caught in the same plight in which they, and even the victim, were caught, because they all knew the family. When we arrived at the hospital, we did indeed have to report the incident, and I and a friend of the woman who came along were registered as witnesses. The victim continued to be reluctant to say who the driver was, and the friend insisted to her, "Say it was him, X." However, the victim replied, "I don't really care. Just let it go." Her friend answered, "Really? Just because he's rich, the son of so-and-so, nothing's going to happen? That's exactly why you should tell!" Prodded by her friend, the victim finally let slide from her mouth, to her evident distaste, the name of the driver, the name that had been mentioned many times before among the people gathered on the town square. After that, I had to go and make a statement with the police, to whom I described the accident that I witnessed, but—to my great relief (and, this time, I understood much better the plight of the victim)—because I did not see who was driving the car, I did not recognize the car or its owner, and thus I did not have to mention the name of anyone . . .

This event occurred at the end of 1985, and I do not know how the investigation ended. As can be seen, the judicial apparatus is there, but the story illustrates the difficulties in using it. In addition to this case, I can also mention as an example the fact that the town lives with the recognition of some juvenile delinquents, so much so that one sometimes hears "watch out for X" instead of the typical phrase, "watch out for thieves," or, as another example, "I'm going to lock the doors carefully tonight because I saw X in the neighborhood today." Because everyone knows about the "mental problems" of one of them or the use of drugs that they attribute to all of them (accusations that are quite commonly associated with delinquency in general), it is not just the police, but the entire community, that maintains an attitude of tolerance toward the juvenile delinquents. Thus, although the police may get involved, the victims themselves of a theft may also go directly to the house of the delinquents whom everyone believes to be thieves, and ask the family to return their stolen goods! People ask each other directly, and sometimes, again "on the basis of *understanding*," they actually manage to obtain their own stolen goods!

Thus, tolerance for the transgressors of the order is not just a reflection of the social prestige of the family, as in the first case, where the driver was the son of a "rich family." As the case of the juvenile delinquents and thieves indicates, a similar tolerance applies to "poor families" as well. The general complacency with those who violate the law is justified because they are all from "known" families and they know each other as well. Thus, the mirror of familiarity chills the application of justice.

Personal ties also play an important role in local party politics. As already mentioned, the two parties were designated according to the names of the two people who traded the office of the mayor during the previous seventeen years, and many Cunhenses refer to the party "of Osmar" or "of Zelão" as if behind them there was no official party with a platform and series of proposals, but instead as if it the party belonged to *that person*. Until 1985, the two people belonged to the same party, but locally it was as if they belonged to two different parties. To put it simply, the majority of the people voted for the person and not the party; only a minority voted ideologically and showed any concern with the party positions that were behind the persons. Frequently, when I asked, "Who did you vote for?" or "Who are you going to vote for mayor?" I heard the response "So-and-so"; but if I asked, "What party?" I saw doubtful expressions, and the person would ask the neighbor, "What's the party of So-and-so?" or simply would say, "I don't know."

In keeping with the general outlook, the reasons for such choices are of a personal order that are easily recognized in what is called favoritist or clientelist politics: friendship, kinship, or favors and help that had been given, for which one owes gratitude or even an "obligation" and which one repays with a vote. Once the candidate is elected, the voter feels that the tie of friendship and/or the right of obtaining new favors has been reaffirmed. One might also hear that the reason for the choice is that a candidate is (either potentially or proven by experience) a good administrator, but commonly the reason is the "respect and considerateness" that voters have for their candidates; in other words, the candidates maintain the level of personalism. Thus, although there is a system of public municipal services that maintains the roads and streets and the cleanliness of the town through a system of delegated roles, it is nevertheless common for someone to speak personally to the mayor or his aide, or even to ask his spouse to intercede in order to resolve a problem, such as the damage caused by the rain to a street or an access road to a farm, or the installation of a tent during the festival season.

Regarding voting behavior on a state level, the domain of personalism does not function to the same degree. The identification of parties and candidates is clearer, a fact which I believe is a function of the quantity of names and the diversity of choices, as well as of the use of radio and television for advertising. However, as is common in other rural regions of the country, one finds the "directed vote," which functions according to the local political interests and clientelist politics in which one places trust and to whom one owes an obligation. ("Vote *with* So-and-so" means vote for the candidates or party that he or she supports.) Nevertheless, because the state elections take place at a different time from those of the municipality, and because the vote is not officially linked, the influence of the local politicians appears unable to compete with the campaigns of the mass media.

Still, at the local level politics is basically characterized by *persons* and personal relationships. The result is the creation of *factions* based on personal loyalties to the leaders and especially characterized by the coreligionists and close followers of the politicians and local party leaders. These groups, which represent a variety of positions and different loyalties that are worked out in the "local political front," are not exceedingly hostile to one another, as they are said to have been "in the past." Still, there is certainly a litany of mutual accusations, just as there are cases of mutual avoidance and even of broken relationships among the members of these factions. As the people of Cunha often say, criticizing the influence of the mayors and their personal disputes, "What one does, the other undoes, and the city ends up the loser," in the sense that those who take over from a previous administration do not continue the projects that the previous administration initiated.

To give an illustration of this factionalism, I transcribe a note that was published in the newspaper by the owner of a diner that opened in the town. In a strategy evidently aimed at not losing part of the clientele due to the attendance of the other part, the ad offered the restaurant's space to everyone and invited everyone to come: "We want to make it clear to all friends who frequent or per chance desire to frequent this house, that it is open to everyone of whatever religious or political creed as long as it is extremely democratic. . . . We therefore invite all the leaders and their followers of the diverse tendencies of the political parties of our town, to come and sit at our tables and talk, because through dialogue light is born, and, to tell the truth, we definitely could use more of it."[6]

Like the owner of the "Beer Center," I also had to make clear to everyone that I had to talk to everyone, that this was part of my research task, and that people should not cut me off due to my relationship with others. This did not involve simply political factions, but also antagonisms that occurred on other levels, such as those among the neighborhoods and supporters of the soccer teams, as well as other conflicts typical of a small town, such as severed relationships or dislikes for personal reasons and discordances. Although "everyone gets along with everyone else," not everyone "gets along *well* with everyone else." As in the universe of the house, in which everyone "gets along," there are still confrontations and preferred relationships.

Ritual and Temporality in Cunha

Up to this point, I have focused on the ways in which personal relationships have influenced Cunha's everyday life: the forms of naming linked to children, wives, parents, and husbands; the linkage of the names of owners with their commercial establishments or private estates; public spaces that operated as living rooms; treatment in public agencies based on an almost automatic recognition between clients and clerks; credit that is extended on trust; the difficulty of the application of the law to people who are "known"; and the personalism and the consequent factionalism of the local party politics. In this section, I will consider ritual, the rhythms of daily life, and notions of time as they are lived and represented in Cunha, and I will show that just as the relations that dominate the local life are personalized and characteristic of the "universe of the house," the dominant sense of time in Cunha is also the "time of the house."

Beginning with concepts of time, I encountered constant references from people of all ages to the fact that "things used to be better": in a time of *before* certain things were available that one can no longer find, or there was a way of doing things that no longer exists: "Things used to happen here." Cunhenses do not construct the past in this way only for what they view as their "traditions"—festivals, the bands, and ancient mansions, for example— they also think of the past as a time when the town was livelier in terms of, for example, festivals, the movies, dances, and sports. They also constantly refer to the fact that "Here nothing happens" and "Cunha isn't progressing" when they wish to show that, with respect to the present time, there is also a lack of activity (*movimento*). Activity is therefore located *outside*: either in another time or, spatially, outside Cunha.

When I asked when this "before" was, the answers varied from the year before to the past located "many years" ago. And when the question did not leave them simply perplexed, the most common explanations were the dependency of Cunha on Guará and the rivalry between the personal and political factions that keeps the town from progressing. As a local journalist described in an article titled "A Town in Agony," "Here there's no cooperation, simply because the town is divided by the eternal `I'm for So-and-so and against So-and-so'; `I don't do this because I'm against So-and-so'; and `I don't give because I don't belong to the same party.' "[7]

Nevertheless, Cunha was always dependent on Guaratinguetá, and the political rivalries appear to have been even more acrimonious in the past, as

73

Willems notes for the 1940s and Shirley for the 1960s. If these were the real explanations, the "agony" of the town to which the local journalist refers would have already emerged long ago in that "before" to which Cunhenses refer. Likewise, Willems also noted that in the 1940s, when he did fieldwork in Cunha, the people "had the general impression that the festival of Saint Joseph [like the Pentecost] had lost a lot of its old splendor," and Shirley also commented on the "decline of the great festival cycle" (Willems 1961: 186, 204–205; Shirley 1971: 248). Furthermore, both discuss problems in the demand and opportunities for labor, as well as remuneration, in the town (Willems 1961: 29; Shirley 1977: 216–217). Willems, for example, noted, "Today, there is already a youth group that is no longer satisfied with the rare balls of the clubs and the billiard and card games. Like many strangers, they think that `there's nothing to do in Cunha,' and that only trips to Guaratinguetá, São Paulo, or Rio de Janeiro can answer their complaint" (1961: 177). Likewise, regarding festivals, Shirley noted during the 1960s: "Time after time the author heard statements to the effect that, `This is nothing like it used to be in the old days' "(1971: 249).

Thus, this better time of "before," which Cunhenses represent in various ways, has a rather questionable logic, because when we go back to the ethnographies that describe this better time, we find that it in turn is judged in terms of another better time of "before." The logic of this "before" is that of a mythical time, in which everyone, young or old, constructs a more desirable image of Cunha according to their various criteria. The time of "before" runs from "last year," when they closed the movie theater once again, to ten years ago, when the sports championships warmed up the town, to forty (or fifty, sixty?) years ago, when religious festivals were "true festivals," to an even more remote time—the middle of the past century, when the city was full of opulence: "a time glorified by the present-day inhabitants as a period of splendor and richness," or "a time which many local residents remember as Cunha's 'golden age'" (Willems 1961: 26; Shirley 1971: 52). All these times point to "when it used to be better," a time that does not need any precision to be defined, because it is a myth that in turn is fed in various ways and from different perspectives.

"Before it was better" and "here nothing happens"—these are two key images for understanding temporality in Cunha. The first, as we saw, refers to a fluid and mythical time of the past, when things happened as they are supposed to happen. The second, as we shall see, refers to present-day and cyclical time, which is lived according to the feeling that things do not happen. Both refer to the question of activity (*movimento*)—in the sense contrary to stagnation and lack of events—that is believed to have taken place "before" and that they complain no longer continues in effect today.

Because of my long stay in the town, I was able to see that the phrase "nothing ever happens" means "the same things always happen." For those who have only arrived recently and who have not yet had the chance to get a feel for the "local time" that is marked by certain events, indeed many things appear to be happening. But for those who have been in Cunha for a while, the activity is neutralized by the sense of repetition of events that are already known and by the sense that the events are always the "same thing." Although the events that mark this local time—the rains, the harvests, the festivals, the holidays, the weekends—are intensely lived and are experienced as breaks in the daily routine, they nevertheless make up, in their entirety, another level of routine: the cyclical time that is peculiar to life in Cunha.

Cunha is a festive city. The "festivals" mark the life of the community, with one festival always following on the heels of another that has just ended. The words *festa*, *festeiro*, and *festejar* are always in the air; like the festivals themselves, they are reference points in the local life. The term "festa" is for Cunhenses a ritual of an exclusively religious nature, with the most important in the annual cycle being those of Saint Joseph, the Holy Week (Easter), the Pentecost, Saint Benedict, and the Patron, Our Lady of the Conception. These festivals involve the participation of both the Catholic church and the population, which celebrates in the streets. Still within the scope of religious festivals, one must also include Christmas, which has a more intimate character but nevertheless extends into the streets with the celebration of the Three Kings. The "Festas Juninas" (or "June Festivals," referring to Saints Anthony, John, and Peter) are also designated by the term "festa," but they are somewhat distinct from the more properly religious festivals, since the "Juninas" are sponsored by schools or private groups. In addition to all these festivals, there are also the "festivals of the neighborhoods" in honor of their respective patron saints, as well as commemorations of a nonreligious character that are important to the community: Carnival, the Town Birthday, the Seventh of September (the equivalent of the Fourth of July), and the annual Beer Party.

Despite the variation that may occur, all the festivals involve "extraordinary" activity and they create a special time and atmosphere in which everything revolves around the festival. The town swells up and is caught up and inflamed by the festival, which ends up regulating all the activities of the town. The schedules, the flux of time, the happenings and everyday interests are suspended under the influence of the time of the festival, and the spaces of sociability and reciprocity are intensified.

If the festivals are the special events that mark the cyclical time of life in Cunha, "holidays" and "weekends" reproduce on another scale the same scheme, in the sense that during holidays (such as school holidays, the month of July, and the summer months) and weekends the city appears to light up and expand in contrast to the other periods of the year and the other days of the week. An atmosphere is created with the arrival of people from the outside to spend the weekend, the comings and goings to the countryside, visits, travels, religious activities of all types (Catholic, Methodist, Pentecostal), masses, activity on the town square, in the stores, bars, clubs . . .

These are transpositions of the same scheme: during festivals, holidays, and weekends, the town expands and becomes animated and active. It fills up, colorful, like a balloon. Afterward, the balloon deflates during the interval of the day-to-day, until the next festival, holiday, or weekend. As one can see, these situations that oppose the day-to-day all activate the town; they bring to it the activity that so many Cunhenses complain is lacking. Here, I return to the initial point regarding the local representations in which Cunhenses repeatedly say that "things were better before" and "nothing ever happens here." We saw that this "before" could have been better, worse, or the same, but they say that it was better; and likewise we have seen how in Cunha many things do happen, but they say that nothing ever happens. Thus, a mythical and desirable past is opposed to a cyclical and undesirable present. Behind these representations, activity—what is said to have happened in the past—no longer appears to take place because it is lived as repetition. As much as one appreciates and intensely experiences the events that comprise and bring activity, as a whole these events are also encompassed by the idea that everything is always the same—a cycle that will repeat itself and never change.

Thus, beneath the surface, where people call for progress and change, there is a confrontation: tradition to be maintained versus progress, advances, and activity to be implemented. In the local vision it is as if this movement were outside of Cunha: time passes by on the outside, whereas within Cunha life repeats itself. In this evaluation, Cunhenses oppose the time of the world, which goes on—and which is associated with the idea of progress and advance—with the "static time" of their small town. This judgment also situates them with respect to the "mentality of the town," when they complain about its lack of more "advanced" ideas.

Roberto DaMatta analyzes the way in which "house" and "street" function as ordering principles in Brazilian society, as spaces that correspond to specific values and codes, with the life of the house being governed by a cyclical time and that of the street governed by a linear, cumulative time. What happens in the house occurs outside time, like a nest or safe haven; the code of the house opposes change and progress, whereas that of the street is, on the contrary, open to it (DaMatta 1985: 51, 41). From this perspective, we can see how these two codes operate in the representations of Cunha, which appears as a house, with its cyclical time demarcated by special events, in opposition to the outside world, which appear as a street, where time passes and goes forward.

Leaving Cunha

If Cunha is a great house, its street is the rest of Brazil, and Cunhenses seem to enjoy leaving town and taking trips to neighboring towns. As noted at the beginning, Cunha is located between two other, larger towns in the Paraíba River Valley—Parati and Guarantinguetá—both of which are connected to Cunha by road and frequent bus service. Indeed, Guarantinguetá is a constant point of reference for the Cunhenses. Just as people from the rural areas come to Cunha (the town) in order to do business, the people of Cunha go to Guarantinguetá—which is known as "Guará"—for the same purpose. And from Guará they go on to other places. There they can change buses and go to any other city in the valley, to the state capital, and on to other cities in the state and country. Every hour from six in the morning to eleven at night, a bus line between Cunha and Guará provides service for the hourlong trip, and for those who have cars, the thirty-mile trip on a paved road is even easier. When they go, they always have to run an errand for someone: a package to deliver or pick up, a bill to pay, or a ride to give. People often make the trip to Guará to buy something they cannot find locally in Cunha, or to visit a medical specialist, or to take college-level courses. Those who can afford it (the middle and upper classes) also go to Guará for entertainment—to see a movie or to dine out—but during the summer they tend to prefer Parati and Ubatuba, which are located on the coast and have good beaches.

Cunhenses therefore visit neighboring towns for instrumental reasons, but the decision "to go to Guará" or other towns also has a meaning related to the question of personalism. "To go to Guará," to Lorena, or to other towns—beyond being a trip for shopping, dentists, education, movies, restaurants, or weekend dances—also means "to leave": to leave the control of the town where one always sees (and will be seen by) the same people, no matter where one goes. To go to Guará, therefore, is to make the passage from "person" to "individual," to leave the house and to find the breathing room provided by anonymity, but, of course, only somewhat, because in Guará one might still run into someone from Cunha who is looking for the same thing. If Guará is a good place to which one might escape, Parati is even better; it is an open city that Cunhenses, especially the youth, compare to Rio. "Ah! Parati!" they say in a tone of "what I wouldn't give to be there now": "There you can find everything, do everything—it's the opposite of Cunha."

Carnival also provides another opportunity to escape from the control that the city exercises over its population: the great number of masked people, clowns, men dressed as women, women dressed as men, faces covered and completely disguised. The flavor of the event is to challenge others with pranks without having them figure out who one is. In a place like Cunha, where everyone knows everyone else and their activity is absolutely controlled (even the parked car!), this seems to be a typical inversion for Carnival: to become unknown, anonymous, unrecognizable.[8] In the case of women, anonymity also means they may fool around without revealing their identity.

On this topic, Gilberto Velho discusses the question of the possibility of individualization. He points out that when people leave their towns, neighborhoods, homes, and relatives, they reinforce their individuality.[9] To leave for another place, to see and do different things, to see and be seen by different people—these are what almost all Cunhenses hope to find. And in the case of women, the idea that "it is better to become the girlfriend of someone from the outside, who has a different mentality," reinforces this perspective. One even finds, especially among the youth, the desire to leave definitively, to go away, at least "for a while."[10]

The belief that in Cunha "nothing ever happens"—which, as we have seen, means that the same things always happen—also resonates with the belief that one must always live "with the same people." The sense of sameness may also be the reason why Cunhenses pay so much attention to newcomers to their town. As someone who lived for some time in Cunha, I was treated with the same interest and attention that the Cunhenses were accustomed to giving to strangers, attention which is possibly even doubled for those who come from a big urban center such as São Paulo or Rio, and perhaps even more so for Rio than São Paulo because Rio is culturally more distant. Such receptivity appears to be related to a desire for exchange and renewal that can be satisfied through contact with the Other, who simultaneously brings news and is news. This observation is based on the treatment that I received as well as on the testimony of visitors and people who moved to Cunha from other cities. Likewise, friends from Rio and São Paulo who visited me during that period were equally captivated, and captured, by the welcoming treatment they received from the Cunhenses.

If leaving Cunha or establishing ties with people from the outside mitigates Cunhenses' subjection to "sameness" and social control, the threat of this control still hovers in the air, for gossip plays an important role in the town life. People complained a great deal about gossip: "Gossip dominates the town . . . On the town square the main subject is to talk about other peoples' lives"; "Everything in town is gossip"; "Here in Cunha, whatever you do is reason for gossip; I don't know if it's because it's a small town." Likewise, Shirley noted, "The gossip of the town, however, is red hot and also very useful to an anthropologist" (1977: 234). Gossip is motivated by the local sense of morality, and it functions through accusations directed toward those who, in the eyes of the accusers, break with the accepted standards of behavior.[11]

The other side of "everyone knows everyone else" is "everyone controls everyone else," and when Cunhenses brag and complain about themselves, it involves their shared condition as "persons" in a cozy world based on mutual recognition but also on demarcated positions that are controlled and contained by their own rules, a world where one feels comfortable but from which one is also eager to escape. As has been shown, living in Cunha and leaving Cunha involves the desire to flee from the condition of being a person to that of an individual, and thus to leave the world of the house for that of the street. If the big house that is Cunha is welcoming, and if in it people feel wanted and recognized, at the same time it is also oppressive, and people feel controlled and restrained by the rules they must follow and the expectations they must fulfill. The pleasures of personalized treatment, of being recognized and esteemed, cause Cunhenses to adore their town; but the hardships of the lack of privacy, of always being on exhibit and consequently contained and hampered, lead Cunhenses to hate their town. Such are the pleasures of recognition and the hardships of social control, the delight and bitterness of the small town, where personal relations rule: the heaven and hell of personalism.

Acknowledgment

I am grateful to David J. Hess for his assistance in the adaptation of my original text into the current essay. Not only did David translate it into English, but he also contributed by making important comments and suggestions.

Endnotes

1. The project was titled "The Impact of Television in Rural Brazil" and directed by Conrad Kottak. It covered six different communities and resulted in the book *Prime-Time Society* (Kottak 1990). A "novela" or "telenovela" is a prime-time serial about Brazilian subjects that appears every night and is produced by the national television networks, with Brazilian actors, writers, and producers.

2. Although I refer to Cunha as a "Brazilian small town," I believe that many of the characteristics and representations described here might apply to other small towns in other societies. In fact, I have seen many similarities between Dundee, Michigan, and Cunha, and my dissertation (Prado 1993) discusses the extent to which and in what ways these similarities have a different meaning with respect to the broader culture of American society.

3. From the 1980 census by the IBGE, the Brazilian Institute of Statistics and Geography.

4. The "Cruzado Plan" was a measure adopted by the Brazilian government that attempted to reduce and contain inflation by means of a wage and price freeze.

5. It is worth noting, for example, that the priest also plays an important role in the discussion of local issues. He is the only priest in the whole town, and in terms of the theme of personalism, it should be noted that the *person of the priest*—his personality as it is reflected in the direction he takes with respect to the church—is strikingly influential, and the people also recognize his important influence. The way that Cunhenses refer to the priest and how they relate to him makes it clear that it involves a *person* who is in that position: Padre Mauro. In the same way they refer to previous priests: Padre Geraldo, Padre João, etc., who also made their personal mark on the conduct of the parish.

6. *Voz Popular*, no. 25, August 8, 1982.

7. *Voz Popular*, no. 5, July 8, 1981.

8. On Brazilian Carnival as a ritual that highlights the inversion of the everyday life, see DaMatta (1991).

9. He also calls attention to the possibility of the "emergence of situations in which the individual as a moral subject is highlighted and where an individualist *ethos* can exist even when it is subordinated to the dominant holistic order" (1981: 48).

10. This necessity to leave, or desire to leave, particularly on the part of the young people, is also noted by Milanesi (1978) for the town of Ibitinga and Abreu Filho (1980) for Araxá.

11. Because the standard of morality is even more rigid for female behavior, women are the privileged focus of "commentary" and consequently of social control, and thus they tend to complain more about gossip. As a result of my research on the reaction of women in Cunha to female characters on the Brazilian soap operas (*telenovelas*), it became clear that regardless of their social status, the local women admired the characters, whom they saw as "free." The women's evaluations of the television characters frequently involved an opposition between control and freedom (or dependence and independence). Whatever they devalued, complained about, or did not like tended to be expressed in terms of control, and likewise whatever they valued or found attractive and pleasing was expressed in terms of freedom.

References

Abreu Filho, Ovídio
　1980 "Raça, Sangue, e Luta: Identidade e Parentesco em uma Cidade do Interior." Master's thesis, Graduate Program in Social Anthropology, National Museum, Universidade Federal do Rio de Janeiro.
Cunha, Mario Wagner Vieira
　1944 "O Povoamento do Município de Cunha." *Anais do Congresso Brasileiro de Geografia* 9(3): 641–49.
DaMatta, Roberto
　1985 *A Casa e a Rua*. São Paulo: Brasiliense.
　1987 "The Quest for Citizenship in a Relational Universe." In J. D. Wirth, E. O. Nunes, and T. E. Bogenschild (eds.), *State and Society in Brazil*. Boulder, Colo.: Westview Press.
　1991 *Carnivals, Rogues, and Heroes*. Notre Dame: University of Notre Dame Press.
Dumont, Louis
　1980 *Homo Hierarchicus*. Chicago: University of Chicago Press.
Gluckman, Max
　1962 "Les rites de passage." In Max Gluckman (ed.), *Essays on the Ritual of Social Relations*. Manchester: Manchester University Press.
Kottak, Conrad P.
　1990 *Prime-Time Society: An Anthropological Analysis of Television and Culture*. Belmont: Wadsworth.
Milanesi, Luiz Augusto
　1978 *O Paraíso via Embratel*. Rio de Janeiro: Paz e Terra.
Prado, Rosane
　1987 "Mulher de Novela e Mulher de Verdade: Estudo sobre Cidade

Pequena, Mulher, e Telenovela." Master's thesis, Graduate Program in Social Anthropology, National Museum, Universidade Federal do Rio de Janeiro.

1993 "Mitologia e Vivência da Cidade Pequena nos Estados Unidos." Ph.D. dissertation, Graduate Program in Social Anthropology, National Museum, Universidade Federal do Rio de Janeiro.

Shirley, Robert W.

1971 *The End of a Tradition*. New York: Columbia University Press.

Velho, Gilberto

1981 *Individualismo e Cultura*. Rio de Janeiro: Zahar.

Velho, Gilberto and Luiz Antônio Machado

1977 "Organização Social do Meio Urbano." *Anuário Antropológico 76*. Rio de Janeiro: Tempo Brasileiro. Pp. 71–82.

Willems, Emilio

1961 *Uma Vila Brasileira: Tradição e Transição*. São Paulo: Difel.

Two

Race, Class, and
Gender in a
Changing Society

⊠

As in many other countries, in Brazil race, class, and gender are central to the dynamics of social structure, particularly in the context of social hierarchy. However, race, class, and gender are not structured in exactly the same ways in Brazil as they are in the United States, nor are they changing in the same ways. The essays in this section explore from a cultural perspective some of the complex dynamics of the triad in Brazil.

Coelho's essay is a study of two scandals, that of Aída in the 1950s and that of Mônica in the 1980s. Both involved rape-murders of young and innocent teen-age women, and both became scandals because they violated the sense of security among the middle class. Coelho draws on newspaper documents, backed up by her own experience as a woman who grew up Rio de Janeiro, to explore changing gender patterns as well as the nature of class relations as expressed in public scandals. Regarding gender patterns, she shows that the scandals reveal dramatic changes in sexual morality: Aída is seen as a symbol of purity and innocence, whereas Mônica is seen as a healthy teenager who has boyfriends. In terms of the theme of hierarchy and personalism, Coelho also shows dramatic changes. The society of the 1950s had stricter gender roles, and its media configured the scandal in terms of the opposition between the bourgeois, Catholic family and deviant youth. By the 1980s there was a more relaxed attitude toward women's sexuality, and the scandals also revealed a greater sense of diversity and individualism. However, the very fact that the cases occurred and were so similar, notwithstanding a gap of thirty years, shows underlying similarities in Brazilian culture across the two time periods. For example, in both cases women are still viewed as passive with respect to men, and men are seen as relatively wild and uncontrolled. Brazil, like the United States, was and is a patriarchic society.

Coelho also shows how class relations articulate with the changing gender patterns. Both scandals were about the middle class, although in slightly different ways. Aída became a specific symbol of the traditional bourgeois Catholic family, whereas Mônica became a more a general symbol of the threatened middle class. Coelho also situates the two middle-class scandals in terms of the relationship between the middle class and the media. She argues that members of the middle class are persons in the sense that they are news. In contrast, the poor are anonymous individuals in that they are not even considered newsworthy. In other words, even though there are many rape-murders, the Aída and Mônica cases became scandals because they affected the middle class.

Whereas Coelho considers gender and class in the case of the middle class and public scandals, Sarti considers gender and class for the lower classes and family relations. Sarti's essay is noteworthy for exploring how the traditional patriarchal Brazilian family is changing among the poorer urban classes. This family is characterized by a number of hierarchical relationships, including male over female, old over young, and richer families over poorer families. Sarti shows that changing circumstances in the city are working to bring about variations in the traditional pattern. Especially when women are working and their children are older, the traditional hierarchical relationships are more likely to be changing, although not always. For example, when women and men are both working, the woman is likely to provide the secondary income, a situation that is also true for women of other classes. As Sarti remarks, in this type of situation "women's work is embedded in a patriarchal code that cuts across classes."

Sarti also shows how attention to hierarchy can contribute to an understanding of social classes. In standard class analyses, the poorer classes are usually identified according to their economic relationships, such as the working class and the underclass of the informal economy. Sarti shows that in the neighborhood she studied, the poor divide themselves up according their own scheme of class hierarchization: those who live on the upper street, the middle group with homes, the poor in *favelas* (shantytowns), and the poorest, who live under the bridges. Thus, a cultural perspective that begins with the community's understandings can add new ways of looking at classic sociological problems such as poverty by pointing to how local cultures conceptualize class.

Silverstein's essay involves changing patterns of race relations, but at the same time the race relations are interwoven with class, gender, and religion. Her case study focuses on the "liberation" of the African religions of Bahia, which took place in 1976 and which she witnessed. Brazilians like to think of their country as a model for race relations, and indeed Brazil has not suffered from the level of animosity and violence that is found in countries such as the United States or South Africa. Brazilians point to the intermingling of the races and the many mulattoes (mixed African/European descent) and mestizos (mixed Amerindian/European) as evidence for their harmonious blending. They also point to the syncretism, or identification, of African *orixá* (oo-ree-shah') spirits and Catholic saints as additional evidence of the harmonious mixing of races in religion.

The reality, however, is far from the idyllic ideology of racial harmony and mixing. As Silverstein notes, until the 1970s the African religions of Bahia were under the jurisdiction of the police, and at some times they were violently closed down. Likewise, Brazilians of primarily African descent have always been barred from the upper echelons of Brazilian society, whether through marriage, public office, or economic opportunity. As for the United States, the legacy of slavery still weighs heavily on Brazilian society, and race relations constitute perhaps the most evident way in which the society can be described as hierarchical.

At the same time, however, there are some dramatic differences between race and racism in Brazil and the United States. One of the most evident differences is the extent to which Brazilians of primarily European descent believe in spirits and the supernatural world associated with African religions. Whereas North American Protestants tended to weed out African religion as devil worship or superstition, Portuguese Catholics were more willing to believe in the powers of the African priests and priestesses, both to heal and to do harm. As a result, African culture has come to have a particularly important place in Brazilian society. Today, African culture is recognized as having an economic value as well, for it has become part of the tourist industry. Because the African religions are led by women, whereas the Catholic church is led by men, the race/class dynamics have a gender dimension as well.

Silverstein's exploration of Bahian religion shows how race, class, gender, and religion all form a complicated web in which relations of hierarchy are capable of inversion. In other words, powerful white men may seek out the help of poor, black women. Those women occupy a position of leadership in their communities, and they are also revered as having special supernatural powers far beyond those of the white men. In this sense, attention to culture and hierarchy again leads to complexities that a standard Marxist analysis of domination cannot achieve. To some extent, there is an element of cooptation involved, for the white political leaders, tourist industry, and culture industry have all recognized the payoffs of recognizing the African religions. However, as Silverstein also shows, because of the Portuguese traditions of folk Catholicism the situation is more complicated, for the dominant groups also believe in the power of the African religions.

Chapter Four

Rituals, Scandals, and Sex Crimes: Attempted Rape-Murders Across Two Generations

⊠

Maria Claudia Pereira Coelho

Mônica Granuzzo and Aída Cúri: two Brazilian women killed while trying to defend themselves from attempted rape. The cases of Mônica and Aída Cúri: two scandals that mobilized Carioca (Rio de Janeiro) society and, in the process, also revealed it. Structurally similar, and with the peculiarity of having been transformed into newspaper stories, these two cases invite comparative analysis.

Aída and Mônica were both young, middle-class women of the South Zone of Rio de Janeiro. They died from falls from high-rise apartment buildings in the South Zone, the first in 1958 and the second in 1985. In both cases, the reasons why they had entered the buildings remain obscure points in the investigations (and, as will be demonstrated below, points of great relevance). The families of Mônica and Aída did not know the suspects, who, by coincidence, numbered three in both cases. The prosecution argued in both cases that the two young women died in an attempt to defend themselves against sexual violence. Thus, they would have fallen or jumped from the buildings. In short, these are two cases of women who died during attempted rape, cases that have as protagonists people of the middle-class South Zone of Rio de Janeiro. Beyond these elements, there is a factor of highest importance that is the basis of this study: both cases became public scandals, causing headlines in the major media, scandalizing and mobilizing cultural values, and detonating acrimonious questions regarding the cases.

This study considers two basic dimensions. The first involves the sexual aspect of the two cases. In the hypotheses that were put forward to explain the events (Mônica/Aída fell? They jumped? They were thrown?) as well as to explain why the victims were in the buildings from which they fell or were pushed (flightiness versus innocence), one finds a clear expression of the conceptions of masculine and feminine sexuality in the two periods. The second dimension refers to the societal aspect of the two cases, evidenced by the public scandals that emerged. The basic idea here is that the people involved were transformed into stereotypes of social groups. The cultural values and media representations involved in this transformation thus had a double character. First, there was an exacerbation of the emotions present in the cases, giving them a personal character, and second (and possibly because of this), the entire society became involved in the cases through discussions and debates about who was guilty and responsible . . . in other words, who was scandalous.

The notions of myth and ritual are basic to understanding the nature of these scandals. Both myth and ritual can be taken as texts, narratives, or moments in which society speaks about itself. They are thus firmly situated in the everyday world and made of the same essence as this world: in a sense, they are a type of window through which society dramatizes what is most important to it. As Roberto DaMatta states,

> The study of rituals, then, is not and should not be an attempt to search for the "essence" of a special, qualitatively different moment. Rather, it should be an attempt to see how trivial elements of the social world can be *dislocated* and thus transformed into *symbols* which, in certain contexts, help to construct a special or extraordinary moment.
>
>   Like every symbolic discourse, ritual highlights certain aspects of reality. One of its basic features is to render certain aspects of social reality more present than others.   (DaMatta 1991: 53–54)

Even if ritual and the daily world share the same "essence," they are not confused, because ritual *dramatizes* social life and makes the members of a society aware of themselves, their values, and their ideologies. In a phrase, it is by means of drama that societies distinguish themselves and create an identity (DaMatta 1991: 20–21).

This drama, however, does not happen in just any way. It is contained in two basic mechanisms: displacement and condensation (Leach 1976: ch. 8). By taking something drawn from everyday life and displacing it, the everyday is transformed into a ritual drama which can *concentrate* and highlight attributes that remain hidden in daily life. This essay will discuss the notion of a media-generated "scandal" as a particular type of ritual: a drama that constructs a narrative about a society by condensing and displacing elements of daily life. But this narrative is constructed around history: it is an episode drawn from the daily world whose characters are displaced and condensed, transformed into paradigms that discuss social questions (see DaMatta 1991: 23–25). The scandals that emerged out of the stories of Mônica and Aída have all of the ingredients that make up ritual: the use of everyday elements in a drama (a real story that is retold and transformed into a paradigm), the displacement and condensation that occurs in the portrait that is drawn of the actors, and the symbols/characters that the mass media construct.

The mythical quality of these events should not be ignored. Umberto Eco (1976), in an article about James Bond novels that used a method similar to that of Lévi-Strauss (1963) for the analysis of myths, called attention to the possibility of thinking of the culture industry as a contemporary space where myths are produced. At least two of the premises used by Lévi-Strauss for the study of myths appeared here clearly: the idea of myth as narrative that says something about the society that produces them (for example, as was evident in the social mobilization that occurred around the two cases of attempted rape, as if society recognized itself in these stories); and the logical development of the first premise, the idea that all myths must be understood in relation to the other myths of the same society (which occurred in the insistent associations that the media made between the two cases of Mônica and Aída, and eventually with other scandals involving sexual crimes).

I will therefore treat scandals as both myth and ritual. By approaching scandals from this perspective—as moments in which society speaks about itself—I will show how the two dimensions of gender and cultural values discussed above are found to be intimately articulated. It is due to the scandal that is produced around these two cases that discussion about the sexual behavior of the victims and the suspects achieves the level of moral prescription and reveals the gender roles that exist in the society. The space of thirty years that separates the occurrence of the two very similar cases opens, in its turn, the possibility of discussing changes and continuities in sex roles. Thus, this essay is divided into three parts. In the first part, I review briefly the case histories such as they were narrated in the press. Then I discuss the question of the sex roles that are implicit in the commentaries made about the cases, with the goal of understanding how conceptions of Brazilian sexuality and sexual morality changed during the thirty-year period. Finally, I discuss the cases as scandals by examining the role of the mass media in their production as scandals.[1]

In this essay, I have avoided a sociological discussion of terms such as "lower," "middle," and "upper class," and instead I have used them as "native categories" or "representations" encountered in the sources. Thus, the two cases involved members of the middle class (both victims and suspects) and, as ritual dramas, the scandals make the middle class their great protagonist. Cases of attempted rape, with subsequent death, occur frequently in the lower-class Baixada Fluminense region, a large area in Rio de Janeiro that is known for its high rates of violence and misery. However, these cases hardly get more than a mention in the newspapers. These are cases that involve those "individuals" whom Roberto DaMatta has so well identified, when he notes that the word "individual" can be used "in harsh police reports to highlight absolute and negative anonymity" (1991: 182).

In terms of DaMatta's individual/person opposition, the middle class would be, at the beginning, made up of persons in the sense that they do not emerge from police reports as anonymous individuals. In other words, as "persons," members of the middle class are "news." But there is another side to the question. The middle class can be viewed as "persons" in the sense that its members are not anonymous like the people of the lower classes, but they are individuals in the sense that they do not have the prestige to impede the reporting of a sometimes undesirable scandal. In other words, they are reported in the press as a category in between the lower and the upper classes: they are interesting as news, but they have no control over it.

This question makes it possible to perceive how the emotions of the persons of the middle classes appear in the media in contrast to those of the lower classes. On this point, Luís Reis and Haroldo Barbosa made a fine observation in a song entitled "Newspaper News," which tells the story of a poor mulatta woman who attempts to kill herself because a man has rejected her. In this song, the authors comment on the coldness and lack of accuracy of the newspaper report, which does not describe the human suffering involved, as is frequently the case. In the first part of the lyrics, the authors narrate the suicide attempt as it is registered in the newspapers; they portray clearly the situation of total anonymity in the names of the protagonists: Jane Doe (*Joana de tal*) and John Doe (*um tal João*). The existence of two parallel "levels" of reality (the personal level of the drama of Jane and the social level involving the cruelty of the newspaper coverage) can be detected in the line "here the news lacks exactness" (*aí a notícia carece de exatidão*). After this phrase, the song makes a transition that demonstrates the extent of the personal drama that is not reported, a drama which the song summarizes in the phrase "our pain isn't in the newspapers."

But there is a fundamental detail: in mentioning Jane's "humble shack," the songwriters situate the case in the lower class. Could this situation also describe the scandals of the middle class? We all see the way the press besieges the friends and relatives of the victims, the moments of tears and the brutal and obvious questions that reporters often make. In cases such as those of Mônica and Aída, the pain and emotion of the relatives are basic ingredients in the scandals, and they are often exacerbated by the press. We could thus say that the pain of the middle class *is* in the newspapers, but much more than they would like to see, precisely because the middle class is caught in the dilemma of being news and not being able to escape it.

The Cases

Aída Cúri died at 9:30 p.m. on July 14, 1958, as a result of a fall from the Rio Nobre Building, located at Avenida Atlântica 3388 in the neighborhood of Copacabana. On the first examination, the police investigation stated that there were signs of fractures and of violence (principally on the breasts, where there was a mark produced by suction). The brassiere was also torn.

It is important to note that on the first two days, the newspapers insinuated that Aída was a thoughtless and flippant person. However, such insinuations disappeared on the day the police accused two men whom they believed to be guilty of the death of Aída: Cassio Murillo Ferreira da Silva (who lived in the building) and Ronaldo Guilherme de Sousa Castro. Both were accused by Antônio João de Sousa, a porter of the Rio Nobre Building and himself also a suspect. Aída's family was not aware of her relations with the suspects, which was an obscure point in the inquiry.

The defense claimed that Aída had killed herself, and it supported this hypothesis with the following arguments: 1) She would have gone spontaneously and of her own free will into the apartment; 2) She did not suffer any physical violence; 3) She jumped from the window without any apparent motivation, and the people accompanying her were unable to stop her; 4) The reasons for suicide were related to her life history as a young woman with nervous disorders or psychological complexes.

The examination of the body disclosed fingernail marks, bites, and diverse excoriations, and it also disclosed that Aída had died a virgin. The investigation arrived at the conclusion that Aída, having suffered from attempted sexual assault (as the wounds on her breasts and the ripping of her inner clothing proved), was thrown over the walls by the aggressors. The final conclusion was that Aída was wronged by the boys, who took her to the top floor of the building, their action covered by the porter Antônio João. There she suffered attempted rape, after which she was killed.

Cassio Murillo, considered the principal party responsible for the crime, was involved in the trial only as a witness because he was a minor at the time of the crime. He was placed in the Service of Assistance to Minors and allowed to go free in 1962. Ronaldo Castro was given a prison sentence of thirteen years.

Mônica Granuzzo Lopes Pereira died on June 16, 1985, at about 7:30 p.m., from a fall from the apartment at Solar Santa Margarida Building, located in Fonte da Saudade, a neighborhood in the middle-class South Zone of Rio de Janeiro. On the afternoon of the following day, the police discovered her body, wrapped in a red blanket in a ravine between Vista Chinesa (Chinese View), located in the hills of Rio de Janeiro. On the afternoon of the sixteenth, Mônica went out to have ice cream with Ricardo Sampaio Peixoto, whom she had met the day before in the discotheque. Before going out, she left his address with her mother, Marieta Granuzzo. Since Mônica did not return, her mother filed a complaint with the police the next morning. After finding the body, the police went to Ricardo's apartment, where he was taken into custody along with two friends, Renato Orlando Costa and Alfredo Patti do Amaral.

The examination of the body revealed that Mônica had died a virgin, but that she was brutally beaten prior to dying, because her body showed lesions that could not have been produced by the fall. The police concluded that Mônica threw herself from the window; however, according to the district attorney, that would not lessen the guilt of Ricardo, who would have brought about the suicide through his aggressive conduct. The judge accepted the accusation of the district attorney and charged Ricardo of the following crimes: qualified homicide, hiding the body, fraudulent abduction (Mônica was a minor and was induced to go into the apartment on the pretext of picking up a jacket), trafficking in drugs (the police found residues of marihuana in Ricardo's apartment), invasion of a domicile (Ricardo hid in the neighbor's apartment, which was empty, when the police arrived), and destroying evidence (cleaning blood stains). Alfredo was charged with hiding the body and destroying evidence, and Renato was charged only with hiding the body.

In 1990, Ricardo received a prison sentence of seventeen years and some months, but the sentence is not final. Both the defense and the prosecution appealed, the former to shorten the sentence and the latter to lengthen it.

Sex Roles

As examples of the play of cultural values, the cases offer innumerable themes for analysis. In this section, I will discuss the different conceptions of sexuality that are implicit in the repercussion that the cases had, then I will describe and compare the feminine and masculine roles articulated in the two cases. It is necessary to emphasize, however, that such an analysis is only valuable insofar as the repercussion of the cases does in fact reflect cultural values, with the sexual behavior attributed to the characters in the cases reflecting socially established standards that, when broken, constitute the basis of scandals.

Before starting I would like to point out two directions that this analysis could take. In order to do this, it is necessary to make a distinction between sexual morality and the conception of sexuality. Sexual morality, the conception of sexuality, and their relationship involve a logic similar to Geertz's concepts of ethos and world view (1973). Ethos involves the evaluative elements of a given culture, whereas world view is related to the cognitive dimension. Sexual morality is thus part of ethos; it refers to the evaluative elaboration of sexuality, defined as right or wrong, proper or improper forms of behavior with respect to gender. Likewise, the conception of sexuality is part of world view; it belongs to the natural and involves the legitimating search for biological explanations, but it, too, does not ignore distinctions of gender.

The hypothesis which I will defend here (with respect to these two notions and the cases of Mônica and Aída) is that whereas sexual morality changed dramatically in the direction of greater liberality from the 1950s to the 1980s, the conception of sexuality remains unchanged in terms of its underlying and basic constructs: instead, there is only a diverse balancing of feminine and masculine sex roles. As I will demonstrate in the next section, Aída was described throughout the scandal that developed around her death as a model of purity and virtue. However, at the beginning of the coverage, a comment in the newspaper *O Globo* revealed some aspects of the sexual morality of the period. (All quotations in this section are from *O Globo*.)

In it (Aída's notebook) are the names and addresses of men, in shorthand, with allusive phrases that demonstrate the youth's familiarity with these people. These notations permit one to conclude that the girl did not maintain a regular life, and they even give the impression that she was a little flighty (7/16/58, p. 6).

Thus Aída is suspected of being flighty because her notebook contains the telephone numbers of some men.

Such suspicion is in sharp contrast with a declaration by Mônica's mother.

It was there (in Iguaba Grande) that she met Serginho and Marcelo, two boys who wanted to be her boyfriend. She was indecisive at the time, because the two wanted to be her boyfriend and she had never had a boyfriend before (6/30/85, p. 27).

Mônica's doubting with respect to two boys who were flirting with her is, on the contrary, a sign of her normality as an adolescent who is having her first contact with a boyfriend.

A similar contrast can be made between the following two passages:

Ronaldo also declared that the report of Aída's friend Ione Gomes to *O Globo* was true, making an allusion to what Aída Cúri herself must have told him, namely that her brother is said to have subjected her to rigorous control, forcing her to be at home every day before 9:00 p.m. (7/18/58, p. 6).

Mônica said that she met a boy the day before and that he lived in Fonte da Saudade. She was an innocent and ingenuous girl, a girl-woman. She did not see any reason not to go out with Ricardo and to go with him to his apartment (Mônica's grandmother's declarations, 6/20/85, p. 17).

Here is a new contrast: Aída's brother watches over her rigorously, making sure that she is always home before 9:00 p.m. Mônica, in turn, has the liberty to go out with someone she meets the day before, and she does not see any harm in going with the boy to his apartment. With respect to the time of the day, a curious detail emerges.

"At that time (when Mônica went to the discotheque)," Mônica's father recalls, "I took her myself, together with three other friends of hers. Afterwards I returned to pick them up at three in the morning. They set the time, since they didn't want to leave any earlier" (6/21/85, p. 11).

In other words, fourteen-year-old Mônica has the freedom to choose the time when she will return home—she can stay out until three in the morning—whereas eighteen-year-old Aída's schedule is controlled by her brother.

These examples confirm the commonsense notion that the sexual morality of the 1980s was much more liberal than that of the 1950s. A few other examples from the Mônica case can be cited.

"Things were going well, and we were kissing and hugging." (Declaration of Ricardo on what happened between him and Mônica while they were in the apartment, 6/18/85, p. 12.)

"She only wanted to kiss. She grabbed me and messed me up all over." (Declaration of Ricardo about Mônica, 6/19/85, p. 15.)

One does not find any corresponding observations in the Aída Cúri case. However, the total absence of such data on the physical contacts between Aída and the defendants is in itself eloquent enough testimony for the clear modification in the sexual morality of the two periods: Mônica went to the apartment of a boy she met the day before, and she is said to have exchanged kisses and hugs, without this providing evidence against her. On the contrary, it is considered normal behavior. In contrast, Aída is exalted as "the youth sacrificed in the holocaust to virtue" (7/26/58, p. 6).

One last datum supports this idea of greater liberty in sexual morality in the 1980s with respect to the 1950s. The previously cited quotation continues as follows:

"She only wanted to kiss. She grabbed me and messed me up all over. I thought it was strange and I began to feel sick, imagining that she was a transvestite." (Declaration of Ricardo about Mônica, 6/19/85, p. 15.)

In other words, the sexual morality of the 1980s admits that it is possible to find abnormal the fact that a woman does not permit any kind of intimate contact, beyond kisses, to someone whom she meets the day before. It is clear that I do not intend to discuss here if the version of the accused is true or if it is serving his interest, but instead it is only necessary to remember that as a narrative Ricardo's story itself highlights the reigning sexual morality.

I now wish to develop the second argument stated at the beginning of this section: that the conception of sexuality has remained unchanged from one period to the other, and instead that it has presented a diverse balancing of feminine and masculine sex roles. The conception of sexuality that remains unchanged has two basic characteristics: the attribution of a passive role to the woman, contrasted with the opposite and complementary initiative of the man, and the conception of masculine sexuality as uncontrolled and irrational. However, although these characteristics are present in the two periods studied, they show modifications that one might, at least as a beginning, call "modifications of intensity."

The attribution of initiative to the man becomes clear in the Aída Cúri case with the assumptions regarding the reasons why she would have gone up to the top floor of the building, all of which involved speculation about the ruses that would have been employed to get her to do this. At no place does anyone consider the hypothesis that she might have wanted to go up, because this would not be consistent with the profile of her as a decent and modest girl.

The girl was lured up to the top floor of the building. She must have been the victim of a terrible trap. The criminals must have used disconcerting artifices to induce Aída, an inexperienced and modest girl, to that adventure of such tragic consequences (7/24/58, p. 15).

We cannot accept the fact that our dear Aída has been transformed into a flighty girl from one day to the next. We, who knew her for so long and were close to her year after year, believe firmly that she was forced under threat to follow the criminals. Otherwise, she would not have gone into that apartment (testimony of friends from high school, 7/24/58, p. 15).

This attribution of initiative to the man, complemented by suppositions regarding the ingenuousness of the woman, also appears in the Mônica case.

Mônica didn't see any harm in accompanying Ricardo and going with him up to his apartment. And this is what cost her her life (testimony of Mônica's grandmother, 6/21/85, p. 11).

She was a candid, innocent girl, and she didn't see the evil in people. That's why she must have gone with him . . . That's why I say that she was tricked into going up into the apartment, certainly believing that his relatives were in the apartment (6/21/85, p. 11).

The second basic characteristic of the conception of sexuality in the two cases is the treatment of masculine sexuality as instinctive and uncontrolled. However, such a characteristic is subject to what was called "modifications of intensity," inasmuch as with Ricardo such behavior is criticized as sexual mania and abnormality.

Aída's executioners used disconcerting artifices to mislead her and attract her to the site, and when she resisted their savage impulses in a desperate struggle that left her exhausted and apparently dead, she was thrown into space (8/2/58, p. 6).

. . . from the porter who affirmed having witnessed violent scenes when Cassio tried to press the poor student against the wall of the top floor in his anxiousness to satisfy his instincts (7/24/58, p. 12).

Maria [Mônica's maid] said that Ricardo was not Mônica's boyfriend, but he was a degenerate and a maniac whom she met Saturday in the discotheque (6/19/85, p. 15).

While such characteristics remain unchanged between the two periods for masculine sexuality, the female sex role presents some relevant modifications. Characterized by a total passivity with respect to the initiative attributed to men, in the time of Aída Cúri any vanity could be interpreted as an attempt at seduction, since this also would run counter to the ideal of passive behavior.

On the day of her death, when Aída stopped by her house after work and before going to Copacabana, Dona Jamila (her mother) admonished her for using too much lipstick (7/16/58, p. 6).

On the other hand, what is condemned in Aída is valorized in Mônica as a sign of her maturity as a woman.

When she returned, she gave the appearance of having stopped being a girl and having awakened to life: she began to prepare herself better; coquettish, she asked for clothing that was in style and went out with her girlfriends from high school (testimony of Mônica's father, 6/21/85, p. 11).

Various other statements and commentaries made with respect to the case point to a decline in the passivity of the feminine sex role. I would like to cite here two statements—one attributed to Aída herself and the other from Mônica's father—that raise this question from another perspective.

Our coverage of the case revealed that Aída had once commented to her mother on the lifestyle of certain youths, saying, "You don't need to worry about me. I would kill myself before I would let you be ashamed on my account" (7/17/58, p. 6).

But Mônica also had a clear mind and a good personality, and she would never do what she didn't want to (6/21/85, p. 11).

Thus, in contrast to Mônica, Aída was capable of killing herself so that her mother would not be ashamed of her, but not capable of reacting of her own will. On the one hand, the sense of dignity and modesty are in a certain way associated with submission, inasmuch as the preference of death presupposes the impossibility of reacting; on the other hand, there is the affirmation of the woman's will against that of the other, which implies a relationship of equality.

Two other observations clearly show differences between Mônica and Aída on this question of passivity. Aída is exalted as "the youth sacrificed in the holocaust to virtue," with her virginity representing her triumph, her victory over her defendants (7/26/58, p. 6). In contrast, Ricardo, in his version of the event, makes a very telling comment about Mônica.

. . . until it reached a point that I couldn't stand it any longer and I asked her, "Are you a transvestite?" She lowered her head shyly; maybe she thought I was asking if she was a virgin (6/19/85, p. 15).

In other words, while Aída's modesty and virginity are two of the principle factors leading to her exaltation, it is implied that Mônica might have been ashamed of being a virgin.

One last detail helps complete the picture that I have tried to sketch up to this point. One of the characteristics of Aída as an exemplary youth emerges in a description of her with respect to sexual matters.

Everyone testified that she was a youth who practiced diligently the tenets of the Catholic faith . . . and that she never was heard to speak about a possible boyfriend, nor to make comments of any type about the pure and simple sentiment of love (7/25/58, p. 10).

In contrast, the conversations between Mônica and her mother about boyfriends, and the knowledge that the mother had of Mônica's meeting with Ricardo, are signs of her normality and maturity (6/30/85, p. 27). Thus, within a framework in which the basic characteristics remain unchanged— female passivity versus male initiative and the instinctive character of masculine sexuality—there emerge differences that point to a process of transformation between conceptions of sexuality and sexual morality as well as the consequent delimitation of sex roles in the two periods.

The Production of the Scandal

Two basic interpretive analyses are needed in order to understand "how to produce a scandal": first, the analysis of the positioning of the mass media themselves with respect to the communication of the facts, commentaries, and observations made about the scandals, and even the mode of narrating the stories; and second, the interpretation of the facts as they were presented, in an attempt to perceive what there was in these two cases that was so peculiar that they were able to provoke scandals of such proportions, and what the reaction of society was that permits us to classify such cases as scandals.

One of the most striking characteristics of cases such as those of Mônica and Aída is that there appears to be a certain involvement of the mass media in the unfolding of the event itself. For example, the media attempted to collaborate with the investigations by looking for clues and proofs that might help elucidate the cases. This attitude appears in the coverage of *O Globo* in the Aída Cúri case. In addition to participating actively in the search for the infamous green sweater that belonged to Cassio, which would have helped solve the crime, and attempting to verify Ronaldo's alibi by locating the girl who confirmed it, the coverage of *O Globo* showed participation in the investigations in other ways, as becomes evident in the following passages:

As the coverage revealed, Cassio Murillo has led a wild life, being known as partly responsible for the disappearance of two firearms that belonged to his stepfather's collection, as well as the theft of a motor scooter, which he later abandoned on a public highway. . . .

Other information that has come to our attention revealed that Cassio has been expelled for various reasons from several educational establishments (*O Globo*, 7/22/58, p. 6).

Such an attitude can also be found in the Mônica case, for example in the transmission by Rádio Globo of a tape in which District Attorney Jorge Vacite questioned the validity of the investigation completed by the Instituto Carlos Éboli, pointing out a series of irregularities in the investigation and affirming that he would demand its annulment or he would ask to be dismissed from the case. Rádio Globo aired the tape, which led to a series of discussions about the authenticity of the tape and generated accusations between the press and the civil police. On the day after the radio transmission of the tape, an editorial was published (on the same page on which the daily coverage of the case was appearing), defending the radio's action. Such facts represent the press's recognition of its involvement in these cases.

Before going any further, I would like to observe that the press involvement is more easily perceived in the Aída Cúri case, due to the type of journalism practiced at the time, when it was more common for reporters to state opinions and relate their participation in the coverage of the facts, which clearly shows media involvement in the case. For example, in the report on the reconstitution of the moments between Aída's arrival on the top floor and her death, the reporter from *O Globo* registered the following declaration from Cassio:

"You are guilty of having put me in stripes at the Service of Assistance to Minors. You are also responsible for that furious crowd that has gathered around the building." Cassio was really despondent, and it was at that moment of melancholy that the delinquent cried. (The reporter looked at his watch—1:30 a.m.) (8/1/58, p. 6).

Also related to this question of the positioning of the media with respect to the facts is another interesting detail that appears in both the reports of Mônica and Aída: when the accused give their versions of the event, if the media do not transcribe literally their statements and instead narrate them, one often finds expressions that incriminate the accused and therefore make it logically improbable that they would have in fact used such expressions. This process provides more evidence in favor of the hypothesis that the mass media are highly involved in the cases; a further example comes from a passage in Cassio's testimony.

He returned to the terrace, but he could not find the unfortunate Aída Cúri. Immediately, he ran to the wall of the top floor and, seeing the street, found the corpse of the poor victim extended on the sidewalk (7/23/58, p. 6).

It is highly unlikely that Cassio used the expression "poor victim," which presupposes a crime for which he himself is one of the accused. Thus there was a mixture of the discourse of the accused with that of society as expressed through the media.

Something similar occurred in a report of Ricardo's declarations, which also appeared in *O Globo*. Running parallel to the reproduction of his words, there is a description of his emotional state that appears to contradict his words and that, in the final analysis, has the similar effect of discrediting his testimony.

Ricardo repeated yesterday that, since their first meeting on Saturday at three in the morning at the door of the discotheque Mamão com Açúcar, he had the impression that the girl was a transvestite. But he stuttered, became upset, made several gestures, and did not manage to explain the reason for this supposition, because Mônica, despite being only fourteen, had the body of an adolescent and the face of a girl (6/19/85, p. 15).

The depiction of emotions of the people involved in the cases in the newspapers and magazines is another topic of relevance for this analysis. In the introduction, I referred to the sense of disgust that these emotions caused among the public who followed the cases. It is undeniable that these emotions are a fundamental ingredient in the production of the scandals, because the sense of drama and the transmission of the pain of the relatives and friends of the victims are a major factor in the public involvement in the cases. Thus, I would like to show how these emotions appear in the media in a process that I term the "exacerbation of the emotions." The contrast between the pain of the relatives of the victims and the "cynicism," "coldness," and "indifference" of the accused becomes fundamental to understanding the social dimension of these cases.

On the day after the first report of Mônica's death (a simple and dry police report), the newspaper *O Globo* ran a front-page photo of Mônica's burial, showing her father as he stood crying next to the coffin. The same photo appeared in the magazine *Veja*, with the following caption: "At the burial of Mônica, the despair of her father, Nilson." *Veja* also published a close-up of Mônica's father crying (6/26/85, p. 103), and a few days after the death of Aída, *O Globo* ran a first-page photo of her mother with the caption "Dona Jamila Cúri, mother of Aída, during the mass of the seventh day" (7/24/58). Furthermore, the magazine *O Cruzeiro*, in a long report on the case, devoted an entire page to the photo of Aída's mother as she contemplated a picture of her daughter, with the following caption printed beneath the photo:

There is no price for a mother's suffering. Dona Jamila Jacob Cúri, with a touched and longing look, remembers her daughter, who was brutally murdered. The criminals will be punished, but no one will restore the mother to her life together with her lost daughter (*O Cruzeiro*, 8/16/58, p. 30).

A similar process occurs in the Mônica case:

"What have they done to my daughter?" asked Mônica's father, Nilson Lopes Pereira, 38, between sobs, upon seeing his daughter buried yesterday afternoon in the São João Batista Cemetery. The mother, Marieta Granuzzo, had a nervous crisis and did not attend (*O Globo*, 6/19/85, p. 15).

The relevance of the "exacerbation of emotions" in turning the cases into scandals becomes even clearer when one compares them with the emotions, or absence thereof, attributed to the accused.

The lawyer Técio Lins e Silva, contracted by the family of Mônica Granuzzo Lopes Pereira, revealed yesterday that the three boys involved in the death of the youth . . . were seen in the discotheque . . . on Sunday night, after the body was hidden.

"They danced until three in the morning, as if nothing had happened," said the lawyer (*O Globo*, 6/24/85, p. 8).

The reconstruction of the event, as we described yesterday, had some dramatic phases. However, what was most impressive was Ronaldo Castro's calmness, impassivity, and lack of reaction—he who was responsible for the girl's presence on the top floor of the building, he who had a most intense and irresistible attraction toward her and, disappointed with her refusal, submitted her to the worst abuse, even to the point of physical aggression, slapping and hitting her. Likewise, the cynicism of Cassio Murillo, who appeared indifferent to the discussion of his crime in all of its hideousness, was deeply impressive to everyone present. He who, according to all indications and, above all, the police investigations, impelled the young girl to her death, did not appear to feel, even at the scene of the tragedy, the cruelty and immensity of his crime (8/2/58, p. 6).

Other examples can be cited—such as the headline in the magazine *O Cruzeiro*, which stated, "Cold and cynical Cassio Murillo and Ronaldo reproduce, in part, the tragedy of the young Aída Cúri: the final act" (8/16/58, pp. 33–34)—but these examples are sufficient to show the media's attempt to characterize the accused as affronting a pain that, in the final analysis, was that of the whole society.

Thus, the narration of the emotions involved in both parts of the cases contributed decisively to their transformation into scandals, not only because the public was captivated and made to feel solidarity with the pain of the victim's relatives, but also because it was made to feel challenged by the indifference and cynicism of the accused. There is thus a clear polarization between the victims and the accused. However, such polarization has an importance beyond that of making the public feel solidarity with the victims' families: this polarization constitutes the essence of the transformation of the cases into scandals, because it makes possible the identification of society with the victims, which then allows the accused to become transformed into a type of "public enemy number one." The form in which such a polarization takes place is the next point to be discussed, and it is fundamental to understanding why these cases became scandals.

In following the coverage of cases such as those of Mônica and Aída from an interpretive rather than an event-oriented perspective, a constant quickly

makes itself felt: the linking of the victims with the values considered culturally positive and a complementary and opposing linkage of the accused
with everything condemned by that same social group. We have, therefore,
a development of the polarization of emotions, a Manichean polarization
between the victims and the accused, who are transformed into symbols of
opposing values. It is this process that touched off the scandals, as I will show
in the following pages.

At the beginning of the Aída Cúri case, a series of speculations about the
character of the girl was made in an attempt to uncover the reasons why she
would have gone to the top floor of the building from which she fell. Besides
the already cited passages about Aída's notebook and her use of lipstick (*O
Globo* 7/16/58, p. 6), there is another passage worth discussing:

In contrast to what she told her mother, Aída did not go to the English school,
since it was closed for the holidays (7/16/58, p. 6).

Such comments appear at first to contradict my hypothesis regarding the
link between the values of the victim and those of society. However, a few
days after this, new comments appeared that eulogized Aída's character,
some of which even contradicted the first comments. Thus, the hypothesis
remains supported because Aída was soon transformed into the incarnation
of the cultural values of the period, values such as "purity of body and soul,"
Catholic religiosity, maturity, and attachment to her family.

Aída studied with us for twelve years, and of the twenty-five years that I have
been a teacher in that school, I have never had a better student. She was the first
in everything. Her behavior was exemplary and her grades enviable. There was
no one who didn't know her. We never said to any of the girls that she should
wear the habit, and we always warned them that the world is treacherous. Aída
was a girl who was made to live in heaven. The world didn't deserve her (statement of one of Aída's teachers, *O Globo*, 7/17/58, p. 6)

I affirm, as Aída's confessor, that she was pure of soul and body. If the truth were
otherwise, I would not hesitate to say so, without breaking the secret of confession. But it wasn't. . . . From what I could deduce from the details of the tragedy,
I am absolutely convinced that Aída has killed herself or was killed in the defense
of her virtue as a virgin (statement of Aída's confessor, 7/25/58, p. 10).

Everyone testified that she was a youth who practiced diligently the tenets of
the Catholic faith, that she was exclusively interested in finding a good job in

order to help her mother, and that she never was heard to speak about a possible boyfriend, nor to make comments of any type about the pure and simple sentiment of love (7/25/58, p. 10).

Aída is thus identified with all of the typical values of the bourgeois Catholic family (religiosity, dedication to the family, seriousness, and purity), so much so that one encounters paroxysms such as the comparison with the Saint Maria Goretti.

It is only a coincidence, but Aída died during the same week that the Church commemorates the holiday of the martyr Saint Maria Goretti, a young Italian who preferred to be killed than to sacrifice the purity of her body (*O Globo*, 7/24/58, p. 6).

Innumerable have been the manifestations in memory of the young girl sacrificed in the holocaust of virtue. Among them there is now an "Ave-Maria" composed by Heriberto Muraro (7/26/58, p. 6).

Aída is thus a symbol of the bourgeois Catholic morality: serious, responsible, a fervent Catholic, dedicated to her family, and a virgin.

And Mônica? What values does she represent? The exaltation of Mônica developed in a way that was structurally identical to that of Aída, although it is obviously linked to different values. Thus, during the first days after the event *O Globo* insinuated that Mônica lacked parental guidance, that she was free to do whatever she wanted, and that, up to a certain point, she was even flighty.

Mônica was alone on Saturday, seated near the small wall close to the exit door of the discotheque, when she met Ricardo. It was three in the morning, and after a quick exchange of caresses and telephone numbers, she went home alone, walking along the Rodrigo de Freitas Lagoon to Largo dos Lees, in Humaitá (6/19/85, p. 15).

Just as in the Aída Cúri case, such information disappears completely as the coverage of the case develops, giving way to a series of character witnesses that eulogize Mônica and her ties with her family.

Mônica had no motive whatsoever to kill herself; she was waking up to life . . . She was a marvelous child. She never gave me any work . . . .
I work in Bahia, but Mônica continued going there [to the discotheque], always taken either by her mother or by the mother of one of her friends, who would also return to pick them up (statement of Mônica's father, 6/21/85, p. 11).

Mônica was like any other girl. She was a friend and schoolmate of my two daughters, and I knew her well: a child full of doubts, of dreams to be realized, all daydreams proper to a girl of her age (statement of the father of a friend of Mônica, 6/19/85, p. 11).

Mônica is thus innocent, candid, healthy, happy, strong-willed, and, above all, normal. If Aída is the synthesis of the positive values of middle-class groups, Mônica is, in a way, the middle-class itself, insofar as her great merit is her normality.

And the accused? What opposition is established between Aída/Cassio and Mônica/Ricardo? At various points in this essay, I have cited passages that contained different criticisms of Cassio Murillo, the main suspect accused of Aída's death. I would like now to highlight these passages and characterize Cassio as he is described in the media, which in turn reveals the values that threaten those for whom Aída is a symbol.

Cassio always asked for the key to the empty apartments so he could take women there. When I didn't answer, he even broke into empty apartments. Coronel Adauto himself recognized that Cassio was terrible and that only he would be capable of breaking into apartments to take women into them (statement of the porter Antônio José de Sousa, 7/29/58, p. 18).

Likewise, Ronaldo was not immune from similar accusations.

As the report from this capital (Vitória) added, Ronaldo Castro disgusted his mother since he was ten. Later, becoming a carouser, he would even steal to support his tastes. One of his adventures even involved appropriating the car of Deputy Osvaldo Zambo (7/24/58, p. 15).

I believe it is not necessary to conclude that Cassio and Ronaldo are described as authentic representatives of "deviant youth," the great antagonist of the bourgeois Catholic family. However, before examining how this helps explain the "production of the scandal," I would like to examine the description of the accused in the Mônica case.

Ricardo, the main suspect, was also the media's main target; he was accused of violence, promiscuity, and illegal activities such as marihuana-smoking, extortion, and theft.

Yesterday, while the police were reconstituting Mônica's death behind closed doors in Ricardo's apartment, a maid who worked in the Solar Santa Margarida

Building told journalists that "Many people know that he beat his mother when they lived together, because he couldn't stand to see her with the boyfriend whom she later decided to live with" (*O Globo*, 6/22/85, p. 12).

Técio Lins e Silva affirmed that the three suspects were accustomed to extort money from homosexuals. He revealed that he had received phone calls from people who had suffered violence from the suspects in attempts at rape and extortion. According to the lawyer, women, homosexuals, and transvestites told stories about a "perverted relation of hatred against minority groups" (6/24/85, p. 8).

In a conversation with the District Attorney, Alfredo told about a dialogue that he had with Ricardo.

"Women have to be treated with care and tenderness, without violence," Alfredo said.
"With me there's no care. It's all slaps," Ricardo responded (6/26/85, p. 5).

Ricardo worked for a week in the boutique Yes Brazil, but he was dismissed because he was suspected of having stolen clothing from the store (*Veja*, 6/25/85, p. 103).

Alfredo and Renato are also described as marihuana smokers (*O Globo*, 6/19/85, p. 15), and Renato is suspected of theft.

The police intend to clarify this morning if Renato Orlando Costa, one of the suspects imprisoned for the death of Mônica, was dismissed by the boutique . . . where he worked for two months, because he had stolen clothing. The police received the tip from an anonymous call, and it was not possible to verify it yesterday (6/20/85, p. 17).

Thus, we have closed the cycle of Manichean polarization between the victims and the accused in the two cases. In the Aída Cúri case, the victim is turned into a symbol of all of the values (chastity, family, honesty, seriousness, religiosity) that are threatened by the values represented by the accused; in other words, the opposition between the bourgeois family and deviant youth emerges clearly. Mônica, on the contrary, is not made into a symbol of any specific social value, and the forcefulness of the scandal that developed around her death resides precisely in this idea that, being normal, it could have been her or any other woman. Likewise, the accused assemble together everything that is marginal, from violence to promiscuity, passing through theft and extortion.

In the Aída case, we thus have a transformation of the personalities into stereotypes of antagonistic social groups, which accounts for why there was such a social mobilization around this case: the Aída case is a scandal because it reflects a latent social conflict between the bourgeois Catholic family and deviant youth. Thus, it is not the death itself of Aída that is moving to the public, but the symbolism in which the death is invested as a victory of deviant youth over the bourgeois Catholic family. The scandal does not emerge as solidarity with the Cúri family but instead as a defense against the general threat to the family that is concretized in the case. It is thus not by accident that *O Cruzeiro* gave the following headline to a report on the case: "The Death of Aída: The Crime of a Lost Generation" (8/16/58, p. 28).

In comparison, the force of the Mônica case as a scandal does not reside in her association with a specific group of cultural values, but instead in the diversity of social types that she represents. Likewise, Ricardo is not the stereotype of any specific social group, but instead a synthesis of all the dangers that threaten middle-class society. However, as for the case of Aída, social conflicts emerge because Mônica is so "normal" and therefore can serve as a metaphor for everyone who is threatened by deviants, in turn symbolized by Ricardo. The case therefore dramatizes the general climate of violence in Rio and the feeling that no one is safe. The Mônica case thus expresses a social conflict just as the Aída case does; however, the difference is that now the identity of the opponents is not so clear.

On this point, there is a declaration by Mônica's uncle, who, making an appeal for people to speak if they knew anything that might help elucidate the case, remembered the following:

Before it happened, I never imagined that my niece would be killed in such circumstances. Tomorrow, it could be the daughter of anybody (*O Globo*, 6/24/85, p. 8).

This is what I call the "social dimension of the cases": the fact that the cases constitute themselves as a type of paradigmatic expression of social conflicts, either as an evident antagonism or as a general danger that threatens everyone indiscriminately.

One final point corroborates the analysis presented here: the debates linked to the themes that emerged from the two cases. The Aída Cúri case generated two major discussions about the questions of penal irresponsibility and deviant youth. The first theme is related to the fact that Cassio, as a minor at the time of the crime, was not subject to the penalties that the law assigned to such crimes. Thus, an acrimonious debate emerged about the necessity of lowering the age of penal responsibility (*O Globo*, 7/28/58, p. 6).

The debates surrounding the Mônica case present a heterogeneous assortment of more diverse themes, running from the presence of minors in discotheques to questions of the feminist movement involving violence against women. It is thus that a few days after Mônica's death there was a police raid on the discotheque where she met Ricardo to check for the presence of minors (*O Globo*, 6/23/85, p. 19). On the same occasion, there were several interviews with the youth about values such as virginity and fidelity (*O Globo*, 6/23/85, p. 19). One of the questions that emerged out of the Mônica case is the effect of the separation of couples on their children, given that both Mônica and the three suspects were children of separated parents.

Children should go to the alcoves of their homes and plead with their parents not to separate or divorce, which prejudices their development and causes traumas for the rest of their lives. It can even lead them to vice and to fall into sinister traps, as happened in the Mônica case (6/27/85, p. 14).

Feminists also attempted to raise a series of questions. Their participation in protests is quite striking, and the media highlighted their leadership role (*O Globo*, 6/27/85, p. 14). Psychoanalysts were also called upon to give their opinion of the case (*O Globo*, 6/20/85, p. 17). The parent-child relationship is another one of the themes that emerged, as is demonstrated in the following statement of Dona Marieta Granuzzo, Mônica's mother.

Mônica's death is a result of the violence of the city. I never would have believed that in a discotheque like that she would have met people like Ricardo. I can only say that mothers must have a friendly relationship with their children in which nothing is hidden and there are no secrets (6/30/85, p. 27).

I also had the opportunity to attend a discussion in which the broad diversity of themes surrounding the Mônica case made itself evident. Called "Justice for Mônica," the discussion took place in the Rui Barbosa House on November 6, 1985, and it included representatives from Catholic, legal, psychoanalytic, feminist, and neighborhood associations. Having the objective of increasing public opinion pressure in favor of condemnation of the defendants, according to a representative of the Rui Barbosa House, the discussion even included Mônica's parents. At one point Mônica's father commented that he knew the action would not bring back Mônica, but in losing his daughter he gained thousands of new ones, for whom he was now fighting.

The examination of the debates raised over the Mônica and Aída Cúri cases confirms the analysis made above regarding the social dimension of the cases. Revealing a specific conflict (the bourgeois Catholic family vs. deviant youth), the Aída Cúri case raised discussions about specific themes (i.e., juvenile delinquency). Affecting a wide variety of groups in society, the Mônica case is multifaceted and it permits an enormous array of themes to be raised and debated.

Before concluding, there is one last detail that I consider fundamental, not only because it reinforces the interpretation made here but also because it clarifies the notion of social scandal as it is embedded in these cases. On August 16, 1958, *O Globo* printed on the front page that the Snack Bar, the traditional hangout of the deviant youth of Copacabana, would move up its closing time from 5:00 a.m. to 1:00 a.m. Likewise, on June 23, 1985, five days after the first news of Mônica's death, *O Globo* published the news that a police raid on the discotheque where she met Ricardo was a failure, because it was found nearly empty, being closed due to lack of customers a few days later.

Conclusions

Starting with two basic dimensions—the transformations of the conceptions of sexuality over two distinct periods and the relationship between the scandals provoked by two cases of sexual crimes and the societies in which they occurred—one can draw a few conclusions that, far from exhausting the subject, at least can point to areas of further research. The study of the cases of Mônica and Aída Cúri validates the common-sense notion that sexual customs have become increasingly liberalized in contemporary Brazil. This study also reveals a more subtle aspect of the conceptions of sexuality of the two periods: the maintenance of sex roles attributed to men and women, particularly the male as the initiator and the worldly-wise versus the female as the ingenuous and the passive. However, this constant aspect of the sex roles is accompanied by a counter-balancing factor of increasingly diverse roles, which is necessary to understand why the sexual morality of the 1980s was perceived as more liberal than that of the 1950s.

Regarding the second axis of this study, there appears to be a common ground between the two cases: the fact that both cases became social scandals because they dramatized conflicts in the surrounding societies. Thus, the death of Aída Cúri detonated a scandal that dramatized the plight of the bourgeois Catholic family threatened by deviant youth, who were represented by Cassio and Ronaldo. Mônica, in turn, represented no specific social groups, and likewise for Ricardo. Instead, it is her normality that strikes us, because anyone could be a potential victim of diverse dangers, personified by Ricardo, who is portrayed as the carrier of all the vices and defects that society produces. With respect to the contextual differences, the relationship of case/scandal/society remains the same: the scandal is produced by identifying the protagonists of the cases with broader social categories and cultural values.

The protagonists therefore become paradigmatic heroes and rogues (DaMatta 1991) who condense opposing sets of social values and dramatize social conflicts. As the social groups become involved, the cases are transformed into scandals, which in turn can be interpreted as rituals and read as narratives of changing values of gender, violence, and everyday life in urban Brazil.[2]

Acknowledgments

I would like to thank David Hess, Everardo Rocha, and Ricardo Benzaquem for their helpful comments, and Fernando Rebello for helping me collect data.

Endnotes

1. In this essay, I deal exclusively with the public dimension of the two cases, that is, with how they appeared in the media. Therefore, the issue of who is guilty or what is true is beyond the scope of the paper. The principal source was *O Globo* (July/August 1958 and June/July 1985), the main newspaper that covered the two periods, but I also used the magazines *O Cruzeiro* (July/August 1958) for the Aída case and *Veja* (June/July 1985) for the Mônica case. Unless stated otherwise, the dated newspaper citations come from *O Globo*.

2. In subsequent essays, I have further explored the way in which public scandals serve as rituals/narratives. For example, see Coelho and Helal (1991a, 1991b) on scandals involving the transfer of soccer players in Brazil.

References

Coelho, Maria Claudia, and Ronaldo Helal
1991a   "O Caso Bebeto: Futebol e Identidade Cultural no Brasil." Ms.

1991b "A Troca como Ritual." *Jornal do Brasil* No. 95. April 28, "Idéias/Ensaios."

DaMatta, Roberto
1991 *Carnivals, Rogues, and Heroes*. Notre Dame, Ind.: University of Notre Dame Press.

Eco, Umberto
1976 "James Bond: uma Combinatória Narrativa." In *Análise Estrutural da Narrativa*. Petrópolis: Vozes.

Geertz, Clifford
1973 *The Interpretation of Cultures*. New York: Basic Books.

Leach, Edmund
1976 *Culture and Communication*. Cambridge: Cambridge University Press.

Lévi-Strauss, Claude
1963 *Structural Anthropology*. New York: Basic Books.

Chapter Five

Morality and Transgression
Among Brazilian Poor Families:
Exploring the Ambiguities

⊠

Cynthia A. Sarti

Brazil is well-known as a traditional, patriarchal society. It is also well-known for its vast internal differences. If one goes to São Paulo, a world metropolis that a recent magazine article describes as "vibrating with entrepreneurial energy and prosperity," one could not deny the country's modernity.[1] The ambiguity of being both modern and traditional, individualist and hierarchical, has been stressed as the core of the "Brazilian dilemma" (DaMatta 1991). Brazilians face the difficulty of achieving modernity in a country anchored in patriarchal values and personal relationships. Although tradition has lost some of its foundation, especially economic, it retains an important symbolic power. Brazil is a society that has modernized itself in such a way as not to think of itself as traditional; paradoxically, it cannot dispose of the old structures, especially in matters of morality. The specter of the old "coronel"—the rural patriarch—is alive, if not well, in Brazilian daily life.

Historically, Brazil developed a patriarchal family pattern that has maintained its legitimacy through successive social transformations.[2] Yet, that family pattern and system could not remain unchanged. My concern in this paper is with the continuing influence of the moral code of the patriarchal family and the frequent forms of its transgression. The dynamics of this "changing continuity" are an essential characteristic of social relations in Brazil: traditional patterns are slowly modified through adjustments and negotiations, an assertion that should hardly be surprising, given the fact that Brazilian history is not known for radical ruptures.

My research has been with poor people (to be defined below). In this paper, I analyze how poor people construct moral categories in family life and within the neighborhood where they live. I focus on the construction of rules and on the meaning of their transgressions. My purpose is to see how the construction of moral categories in the particular context of a subordinate group reveals the social logic within which they operate.

Background Comments

The questions discussed here are part of a broader anthropological research project on morality among the urban poor and based on fieldwork conducted since 1980 in a poor neighborhood in São Paulo.[3] The locale is one of the poorest regions of the city (known as the "periphery"); it is characterized by neighborhoods inhabited by a professionally unskilled and relatively uneducated population.

Some initial definitions are necessary. "Family morality" refers to the set of norms and values that organizes family life. Implicit, unspoken, and internalized, these norms and values are seen as "natural" and part of the family life. Thus, my focus is on the symbolic dimension of family life. My perspective on morality emerges from Durkheim's concept of society as a moral order, that is, from a social science perspective.[4] In other words, instead of seeing morality as something rooted in the individual, as in the Kantian tradition of philosophy, I see society as the source and foundation of morality (Durkheim 1924, 1933). Morality in this sense implies the notion of the "Other" and the collectivity. Morality is also socially given and not internal to the individual. From the social science perspective, there is no *a priori* category. Social norms and values are internalized and expressed, not given, at the individual level.

It follows from this perspective that morality is not an absolute "thing" or substance. No act, no rule, has a moral content in itself. Its content is defined in reference to social relations. A moral act is defined according to the interpretation of actors involved, not by any intrinsic content of the act. The same act can be approved or condemned, depending on the existence of the social rules that prescribe its approval or condemnation. Transgression (or immorality) is, therefore, a consequence of the fact that someone has violated an existing rule.

I will use this framework to discuss two levels of reality. The first is the given set of social norms and values that I call the pattern of legitimacy, in other words, the model from which people construct their moral categories. (We know that such reasoning does not just come from anywhere.)

The second level of reality—separated only for analytical purposes—is the way this pattern is expressed at the level of the individual. I try to understand how individuals negotiate social norms. In doing so, I take into account the permanent and insoluble tension between the individual and social norms, because the imposition of norms necessarily implies some coercion on the individuals, who are constantly negotiating norms.

The basic assumption of this framework, one which I share with anthropology, is that there is no theoretical contradiction between action and thought, because both practices and representations are social facts. I see the moral categories that people use to construct their family life as expressed both in their discourse and their actions. My framework draws on both what people say and what they do, because these two levels are manifestations of the same moral order. The discrepancies between discourse and practices are reflections of social identities built into a relational process, in which the individual is subject to cross-cutting identities rather than "contradictions" to be resolved.

This paper analyzes morality among the urban poor, focusing on the neighborhood level. I consider how the poor follow, transgress, or negotiate implicit social rules. I focus specifically on the mechanisms through which people negotiate rules in family life and in the neighborhood. As a result, I focus on the dynamics of values among "peers" in a neighborhood.

I analyze two issues to understand social relations and the dynamic of values in family and local life: 1) peer relations, i.e., relations in daily life in the neighborhood; and 2) authority within the family. I try to show how the people negotiate social norms in these two contexts, keeping in mind of course that the family and neighborhood are part of a broader system. My attempt is always to see what we can learn about the larger society from the particular way that the people experience their lives.

The Sociological Location of the Urban Poor

A few words on the perspective from which I study the urban poor should make clear some of the similarities and differences with the current literature on the subject. I work with a low-income population for which the average individual income of the workers does not exceed two minimum wages.[5] Even though they inhabit a poor neighborhood in one of the poorest regions of the city, they are not the poorest by Brazilian standards. It is important to understand that most are migrants who came to the city of São

Paulo—one of the most developed regions of Brazil—from the poor and backward northeast or other rural areas of the country during Brazil's economic boom of the 1960s and 1970s. As a result, they have experienced relative social mobility along with geographical mobility, because they are exposed to job and educational opportunities that they did not have where they grew up. They live in residential neighborhoods—the so-called "periphery"—that are distant from the city center, in precarious urban conditions and with much uncertainty about the legal title to their land. Indeed, they have been able to buy the land and build a house because those conditions make it affordable.[6] Their ownership is an important element in their social identity, differentiating them from other "poor people."

I call this population "urban poor," a term which may seem less precise than the concept of "working class." However, I do so because I do not take their working conditions as the principal starting point, as is implied in the concept of class. Furthermore, I focus on interactions within the family and the neighborhood, because these are the relevant issues concerning the living conditions of the urban poor.

My approach is ethnographic; my goal is to reconstruct the social universe in a way that is similar to how these people construct it. Thus, I try to construct the sociological definitions derived from the "natives' " own categories. That does not mean I explain society through the informants' categories, a trap especially for researchers who identify politically with the people they study. Rather, it means that I base my explanation on my informants' categories, which implies a degree of detachment. The poor, like everyone else, think about the values, the norms, and the codes in which they are socialized (through education, religion, political organizations, state agencies, and work), to which they are exposed, and which they internalize at all levels of social life. In short, they interpret their lives. I try to follow their interpretations.[7]

In the way the urban poor represent the social order they clearly see themselves as "poor" as opposed to the "rich," the ones who live "over there" in the "center," or "there in São Paulo" (phrases that reveal their sense of exclusion). The term "rich" also refers to anyone who has a postsecondary education, who is therefore a *doutor* (someone with a university degree). That constitutes the basic, structural opposition in their perception, but it is not the only one. They construct their social identity by thinking in terms of oppositions and comparisons. Those whom they consider to be "peers" vary according to the reference point. Thus, the people who are considered equal in one context, for example (when compared with the "rich," i.e., those from the city center as classified by income or by educational level) might be viewed differently in other contexts, when other comparisons are made.

The construction of the categories in which the poor place themselves as a social group implies a continuous process of identification and differentiation, or, more precisely, identification through differentiation. Social identity is by definition relational: it is defined in relation to, in opposition to—that is, always in relational terms. Social identity, therefore, has no fixed context. It varies as the social actors form their identity in relation to their multiple social roles. The "good worker" is defined in opposition to the "thief," the "honest woman" in opposition to the "whore," and so on.[8]

An additional comment is necessary here regarding the notion of class consciousness, insofar as class is understood to imply some essential content or substance. Admittedly, the concept of class is also, by definition, relational. But insofar as its use emphasizes the opposition of classes, it fails to capture the dynamics involved in relations among those who are equal in economic terms. In short, it underplays the dual process of identification and differentiation among peers, which is an essential part of the dynamics of class relations.

The existing literature on the poor, based primarily on the principle of class exploitation and on the conception of the working class as the main force of political transformation, has paid little attention to the importance of peer relations in the process of constructing social identity. As Montes (1983) argues in her revision of the concepts of culture and ideology, Marxist-influenced social science has tended to reduce culture to a question of domination. Culture thus tends to be seen as an instrument of power, without regard to its internal dynamics and logic. The dominated is either "conscious" or "alienated," terms which are considered to be mutually exclusive. This either-or analysis fails to capture the ambiguities and the intermediate categories that go into pluralistic social identities. Anthropology, through its concept of culture, has been the main source of criticism of the class-oriented approach. However, analyses based on the concept of culture often give little weight to the broader structure within which cultural manifestations occur. My goal is to consider morality from a cultural perspective that takes into account the place of morality in a broader structure of hierarchical, capitalist relations.

Although social differentiation takes place on an economic basis, the poor also make constant differentiations that are established in moral rather than purely economic terms.[9] This process of identification and differentiation among peers is as important for the social identity of the poor as is the basic economic differentiation. The process also has important political implications, because it defines the limits and possibilities of a collective identity on which to base political action.

Interpreting from the inside means trying to avoid viewing the poor (because they are deprived) as mere instruments of a perverse society, a perspective one often finds in the literature. Rather, researchers should try to uncover their rationales, their explanations of their choices. How do the poor place themselves as social actors? It is not only in relation to these "others," the "rich," but it is also in the peer relations, in the intermediate relations, in the interstices, that we find important clues to the nature of social identity.

Peer Relations

Peer relations among the urban poor are inherently ambivalent, both within the family and in the neighborhood network. From what I observed, the so-called solidarity among the poor, which the literature tends to emphasize, does not capture the complexity of peer relations, which involve rivalry as well as solidarity.

Within the family this ambivalence is reflected in the attitude toward kinship ties. On the one hand, these ties, with their implied relations of reciprocity and complementarity, are seen as a necessary part of daily life. On the other hand, they are rejected as a burden because they make difficult social mobility, which is seen in individualistic terms (Kottak 1967). When "progress" or "a better life" (meaning a move up from one's group of origin) appears possible, family ties might be seen as an obstacle. Although the poor need family ties for mutual support (which is usually what they can afford), their attitude toward the extended family is ambiguous. They experience a conflicting reality because their lives are structured in terms of the extended family ties, but they also value the nuclear family. If they fail to create a nuclear family, the reason is usually economic: they cannot dispose of the larger family ties. Woortmann (1982) argues that the incorporation of relatives to the household unit constitutes a strategy rather than a cultural value. I do not agree that there is a practical reason ("a strategy") involved in the incorporation of relatives to the household, and I do not think that mere "strategies" can be understood in contrast to "values." Rather, the "strategies" that people adopt are implied in their values. I argue that the poor experience a conflict of hierarchical and individualistic values, as they try to build an independent nucleus in a hierarchical structure of family life, which they also value.

Despres states in his study of Manaus (in northern Brazil) that the formation of extended households "seems not to involve a desire to constitute or maintain an extended family in the fashion of the much-described *parentela* of Brazilian tradition. Rather, they were formed out of a sense of obligation rooted in the mutual affection that members of the nuclear family had for one another" (1991: 165). Thus, in hard times the poor rely on reciprocal family relations to help each other—as in times of sickness or when a newly arrived relative is becoming established in the city. In fact, there is this sense of obligation, but rooted in the principle of reciprocity and complementarity that structures family life and within which affection is developed. Furthermore, this engagement always retains an ambiguous character. As Kottak describes in his study of a community in the Brazilian northeast: "Since . . . their wealth and power are so limited, lower-class Brazilians have come to regard kinship with ambivalence; it offers salvation to the destitute but a threat to the more ambitious entrepreneurs" (1967: 431). This argument applies especially to poor migrants to São Paulo, because the quest for a "better life" is the very reason for migrating. At the same time, kinship ties form the essential network for migrants trying to establish themselves in their new environment, which implies the moral sense of reciprocal obligations.[10]

The same ambivalence can be seen in regard to the neighbors, whom they perceive as analogous to the family. One of my informants said: "Practically, it is like a family, because when we are in need, they are here. When they need us, we are all together, so I think this is a family." Generally speaking, the residents like their neighborhood. They would prefer to be better off, of course, but here at least they have achieved their ideal of owning their house, an ideal linked to their life goal of marrying and having children. They seldom leave the house or the neighborhood, except to go to work. Occasionally, they visit relatives in other parts of the city. Their social life is primarily limited to the family and to their immediate neighbors.

A brief look at neighborhood corner stores illustrates one important feature of that life. There are two types of corner stores where people socialize. One sells daily necessities such as food, cleaning materials, school supplies, etc. Men, women, and children congregate there. The other type of store is a masculine space, a bar, where customers usually play pool ("sinuca") and cards. This second type is divided into two categories, each based on moral values. One is places where "honest people" go on their way home from work or on weekends and days off. Here, "the atmosphere is social," as one informant put it. The second category of men's bar is where the outlaws gather. Here, they plan robberies (to take place usually outside the neighborhood) and they sell drugs. Given their business, they have to guarantee at least the acceptance, if not the complicity, of everyone present. These are the "closed" bars, where gangs assemble and control the customers to ensure the gang's security.

The residents of the neighborhood draw a basic moral distinction between the image of the "worker" (*o trabalhador*, associated with the father, the head of a family) and that of the "thief" (*o bandido*). It is important to stress the symbolic dimension of this opposition, because it plays an important role in the construction of the identity of the worker. The "thief" is the negative point of reference against which the poor situate themselves on the "good side." Nevertheless, in daily life the distinction between the "worker" and the "thief" is much more flexible, shaded, and nuanced, and as a result the boundaries between the two categories are often fuzzy. For example, from the "worker's" point of view, the "thief" is not only someone who "makes easy money" but also someone who does not care about where the money ends up; in other words, the "thief" does not take the money home. In contrast, the "worker" is associated with the role of "provider," the head of the family, and therefore the "worker" is associated with family values. Within this reasoning, a man who gets money through "illegitimate" means (such as robbery) but takes this money home is not necessarily considered a "thief"; at least, he is not a "bad thief" or he is only "a thief by circumstance." Thus, once again it can be seen that the moral categories do not have an essential content; rather, they are relational and their meaning varies and shifts according to the point of reference. If violence—and the fear it infuses among local residents—is said to be part of the local life, then there are rules that render violent acts, although feared, to some extent understandable to the residents. As a result, violence comes to fit into the local rules.[11] "You cannot call a thief 'thief,' " says a 24-year-old male informant. "Obviously, he won't like it. You have to treat him like a person: from one person to another."

The neighborhood itself is divided into an economic hierarchy characterized by three main areas. The upper street ("a Avenida") is where people who are slightly better off have their homes. Down the hill one finds an intermediate area of more precarious homes built on clearly demarcated lots that have been purchased legally (although the titles for this area are in dispute). Descending farther one reaches the squatter settlements ("a favela"), where the residents have invaded the land and built homes without any legal title to the land. Although the difference between the upper street and the squatter settlements is clear, there are less obvious differences in the living conditions among the residents in the intermediate area. Symbolic distinctions therefore are made in terms of moral categories. The most evident distinction the residents make is between their neighborhood and the squatter settlements on the edges of the neighborhood. To live in the settlements means to be in a lower social condition. The squatter settlements embody the residents' basic fears: violence, robbery, sexual indiscretion, and drugs. The head of the family must keep his doors locked and build locked gates around his house. He encloses it in a dual sense: first, to delimit his property (brick walls and iron gates, as opposed to fences and wooden gates, are symbols of social differentiation); second, to protect symbolically himself and his family against their fears, to keep deviation at bay. It is important to stress that these fears, conceived here in moral categories, are constructed as a defense of family values. The risks and the deviations in social life are defined as such because they threaten the pattern of family life.

Deviation has the family pattern as its moral reference point and is defined differently according to family role. Gender roles constitute a significant point of differentiation, because men and women are defined as being in different moral categories. In the case of sons, the main risks are drugs and banditry (normally understood to include robbery and murder). In the case of daughters, the risk is prostitution, i.e., a life that would divert her from marriage and the creation of a family. Good behavior is mainly defined in terms of work values for a man and family values for a woman. Accordingly, the principle accusation against a woman is that she is a "whore" ("uma puta"), referring to her sexual behavior; and against the man that he is a "bum" ("vagabundo"), which refers to work values.

Parents locate danger in street life, confirming DaMatta's argument (1985) that the opposition between the house (the family sphere) and the street (the public sphere) plays an important role in the construction of social identities.[12] Thus, the ideal is to keep children inside the house in order to avoid "bad influences." Ideally, the mother should watch the children, which is one of the main reasons why women's working is not favored. It is acceptable if subordinated to the mother's role, as in a part-time job or work that can be done at home. In fact, because mothers often work and their choices are limited, daycare centers are seen as a good solution, or at least a lesser evil, since they keep children off the street.

Because the distinctions among peers are not clear, differences must be continually stressed through the use of moral categories. One of the first phrases I heard in the neighborhood was: "We are poor people, but we don't live in the 'favela.' " When I interviewed people who did live in the squatter settlements, they said: "We live in the 'favela,' but at least we have a roof over our heads. We don't live under the bridge." (I did not interview anyone living under the bridge, but I think it very likely that they would construct some negative point of reference as well, because this is the social logic.) Social hierarchization is therefore reproduced endlessly because it is based not on economic distinctions but on moral values. Thus, residents can always construct a moral spectrum to differentiate themselves from the negative reference point.

Considering that poor neighborhoods in Brazil are mostly nonwhite, race can also be used as a moral category to differentiate people, and thus race becomes another way of constructing an internal hierarchy among the poor. Unlike in the United States, in Brazil skin color is constructed in a way so that it is crosscut by other social conditions. In other words, it is possible that two people who have the same skin color can be considered socially different. A person might be more or less "black" depending on some point of reference other than color, such as the person's economic standing or moral status. Thus, according to the poor people's distinctions, a black thief is darker than a good and honest worker who would otherwise have the same skin color.[13]

Within this logic, to complain about one's neighbor is intrinsic to the local discourse. The neighbor becomes the mirror, the constant positive or negative point of reference against which the residents base their identity as a person worthy of respect. If they see the "rich" to be at the top of the social hierarchy and the squatter settlements at the bottom, they see themselves and their neighbors as equals in being in between. Toward their peers they feel the same ambivalence they feel toward the family.

Constructing a social identity is therefore a dual process. There is a need for peer-group support, because that provides a social identity—the feeling of belonging to a group—but there is also a need to differentiate, which gives a sense of being respected as a unique person. The construction of moral categories is thus essentially relational: to ensure that one is in the "good" realm, one has to construct an "evil" realm and place counterparts there. Because peers are so close, they are a constant point of reference in the process of identification and differentiation, which is inherently ambivalent.

Authority Within the Family

Moving now from neighbors and peer relations to the family, one finds the source of the hierarchical structure of social relations that is based on the family values of complementarity and reciprocity. Understanding the structure of poor families and the importance given to family relations by the poor leads to understanding how family values shape not only life within the family but also the family members' ideas about what counts in the outside world. Family values are always a central reference.

The pattern of authority within the urban poor family is patriarchal, characterized by the man's authority over the woman and the elders' (parents') authority over the young. As discussed above, the patriarchal family is a longstanding Brazilian family pattern that has been described in the literature since Gilberto Freyre (1980) first applied the term to the Brazilian case and argued that this legitimating pattern of family authority furnished the reference point for all of Brazilian society.

My focus is on how this pattern is experienced by the poor and how changes in their experience of it relate to their position in the larger picture. In my view, there is no pattern of family authority unique to poor families. They translate in their own terms the traditional family pattern in Brazilian society. I will try to follow the particular way that they translate this legitimate pattern of family authority.

The fact that the man is the prime authority figure does not mean that the woman totally lacks authority. The man and the woman share authority in different domains. She has a domestic authority defined by her social role: she manages family life, she takes care of the whole family, she controls the money that (in the ideal model) the man brings home. In short, her share of authority is based on her role as mother. All family organization in this context is based on a traditional division of gender roles: man is the provider (the breadwinner) who furnishes the food and a roof, whereas the woman takes care of the house, her children, and her husband.

The roles are therefore defined in reciprocal and complementary terms, with each side having a different role to play. The woman is considered the "head of the household," whereas the man is considered the "head of the family." That order implies a hierarchical difference: the man retains authority at a higher level, following the precedence of the family over the household in their hierarchy of values. Within this picture, the wife's domestic authority makes the internal dynamics of family relations more complex than a superficial understanding of the patriarchal pattern might suggest. Although subordinated by virtue of her gender, she is respected and valued as a mother (women of this social stratum are valued as such only if they are mothers).[14] The internal family dynamics therefore reveal negotiation and compensation based on this division of authority.

Although the Brazilian family is patriarchal—with the man representing the highest authority—it has some special features when compared to other male-dominated societies. As a hierarchical structure, the Brazilian family is based on the principle that the subordinate receives protection (although because it is hierarchical, abuse is always likely to take place). Regarding the question of protecting the subordinate, the Brazilian family—as for any hierarchical structure—resembles feudal society more than the individualism of capitalist society. It is a protection based on the principle of reciprocal obligations, not on the competitive principles implied in the notion of the individual in capitalist culture. Although in Brazilian society the protective relationship occurs primarily within marriages (with the husband as protector), it also occurs in consanguineous (blood) relations when conflicts between affines (in-laws) take place.[15] It is especially frequent in cases of divorce (or de facto separation, since legal divorce is not a common practice), when women return to the protection of their father and/or brothers.[16]

Considering the important role of authority performed by women in poor families, how can one define male authority within the family? The authority of men and women are founded on different grounds. The man embodies the notion of authority. He is responsible for the external image of the family. As father, it is his job to guarantee his family's respectability. Man's authority within the family is therefore mainly defined in terms of the family's relationship with the outside world, rather than in terms of intrafamily relations. He mediates between the family and the public sphere. Thus, male authority is based on a social representation, rather than on the control of resources within the family. Male authority is mainly supported by a gender system that places the woman in a subordinate position. When she occupies a masculine role, such as supporting economically the household, she does it in different conditions defined by her gender.

The conception of authority embodied in the man leads to the question of female heads of households. The incidence of such households has been stressed in the literature on the urban poor, and it has been central to uncovering the important economic role of women in poor households (Barroso 1978, Castro 1989). However, misunderstandings may arise if one does not take into account that even when a woman becomes the household's principal economic supporter, the man's identification as the authority figure does not necessarily change. Although male authority is based primarily on the man's location in the gender system, rather than on his role as breadwinner, the latter obviously reinforces his position: his authority is undermined if he does not guarantee his family's support. Still, if the woman becomes the breadwinner, it is not sufficient to make male authority collapse, because of the strength of the symbolic identification of the man with the idea of legitimate authority within the gender system. In this case, often the male authority role is transferred to men in the wife's family of origin or to her oldest son.[17]

The changing pattern of family dynamics observed in this research on São Paulo's periphery occurs primarily under two conditions: 1) when women work for pay, and 2) when the children are no longer young. At the minimum some of the children (the older ones) have to share in the domestic work and/or paid work. (Nuclear families with small children more often follow the traditional pattern of authority, because the mother's responsibilities can hardly be shared at that stage of the family's life cycle). Those two conditions can produce a changing pattern because they enable the woman to claim a share of authority and place her in a more equal position. More precisely, they are preconditions. As mentioned above, male authority is not necessarily undermined by the changing economic status of women, because the man's authority is grounded not only in his status as breadwinner but also in the social representation of the man as the head of the family. Thus, values do not automatically change in synch with changing social practices.

It should be remembered that wives in working class families or low-income families have always worked, at least intermittently. That is not a new phenomenon, as it is for upper-middle class women in Brazil. However, poor women get the worst jobs, especially in comparison with the opportunities given to women of higher social strata (whose jobs are nonetheless inferior to men of the same stratum). In households with multiple incomes, the wife normally has a lower-income status (Despres 1991, Schmink 1979).

Even when she has more education, which happens frequently, she is not paid accordingly.[18]

Furthermore, within the patriarchal pattern men's and women's work have different meanings. Women's income is lower and it also has a different end: the man provides the basic needs, while the woman provides the "extras."[19] Because the wife's work is conceived as secondary, the fact that she works for pay does not necessarily change the man's authority. Rather, the conditions under which she works—low-paid and unskilled jobs—help reinforce this conception. Thus, for the low-income, low-education population, women's work is embedded in a patriarchal code that cuts across classes. The fact that poor women work primarily in unskilled and badly paid activities makes the experience less than gratifying. It also jeopardizes the idea of self-assertion through paid work. Nevertheless, even under these conditions, many women who were interviewed expressed the desire to work, in order to earn "a little money of my own" and also to get away from household chores, both of which would compensate for the difficulties.

It is worth reiterating that the gender system attributes a different moral status to the man (husband) and the woman (wife) within the family. In the poor neighborhoods of São Paulo, the duty for raising a family is in the man's hands. He understands the role and the woman expects him to assume it. If the marriage fails, she feels he is responsible. Thus, when the project of raising a family is not achieved as ideally planned, the man—who represents ultimate authority—is judged more severely than the woman, who has a secondary position as moral actor.

Much the same holds true for betrayed husbands. Of course, this moral code does not sanction female infidelity. However, in cases when the man "deserved it," female infidelity is tolerated and justified. Sometimes the husband's behavior does not make him worthy of "respect" (for example, when he is frequently drunk, beats his wife, does not take his money home, or has other women). "Respect" and "responsibility" are categories often used in man's discourse about the family. For both the man and the woman, marriage implies "responsibility," which is based on the principle of reciprocity and complementarity. To be "responsible" means to play the reciprocal roles this decision implies for each gender: father-mother, husband-wife, provider-housewife. Even though both have moral obligations according to these roles, in this hierarchical structure the man is ultimately responsible for the "respect" of the family. Thus, if the woman behaves in a reprehensible way, the man is blamed for not having guaranteed her "respectability." How-

127

ever, blame generally does not flow in the opposite direction; a woman is not considered to be equally responsible for her husband's behavior. Yet, when children commit transgressions, the woman is judged severely, because the role of the mother is at stake. As mother, the woman shares authority and therefore blame.

Women internalize the idea that they are not moral actors (as we have seen with way they understand the word "responsibility"), and instead they tend to see themselves as victims. This self-image becomes clear when they commit what is considered to be a transgression. They talk about it as if it were something done to them, thus refusing to recognize themselves as "responsible." However, passivity can also be a defensive reaction that women have available to them when they are found to have committed a disapproved practice.

Because individual discourse on morality is couched in defensive and relational terms, it is important to define the speaker's perspective. The one who speaks places himself or herself on the "good side," constructing some "other" on the "bad side" according to the relational mechanism already described. In other words, the speaker explains a transgression within the family code—such as premarital pregnancy, abortion, drinking, and infidelity—by constructing a reference point that justifies it or mitigates its meaning. For example, if a single mother is a woman to whom the speaker is related—a daughter or a sister—then the speaker's discourse becomes defensive and reveals a flexibility not found for others in a similar situation. In other words, there is always a reason to explain the circumstances. Because the speaker can always find a compensating factor, moral discourse becomes very flexible.

What is striking is that when using these mechanisms of compensation (or negotiation), the speaker remains within the patriarchal pattern of morality. In fact, the transgressions are defined with reference to this pattern. They therefore do not suggest that the patriarchal code is becoming obsolete; on the contrary, as in cases of disobedience, they constitute the other side of the same coin.

Concluding Observations

This study suggests that changes in family practices are not necessarily followed by changes in values, because those practices do not necessarily affect the patriarchal structure that shapes norms and values in the poor family's life. Of course, to some extent adjustments and negotiations modify the old pattern, but it retains its symbolic power. We must therefore acknowledge that there is a degree of relative autonomy in the symbolic sphere. Because social values are internalized in a nonconscious process, they influence people's choices and decisions at every level. The result is a complex dynamic in the interrelation of the old internalized norms and values with the apparently incongruous new practices, creating a multifaceted and ambiguous process of social change.

Studying the symbolic dimensions of social reality is important because despite the fact that they constitute an underlying mechanism—implicit, hidden, and often unspoken—they directly influence individual conduct in private and public life. In sum, they involve the very definition of people as social actors on every dimension they are required to act: as family members, as workers, as political actors, and as citizens.

Poor people are not merely deprived, exploited, or passive victims; rather, they are actively engaged in social life on their own terms and according to values that shape and orient their actions. They translate the social order into their own moral terms, thus restructuring the language in which they communicate and giving meaning to the social universe in which they are situated. Thus, it is worthless to be rich without generosity, the moral quality that should accompany wealth. Because poor people recognize a moral order as the foundation of social life, their actions, projects, and ideas have a moral basis that can be translated into the political domain.

Acknowledgments

This article was written during my stay as a residential fellow at the Kellogg Institute in the fall of 1991. I am very grateful to the staff of the Institute for its support of my work, and I would like to thank Roberto DaMatta in particular. Jo Ann Martin always provoked stimulating discussions, as did Thomas Skidmore, who read the manuscript and made important comments and editorial suggestions. Caio Blinder also provided important comments.

Endnotes

1. "Brazil: Drunk, Not Sick." *The Economist*, Dec. 7, 1991.
2. Beginning with Gilberto Freyre (1951, 1980), there is an extensive literature on the formation of the patriarchal family as a social system in Brazil, such as the works of Holanda (1963), Candido (1951), Willems (1954), and Wagley (1964).

3. This research was completed for my Ph.D. dissertation in the Department of Anthropology at the University of São Paulo. I did field research during 1980 and 1982 for a master's thesis (1985). Eight years later I went back to the same neighborhood to continue fieldwork. It began in 1980 with an extensive "survey" (done in collaboration with Teresa P. R. Caldeira) and including taped interviews (around thirty in each of the two research projects). I have written down my observations in my fieldnotes, which are the principal source of data for my analysis. My previous experience in the neighborhood has provided me with a valuable basis for comparison over time.

4. According to Durkheim (1933), society is a kind of moral entity; in other words, it is seen from the standpoint of its integration—organic solidarity—through norms and values that tie individuals together and orient their action. Following Durkheim, I analyze society in terms of values, in contrast with the Marxist perspective that emphasizes the economic determination of social relations and values.

5. According to the "survey" done in the neighborhood and mentioned before, the average income was 2.1 minimum wages in 1980. In Brazil, the payment of a minimum wage is enforced by a national law and it is defined as the minimum amount that is supposed to be necessary to cover the basic needs of a worker's family. The average minimum wage in Brazil during recent years has not exceeded $100 per month. Given the context of high inflation, wages fluctuate a great deal. Although wages are adjusted in accordance with wage policies, the constant attempt to compensate for the high inflation rate is hardly successful.

6. There is also an extensive literature on the development of the poor periphery as part of the expansion of the city of São Paulo, e.g., Bonduki (1983, 1988), Kowarick (1980), and Rolnik (1981). See Holston (1991) on the land disputes in this region.

7. In a broad sense, this perspective is a current trend in the literature on poor people, as can be seen in Montes (1983) and Zaluar (1985), among others.

8. These terms are not simply opposed to each other; rather, it is the opposition that precedes and defines the terms of the relation. See the similar concept of segmentation in Evans-Pritchard (1940).

9. DaMatta (1991) analyzes these symbolic operations in the essay "Do You Know who You're Talking to?"

10. This point is somewhat different from Kottak's argument (1967) that there are different functions for kinship according to socioeconomic class and that the extended *parentela* is a strategy to have access to resources and power for the upper-class Brazilians. I think the extended family, as it is already established in the city, is also an important means for the poor to have access to resources (not to power, since they do not have it), based on their value of reciprocity.

11. Zaluar (1985) found the same opposition between "workers" and "thieves" as an important element in the definition of the "worker's identity" in the poor neighborhood that she studied in Rio de Janeiro.

12. Within the same framework, the counterpart of the parents' fears is the children's fear of the alcoholic father, expressed mainly in the teenagers' discourse. (I owe this observation to Felícia Madeira.)

13. For a comparative analysis of race relations in Brazil and the United States, see Degler (1971) and Skidmore (1974).

14. The value attributed to the mother in Brazilian society reveals one of its paradoxes, considering that it is a country known for the increased presence of "street children" ("meninos e meninas da rua") which has become a social problem. As Alda Marco Antônio, the Secretary of Social Welfare of the State of São Paulo, put it: Brazil is a "poor country that fears its children." On this point, there is a lack of effective social policy for poor mothers and children, a fact which shows how removed social policy is from poor people's values in Brazil.

15. The ambivalent protection women receive in patriarchal structures makes the discussion of feminism in Brazil as necessary as it is complex, because feminist thought is anchored in individualistic values and partriarchal structures imply a different system of values.

16. Social scientists have yet to explore the many contradictory implications of the meaning of increased divorce (which is based on individualistic concepts) in a hierarchical and patriarchal society such as Brazil.

17. I have drawn this conclusion from my own data and from Fonseca's analysis (1987a, 1987b) of the importance of consanguineal ties when marital ties are weak, and also from Salem's analysis (1981) of the "chosen son."

18. Castro (1989) attributes the precarious situation of female heads of households to the status of women as wives, arguing that the former is a consequence of the latter.

19. The "survey" done in the neighborhood in 1980 showed that the income of women is half that of men, as the analysis of Caldeira (1984) and my previous work (Sarti 1985) show. The average income of the workers—which is 2.1 minimum wages—goes up to 2.4 minimum wages when only the male workers are considered, and it goes down to 1.2 minimum wages when female workers are considered.

References

Barroso, Carmen
    1978 "Sozinhas ou Mal Acompanhadas: A Situação das Mulheres Chefes de Família." In *Anais: Encontro Nacional da ABEP*. Campos de Jordão.
Bonduki, Nabil
    1983 "Habitação Popular: Contribuição para o Estudo da Evolução Urbana

de São Paulo." In L. P. Valladares (ed.), *Repensando a Habitação no Brasil*. Série Debates Urbanos No. 3. Rio de Janeiro: Zahar.

1988 "A Crise na Habitação e a Luta pela Moradia no Pós-Guerra." In Lúcio Kowarick (ed.), *As Lutas Sociais e a Cidade*. São Paulo: Passado e Presente, Paz e Terra.

Caldeira, Teresa P. R.
1984 *A Política dos Outros*. São Paulo: Brasiliense.

Candido, Antônio
1951 "The Brazilian Family." In T. Lynne Smith and Alexander Marchant (eds.), *Brazil: Portrait of Half a Continent*. New York: Dryden.

Castro, Mary Garcia
1989 "Family, Gender, and Work: The Case of Female Heads of Households in Brazil (States of São Paulo and Bahia)." Ph.D. dissertation, University of Florida.

DaMatta, Roberto
1985 *A Casa e a Rua*. São Paulo: Brasiliense.
1991 *Carnivals, Rogues, and Heroes*. Notre Dame, Ind.: University of Notre Dame Press.

Degler, Carl
1971 *Neither Black Nor White*. New York: MacMillan.

Despres, Leo A.
1991 *Manaus: Social Life and Work in Brazil's Free Trade Zone*. Albany: State University of New York Press.

Durkheim, Emile
1924 "La détermination du fait moral." In *Sociologie et philosophie*. Paris: Felix Alcan.
1933 *The Division of Labor in Society*. New York: Free Press.

Evans-Pritchard, E. E.
1940 *The Nuer*. Oxford: Oxford University Press.

Fonseca, Claudia.
1987a "Aliados e Rivais na Família." *Revista Brasileira de Ciências Sociais* (ANPOCS) 4: 88-104.
1987b "Mulher: Chefe da Família?" *Revista de Ciências Sociais* (IFCH-UFRGS) 1(2): 261-68.

Freyre, Gilberto
1951 *Sobrados e Mocambos*. Rio de Janeiro: José Olympio. 2d ed. (orig. 1936).
1980 *Casa-Grande e Senzala*. Rio de Janeiro/Brasília: José Olympio/INL. 20th ed. (orig. 1933).

Holanda, Sérgio Buarque de.
1963 *Raízes do Brasil*. Brasília: Editora Universidade de Brasília. 4th ed. (orig. 1936).

Holston, James
1991 "The Misrule of Law: Land and Usurpation in Brazil." *Comparative Studies in Society and History* 33(4): 695-725.

Kottak, Conrad
1967 "Kinship and Class in Brazil." *Ethnology* 6(4): 427-43.

Kowarick, Lúcio
1980 *A Espoliação Urbana*. Rio de Janeiro: Paz e Terra.

Montes, Maria Lúcia A.
1983 "Lazer e Ideologia: A Representação do Social e do Político na Cultura popular." Ph.D. dissertation, University of São Paulo.

Rolnick, Raquel
1981 "Cada um no seu Lugar." Master's thesis, Architecture and Urbanism Faculty, University of São Paulo.

Salem, Tania
1981 "Mulheres Faveladas: 'Com a Venda nos Olhos.'" *Perspectivas Antropológicas da Mulher*. Rio de Janeiro: Zahar.

Sarti, Cynthia A.
1985 "E Sina que a Gente Traz: Ser Mulher na Periferia urbana." Master's thesis, Social Sciences Department, University of São Paulo.

Schmink, Marianne
1979 "Community in Ascendance: Urban Industrial Growth and Household Income Strategies in Belo Horizonte, Brazil." Ph.D. dissertation, University of Texas at Austin.

Skidmore, Thomas
1974 *Black Into White*. Oxford: Oxford University Press.

Wagley, Charles
1964 "Luso-Brazilian Kinship Patterns: The Persistence of a Cultural Tradition." In Joseph Maier and Richard W. Weatherhead (eds.), *Politics of Change in Latin America*. New York: Praeger.

Willems, Emilio
1954 "A Estrutura da Família Brasileira." *Sociologia* (São Paulo) 16 (4): 327-40.

Woortmann, Klass
1982 "Casa e Família Operária." *Anuário Antropológico*. Rio de Janeiro: Tempo Brasileiro.

Zaluar, Alba
1985 *A Máquina e a Revolta*. São Paulo: Brasiliense.

Chapter Six

The Celebration of Our Lord of the Good End: Changing State, Church, and Afro-Brazilian Relations in Bahia

⊠

Leni M. Silverstein

In Brazil, Catholicism has historically been the official religion of the country, with Protestantism and other faiths a small minority. Afro-Brazilian spirit possession cults were categorized within this second group as the so-called ethnic religions of former African slaves who had preserved the traditions of their ancestors. These religions are structured throughout Brazil with particular rites and local names said to be derived from their different African origins: Candomblé in Bahia, Xangô in Pernambuco and Alagoas, Tambor de Mina in Maranhão and Pará, Macumba and Umbanda in Rio de Janeiro, and so on. Many of the followers of the Afro-Brazilian religions also identify themselves as Catholic, historically the official religion of Brazil and still very much the dominant religion. Thus, the relationship between Catholicism and Candomblé involves one special aspect of the question of hierarchy in Brazil: race relations seen as the legacy of the colonial relationship between the dominant European groups and the African slaves.

This paper will focus on the relationship between Candomblé and Catholicism as revealed in the enactment of a popular Bahian street festival, Our Lord of the Good End (*Nosso Senhor do Bonfim*). I focus on an event that occurred in the 1970s: the liberation of the cults from registration with the police department that was required before any public ritual activity could be performed. I analyze this event as a symbolic arena where Candomblé, Catholic church, and Brazilian state interests are played out against a backdrop of race, class, and gender relations as well as national and international interests. I also show how an anthropological analysis at the local level can make public policies comprehensible.[1]

The Basics of Candomblé

In order to understand the ritual of the washing of the steps of Our Lord of the Good End, it is first necessary to have a basic understanding of some of the tenets of Candomblé. The practitioners of Candomblé divide themselves into "nations" according to the presumptive ethnic origins preserved in the rites. Basically, the main sources of the current "nations" of Candomblé have been the ancient African cultures of the Bantu of southern African and the Yoruba and Ewe-Fon of West Africa. The gods and goddesses of Candomblé, the Yoruba *orixás* (oh-ree-shahs'), are identified in the literature with Catholic saints. Jesus Christ is linked to the lead *orixá* Oxalá (oh-shah-lah'), the Virgin Mary to the sea goddess Iemanjá (yay-mahn-jah'), and so on. The priesthood and the organization of rites for the worship of these divinities is quite complex and hierarchical. There is, however, one pivotal religious mechanism, spirit possession or trance, which allows the gods to manifest themselves through the bodies of the initiates during the ceremonies, in order to dance and be admired, praised and worshiped. When incorporated by these *orixás*, the devotees neither speak nor provide council. They are on this earth to seek their pleasure, to eat, and to carouse with their fellow deities.

There is a private and public aspect to Candomblé worship. Candomblé works in an ethical context in which the Judeo-Christian notion of sin does not make any sense. The difference between good and evil basically depends upon the relationship between the follower and his or her personal god, the *orixá*. The initiation is endless, gradual and secret, and occurs in places of worship called *terreiros* (tay-hay'-roes).

Public ceremonies (called *toques*) are open to the general population and mark the end of a period of several days of "obligations" that include the sacrifice of animals, prohibitions on food and sex, and seclusion for those being initiated. The ceremony is performed through song and dance as each *orixá* is honored and summoned to the stage by an identifying drum beat. As each *orixá* is recognized, his or her sons and daughters fall into trance, "receiving" the divinity in their bodies. Thus possessed, they retire, only to return to the dance floor arraigned in the regal garments and regalia of the kings and queens who symbolize the Yoruba past. Assembled before their court, these majestic deities dance an enactment of their history, and eat and cavort throughout the night. These "horses" of the *orixás*, however, do not speak or offer council. This is a night time for pleasure.

The religious learning occurs in seclusion, far from the public eyes, in a separate ritualized space where only the initiated may enter. All activities are guided by oracular consultations through cowry shell divinations. Only the highly-trained "mother-" or "father-of-the-saints" (*mãe* or *pai de santos*) possesses the sacred knowledge to perform this procedure. They are the teachers of the new generation, and they are charged with the preservation and transmission of cult life and lore.

Candomblé priestesses and priests must also cater to a large public demand for their magicoreligious services. In Bahia, there is a large clientele who seek out certain sacerdotes to help resolve the typical problems that life inflicts: love, jealousy, work, sickness, lack of money, suspected sorcery are some of the reasons people, not necessarily devotees, seek out ritualistic means to manipulate their circumstances.

Within the Candomblé traditions, various calendars are operating at the same time. One refers to the ritual calendar of the *terreiro* itself. This includes the weekly commitments demanded by each *orixá*: for example, Monday is Omolu's day, Friday is reserved for Oxalá, etc. In addition, special cere-monies are demanded on the birthdays of the mother- or father-of-the-saint's *orixá*, and those which mark the investiture of important members of each community. Yet another calendar revolves around the initiation cycle which is also determined by the necessities of each group. Whereas the indi-vidual temples are aware of the city-wide celebrations dedicated to certain *orixás*, their decision to participate in such a city-wide ritual appears to be an individual or group decision.

Candomblé and Bahian Culture

During the period of this research (1973–1976), the city of Salvador in the northeastern state of Bahia had a population of approximately one million people.[2] The majority of the inhabitants were said to be tinged with a bit of Portuguese and much African blood, witnesses to the incursions of the slave trade into everyday life. Indeed, there is a nationally held belief that the iden-tity of the Brazilian people is characterized both racially and culturally as one-third Portuguese, one-third African, and one-third Amerindian, a result of the intermarriage of the three most populous occupants of the land.

Nowhere is the native theory of racial mixing a more plausible definition of national identity than in Salvador. The Bahians sport almost every possi-ble complexion tone, with hues ranging from the whitest alabaster to the blackest coal, and thus their phenotype defies the neat categorizations of census takers and social scientists. The miscegenation challenges exact racial and/or color classifications: social class is often a more revealing diagnostic indicator of life chances. Yet, frequent newspaper accounts show, for example, the white, upper-class, male, Catholic governor of the state asking a blessing from a black, lower-class female sacerdote, the mother-of-the-saints of a Candomblé house. Rumors proliferate about high-ranking officials (not to mention their wives) who surreptitiously pay astronomical fees for magical intervention in their personal and political affairs from a holy mother-of-the-saints.

Culturally, this city is frequently called the "Black Rome," a composite idea of the double religious identity to which Bahians frequently adhere. As a Roman Catholic religious center, the city bears witness by reputedly consecrating a church for each day of the year. At the same time, it is the traditional center of Candomblé, the spiritual source for the plethora of Afro-Brazilian cults which flourish all over the country. Over one-thousand *terreiros* (a word that I translate as "temples") were said to be registered with the police in this city alone.

The fulfillment of Candomblé obligations takes place in a setting very much conditioned by the religion's long years of religious persecution.[3] Until the 1960s, both the Catholic church and the state had instigated periodic destruction of ritual artifacts and incarceration of some of the more belligerent sacerdotes. The 1930s were a particularly virulent period for Afro-Brazilian religious persecution, a period which coincides with the economic and political transfer of power from the agrarian Northeast to the Central South of the country. Many Candomblé *terreiros* responded by removing their houses to the underdeveloped outskirts of the city, accessible only to the initiated and the well informed. Individual commitments to the *orixás* were performed within an intimate setting directed by the mother-of-the-saints and her extended ritual family. (See Silverstein 1994 for an extensive discussion of Candomblé hierarchy and social structure.)

A popular saying describes Bahians as a practical people who go to church in the morning, a Spiritism session in the afternoon (that is, a European form of spirit mediumship), and a Candomblé ritual in the evening. Bahians tend to be eclectic because no one knows for sure, of course, which path is the one that will insure the fulfillment of their needs and wishes. Thus, Bahians do not view their options in either/or terms. Rather, an individual manipulates a whole set of culturally prescribed strategies with which he or she can respond to a given situation. Thus, in a particular setting, a person might be Catholic, in another, a tranquil devotee of Candomblé. No insincerity is implied; rather, the Bahian interpretation "who knows what will work" has surely proven to be the most pragmatic attitude to take. In a constantly changing and insecure world—a world in which adroit manipulation of one's available social network could mean the difference between having and not having a job, food, or medicine for one's suffering children—all doors must remain open. Underneath the Bahian's very romantic or playful exterior is an extremely shrewd and calculating person who adopts a realistic strategy commensurate with social status and opportunities for survival. This is obviously a very fluid yet plausible approach to a world in constant transition, a world in which an enemy could significantly hinder one's life chances.

Devotion to Our Lord of the Good End

Within this panoply of religious observation, however, a hierarchy of efficacy does exist in the minds of the people. Although competition for their sorely strained financial, physical, and emotional resources is fierce, a promise to Our Lord of the Good End is one that commands attention. Our Lord of the Good End is a manifestation of Jesus who is also the patron saint of the state of Bahia, and he has always been especially benevolent to his Bahian petitioners. It is not by chance that two state hymns are dedicated to him. They are evoked at all state functions, popular music concerts, and even soccer competitions. In addition, Bahians and others are frequently seen sporting on their wrists the narrow, colored ribbons of satin on which the name of *Nosso Senhor do Bonfim* is inscribed. It is believed that *Bonfim* (bonefeem') will grant the three wishes requested during the three-time knotting of the ribbon if the petitioner wears it until it drops off.

Bahian devotion to Bonfim is infamous. Any visitor who is not from Bahia will immediately note a mystique, a special significance surrounding this sanctuary and this figure. All the books about Bahia speak about Senhor do Bonfim. As Martin M. Groetelaars states in his analysis of the devotion of Senhor do Bonfim from the perspective of the Catholic church's liberation theology,

> A victory of a soccer team provokes a pilgrimage to the church to thank
> Senhor do Bonfim. A group of forty workers are grateful to Senhor do
> Bonfim for a happy solution to their salary dispute. A Bahian writer . . .

requests the protection of Senhor do Bonfim upon describing the public calamities due to a drought, fearing another Canudos. An old philosophy professor of Salvador's largest seminary confessed after 35 years of residing in the city: "Senhor do Bonfim is not Our Lord," and a Cardinal, returning from Rome in 1973, exclaimed upon arriving on Brazilian land, "Hail to this Great Country....and always cherished land of Senhor do Bonfim." Jorge Amado considers Senhor do Bonfim a very Brazilian expression of Afro-Brazilian syncretism and sees in him a cultural symbol of the greatest importance. (Groetelaars 1983: 10-11)

The basilica of Our Lord of the Good End is perched upon a high hill overlooking the city and facing the sea. People seeking cures for their ills flock to the church from miles around to petition the miraculous saint. The aforementioned satin wrist bands are frequently purchased as presents and good luck charms from the street venders who line the roadway surrounding the church. By wearing such blessed talismans, people feel closer to the saint and more confident that their prayers will be answered. In fact, within the church, to the right of the sanctuary where the sacred statue of Bonfim resides, there is a separate room, the Miracle Room, filled with *ex votos* or wooden reproductions of body parts that were placed there by persons grateful for the healing intervention of the saint.

Senhor do Bonfim not only has a church and two hymns dedicated to his honor, but also the Brotherhood of Devotion to Senhor do Bonfim, formed by a group of prestigious men to work toward the further glorification of his name. Initially, these men organized the ten-day street festival for which the high point is a three-mile procession that is followed by a ritual cleansing of the church steps. This event is unquestionably the zenith of Salvador's summer festival cycle (with the exclusion of Carnival, of course). Such a popular religious outpouring is accompanied by the tacit acquiescence of the Catholic church, whose resident priest schedules a nine-day series of masses (*novenas*) during this period, celebrates a special mass on the actual purification day, and allows the entire façade of the building to be decorated with a chain of electric lights that can be seen for miles around. Clearly, in its own manner, the church recognizes Senhor do Bonfim.

Although not an official holiday and, therefore, in theory an ordinary work day that always occurs on the third Thursday in January, most people (the young, students, those with a special relationship or obligation to the saint, those who live or work in the vicinity of the procession, the indolent, and the tourists) interrupt their activities to join in the festivities. What distinguishes this street festival from the numerous other summer celebrations is its marked recognition by the Afro-Brazilian religious (Candomblé and Umbanda) communities, as well. Senhor do Bonfim is a multivocal symbol: he occupies a favored position within the curing orations of popular Bahian Catholicism, locates Bahian state identity, and according to popular belief, is also the "syncretized" version of Oxalá, the West African supreme deity.[4] This saint is, therefore, a powerful symbol of condensation (Turner 1974) for at least three overlapping elements that compose Bahian society: Catholicism, the Bahian State, and Afro-Brazilians. Thus, when the Governor of the State of Bahia ascended the steps of the Church of Nosso Senhor do Bonfim to issue an edict granting effective freedom of religious expression to the Afro-Brazilian religious cults, it is evident that he chose his site with care. Bonfim could be evoked to mean many things to many people.

The Liberation of the Cults

Until the governor "liberated the cults" in 1976, Candomblé *terreiros* and Umbanda centers were obliged to request permission from the police delegation of "Games and Customs" (Delegacia de Jogos e Costumes) whenever they wished to perform public rituals involving drum beating (most of them did) and dancing. Afro-Brazilian religious activities were therefore officially classified as a "diversion," or in other words they were placed in the same category as a circus, a discotheque or a whore house. In addition, this particular police delegation was under the direction of the "Censor," a government position that exercised exclusive repressive powers in the name of cultural control.

With the stroke of the governor's pen, therefore, the Afro-Brazilian spirit possession religions were embraced finally within the spirit of the Brazilian Constitution of 1888. Article X of that Constitution had, in principal, guaranteed the rite of free expression to all religions. However, as with many things in Brazil, declarations of intent and enforcement may reflect different ideas which do not always form a cohesive agenda for action. The following is the decree as read by the governor:

Decree No. 25095 of 15 January 1976

The governor of the State of Bahia uses his office in considering that the expression "Afro-Brazilian societies for acts of folklore" is being used to identify these Afro-Brazilian cult institutions in order to register and control them; these cults being an external manifestation of their religion, considering that the use of this expression is antagonistic to the true meaning of the law, to the constitutional principal which guarantees freedom of religious expression, considering that it is the duty of the public authority to guarantee free religious practices to each and every one and to eliminate whatever obstacles which impede it, considering finally, that it is the duty of the governor to extend to the Societies for the Afro-Brazilian cults the right to their religious beliefs and practices as is common to all other religions,

Decrees

Article I: The societies which practice the Afro-Brazilian cults as an external manifestation of their religion, are not included in the Item 27 of Table I Law #3097 of 29 December 1972 and therefore can exercise their cults, independent of registration, paying a tax or obtaining a license from the public authorities.

Article II: This decree will take effect from the date of its publication, revoking all previous dispositions to the contrary.

> —Palace of the Governor of the State of Bahia
> January 15, 1976
> Roberto Figueira Santos (Silverstein's translation)

A group of unlikely companions gathered together to witness the governor's inauguration of a new era in church/Afro-Brazilian/state relations. On one side stood the mayor of the city of Salvador, Jorge Hage, and the Cardinal of the Roman Catholic Church, Brandão Villela, and on the other side stood two Bahian priestesses of the Candomblé. That such a political act was undertaken on January 15, 1976, is in itself quite an extraordinary event. The fact that this event was embedded within another ceremony, that of the "Washing (*Lavagem*) of Bomfim," the annual Candomblé rite of washing the steps of the Bonfim Church, suggests that a symbolic accord or political truce had been formed among the church, the state, and the Afro-Brazilian religions.

However, because the decree was read on the steps of one of the main churches of the city, one which traditionally closes its doors during this important popular festival, I questioned the forces that had contrived to alter the ambiguity and hostility previously characterizing the relations between these institutions. How the cults were transformed from shunned and persecuted pagan rites into a valued cultural heritage, courted by church and state alike, is an interesting question for all of Brazilian cultural studies because it sheds light on the complexities of the hierarchical relationship between the white, Catholic side of Brazilian society and the black, Candomblé side. I shall answer that question first by examining in some detail the ritual of washing of the steps of the church of Our Lord of the Good End in 1976, and then by examining the history of the ritual.

The Washing of the Steps of Bonfim

During the end of my fieldwork in Salvador, I had the opportunity to witness for the third consecutive time the Candomblé rite of the Lavagem of Bonfim, that is, the washing of the steps of "Our Lord of the Good End." As I show elsewhere (Silverstein 1994), two ritual calendars operate simultaneously to determine Catholic worship in Bahia: the official liturgical calendar as dictated by Rome and the popular Catholic calendar which reflects local traditions and customs. The washing of the steps of Bomfim is ostensibly a popular Catholic festival that is traditionally held annually on the Thursday before the third Sunday of the month of January. Although just one ritual among many on a busy calendar of popular festivities, the washing of the steps of Bonfim is considered the cameo of popular festivals (religious and profane), which begin joyfully on December 4 with the Festa de Santa Barbara (Saint Barbara's Feast Day) and culminate in late February or early March with the exuberant Bahian street Carnival. As conceived by the participants, the ritual of the washing of the steps of the church of Our Lord of the Good End is thought about in terms of a payment of a promise made to the saint. Yet, as I shall also show, by the mid-1970s the ritual was also being transformed into a quasi-official public event that had become part of the tourist industry and had brought together the Catholic church, the state, and the Afro-Brazilian religions in an apparently new order.

The Bonfim celebration starts with a procession from the church of Our Lady of the Immaculate Conception of the Beach, popularly known as *Conceição da Praia*, and proceeds along a six-kilometer (3.75-mile) route to the church of Bonfim. Generally, the procession begins with a large group of dignified, aged Bahianas or Candomblé priestesses who carry water jugs on their heads throughout the journey. The ribbon-draped ceramic water jugs are filled with a mixture of flowers and water from the Immaculate Conception Church fountain, and this perfumed sacred water is used to bless and purify the Bonfim church steps. All the participants dress in white: lace crinolines and bodices for the sacerdotes, and white trousers and crisply starched shirts for the men. In addition, most people don the protective beads (*contas*) and amulets dedicated to their guardian African deities (*orixás*).

Along the way, onlookers join the walk, thereby transforming the solemn procession into a dancing, rag-tag, pied-piper, festive white parade in honor of Oxalá, the *orixá* who is "syncretized" with Bomfim.

In 1976, the state-controlled tourist agency Bahiatursa instigated a number of transformations in the procession and ritual. First, two kinds of subsidies were offered to the people (*povo*) of the Candomblé: support for clothing and transportation. Priestesses were given the opportunity to refurbish their wardrobes in a style which seems reminiscent of fashionable eighteenth-century Portuguese noblewomen. Cars were also donated to transport Bahiatursa staff as well as women too old or infirm to fulfill their obligation on foot. In addition, a competition with two monetary prizes was organized: one for the "best dressed" Bahiana and the other for the most beautifully decorated carriage. The selected carriage was a two-wheeled, donkey-drawn cart which, until very recently, served as the traditional transportation means to the ritual site (*Jornal da Bahia*, December 23, 1975).

The participants are usually accompanied by various Catholic brotherhoods, particularly the one dedicated to the devotion to Our Lord of the Good End, whose members belong to the loosely-defined Afro-Brazilian Cult Federation. The self-proclaimed leader of the federation, Antônio Monteiro, headed the procession this year. In addition to Candomblé and Umbanda believers, the procession included politicians, revelers, national and international tourists, and students anxiously awaiting the results of the Vestibular (the Brazilian university entrance exam somewhat akin to the French baccalaureate). Even the American Consul was reported watching the procession from one of the street overpasses which afford superior views of the scene. Although not an official secular or religious holiday, many people excuse themselves from work to revitalize their relationship to Senhor do Bonfim and to dance, drink, sing, and flirt in the very hot tropical summer sun. Such revelry is facilitated by numerous mobile small stalls or tents (*barracas*) which surround the entrance and patio of the Bonfim church, serving typical spicy Bahian finger foods, alcoholic beverages, and soft drinks. The presence of such stands encourages the crowds to relax, talk, and improvise samba as the huge cortege slowly winds up the sacred hill toward the church steps.

The washing of the church steps itself is somewhat anticlimatic, at least for a Western observer who is accustomed to neatly cordoned-off spaces that delineate and control the observer's distance from the ritual activities. Nothing prepared me for the apparent chaos which marked the purification rite.

Reporters, politicians, priestesses, and friends jostled for positions of proximity to the mothers-of-the-saints, some of whom had finally reached the
church steps. The water, so carefully carried from the city center below, was
tossed haphazardly upon the steps, and it sprinkled the sweating and laughing onlookers as well. A drop of water dedicated to Senhor do Bonfim
seemed to assume the same significance as holy water in the Catholic communion celebration and all wished to partake of its beneficent fluids.
Because there was little room to wield a broom, those Bahianas fortunate
enough to attain strategic positions on the steps sloshed their water about,
occasionally entering into trance or dancing as the spirit moved them. Many
people jostled closer and closer to the few priestesses who were managing to
sweep the steps; others just stood and observed the order in chaos, accustomed to this apparently unruly manner of performing a ritual.[5]

Given the solemnities enhancing the celebration that year, the two
Bahian priestesses flanking the governor bestowed upon him a special honor.
Before spilling their holy water upon the ground, they sprinkled him and
each of his illustrious companions (including the cardinal) with a few drops
of the sacred fluid, presumably acknowledging and sanctifying this legal act
with an Afro-Brazilian stamp.

The ritual/event remains a curious one. How did it come to pass that
what was originally a Catholic devotional practice became reinterpreted
through Candomblé beliefs? What does this ritual of multiple planes suggest
about the process of the interpenetration of beliefs and discourses marking
Brazilian nationalism, Christianity, and West African religions as played out
in Salvador, Bahia, in 1976? To unravel this question, I will explore some of
the history which is written about this religious festival and which, as we
shall soon see, reveals an intermingling of Portuguese and West African origin myths, beliefs and practices. It is my aim to show how cultural symbols
from one culture can be reinterpreted within another context.

A Brief History of Senhor do Bonfim

The devotion to Senhor do Bonfim has its Portuguese roots in an origin
myth. In 1745, according to Bahiatursa brochures and Groetelaars' account
(1983: 28–31), a naval officer, Teodísio Rodrigues de Faria, brought an
image of Senhor do Bonfim to Salvador. This replica was an exact copy of
the one venerated in Setubal, a Portuguese city about thirty kilometers south
of Lisbon, the capital. According to popular belief, the original image was

discovered by a woman among pieces of wood that had been washed up on the shores of Setubal, probably the vestiges from a shipwrecked boat. The herb gardens of this city are considered to have special healing properties emanating from the tradition of strong devotion to Senhor do Bonfim.

In Setubal, today, there are actually two hermitages: one is that of Lord Jesus of the Good Death (*Jesus da Boa Morte*) and the other is dedicated to Senhor do Bonfim and was originally called the "Guardian Angel." The latter was founded by Father Diogo Mendes in 1669, and it soon became one of the great centers of Portuguese national devotion south of the River Tejo. In 1711, the Portuguese King Dom João V fulfilled a promise to worship at this site, which was a center of pilgrimages and commemorative processions. People flocked to the site whenever afflicted by calamities such as tempests, floods, shipwrecks, plagues, and earthquakes. The monastery is decorated with beautiful tiles, extraordinary carvings, and paintings, and the main chapel also holds the famous marble stations of the cross commissioned by Friar Antônio das Chagas in 1728.

Groetelaars (1983: 16–17) distinguishes three different aspects of the devotion to Senhor do Bonfim in Setubal: l) the discovery of the image of the crucified Jesus; 2) a monastery called the Guardian Angel, whose name was changed to Senhor do Bonfim; and 3) a hermitage named for Lord Jesus of the Good Death (*Senhor Jesus da Boa Morte*). In addition, he describes a relationship of "syncretism" between the Guardian Angel and the Crucified Jesus, who was also called Senhor do Bonfim. It is probable that these three devotional elements—the crucified Jesus, the Lord of Bonfim, and the Lord Jesus of the Good Death—were transported to Brazil and condensed in the image of the crucified Jesus.

The principal motive for the Portuguese "captain" Teodísio Rodrigues de Farias to bring the image of Senhor do Bonfim to Bahia was to demonstrate his gratitude to God for sparing his life in a shipwreck on a voyage he took from Portugal to Bahia. With the image, he also brought the tradition of devotion which surrounds Senhor do Bonfim in Setubal, a devotion which includes the washing of the church steps.

Remaining in Salvador for a number of years, the Portuguese "captain of oceans and wars" formed a brotherhood principally composed of white, rich, and powerful men who propagated the cult of the devotion to Senhor do Bonfim. The brotherhood and devotional practices took place with the permission of the archbishop of Bahia, Dom José Botelho de Matos. It took 172 years, however, for the ecclesiastical powers in Brazil to approve officially the "Catholic Association of the Devotion to Senhor do Bonfim" in 1918. (Other reports give 1804 as the first recorded washing of the church.)

During the eighteenth and nineteenth centuries, the faithful were not limited to washing only the churchyard and steps leading to the church itself, as is the case today. Constant quarrels with the Catholic priests led, however, to various prohibitions on the form that this ritual cleansing should take. The first recorded ritual washing was by the Archbishop, Don Luiz Antonio dos Santos, who recorded the washing in 1889, a date which is not surprising because it is also the year when Brazilian slavery was abolished. The archbishop demanded that the Christian space be respected and prohibited the people from washing the interior of the church. In the following year, he enforced his edict through the support of the Civil Guard, who promptly confiscated all the implements used in the purification ritual (*Jornal da Bahia*, January 17, 1974). Other edicts followed, alleging the same motive, and in the process the devotion began to look more and more like Candomblé or African cult worship.

> In the beginning, the worshipers did not have a gathering place from which to begin the procession. Instead, they left in a disorderly fashion from their neighborhoods in trolley cars, wagons, donkeys and horses all decorated with streamers, to join the water carriers. Everyone was dressed in white clothes and the old "Bahianas" exhibited their lace skirts, etc. . . .Surtursa or Bahiatursa did not exist to give medals and pay the daughters of the saint [*filhas de santo*] to accompany the entourage. Liters of colon water were splashed in the inside of the church which was afterward dried off with white laced clothes. (*Jornal da Bahia*, 1/17/74)

In the twentieth century, the *povo* again were permitted to wash the interior of the church, and in 1930 the number of the faithful was said to have been incalculable. In 1940 the Redemptorists (*Redentoristas*)—a group believing in Jesus Christ, the Redeemer, and led by Frei Paulo—arrived in Bahia from the South of Brazil. The multitude insisted upon continuing the old customs within the church, including the churchyard as well. A few years later, however, the successors of the Redemptorists thought that the celebration had become profane in nature due to the presence of the African priests and priestesses, and the Catholic hierarchy once again prohibited the purification of the interior of the church. The people raised a hue and cry and were permitted to carry out the ritual on the church steps. In the 1950s, Juracy Magalhães, then the governor of Bahia and a self-proclaimed Candomblé supporter, succeeded in convincing the church to open the basilica for the washing ceremony. From World War II until today, however, the doors of the church have remained closed to all those who wish to honor Senhor do Bonfim in this manner. From that time to the present, the tradition has continued in a symbolic form, with the washing of the churchyard and stairs.

Conclusions

From this brief description of the context, the ritual, and its history, I have tried to present the elements of the two religious systems which have come together under one rubric at the steps of the church of Our Lord of Bonfim. One might argue that the "liberation of the cults" that occurred in 1976 represented a new pattern of relationships between the Catholic church and Brazilian state on one side and the African religions on the other side. However, I suggest that instead it is more appropriate to interpret the apparent transformation in terms of the longstanding ideology of "syncretism."

Dictionary definitions of "syncretism" suggest that it is a process by which different religious or philosophical traditions are combined or merged. Although many anthropologists today question the extent to which African and Catholic religions have merged in Bahia, the term and concept of "syncretism" still continues in popular usage. Under this definition, the Candomblé *orixás* were said to "hide" behind the images of the Catholic saints. Catholic iconography was presumably selected for its similarity to or fit with the colors, sex, temperament, and history of the African gods, which, after a time, became interchangeable. Worshiping an *orixá* became transformed, so the argument goes, into devotion to the Catholic saints (and, parenthetically) and its teachings of sin and forgiveness.

The concept of syncretism, as used in the historical and popular literature on the relationship between Catholic saints and Afro-Brazilian deities, is one that I and other anthropologists now question seriously. As the term appears in these texts, it is implied that the Catholic traditions have commingled with the African ones to produce a new, composite version of the saints. My research indicates that, contrary to such interpretations, people make a distinct separation in their heads between, for example, Saint Barbara and Iansã (ee-ahn-sahn', the so-called Afro-Brazilian equivalent). True enough, both images share similarities such as the use of red clothing, a warrior-like countenance, and dark hair. However, a new, syncretized version of the deity was not created; St. Barbara remains herself as does Iansã. Their legends, containing some overlapping aspects, still place each one within her own religious tradition, and consequently they have never formed an amalgamated story.

In the case of the washing of the steps of Bonfim, the devotion to Oxalá and to Senhor do Bonfim have only one point in common: a confluence of worshipers and revelers, coming together at the same moment in time, at the same place—deemed sacred to them both—to perform a ritual celebration. Here, the similarity stops, for the elements of the Catholic celebration are quite distinct from traditional Candomblé practice. The popular worship of Senhor do Bonfim contains the following elements rooted in the Catholic tradition:

- a Catholic priest reciting formal *novenas,* prayers for the followers of Our Lord, according to Catholic liturgical practice, and a mass;
- a brotherhood composed of prestigious men of the community who organized a procession and the lucrative street stalls lining the boundaries of the church area;
- a unification of various ritual forms, tendencies, and tensions within the Catholic church: pilgrimages, promises, evangelical and pastoral Catholicism, as well as the more recent popular participation of the Ecclesial Base Communities and the theology of liberation.

Candomblé, on the other hand, reaffirms a West African belief system, cultivates the ancient African gods and kings, and celebrates a time before slavery and the Black Diaspora. From this perspective, we see Afro-Brazilian priestesses, resplendent in colonial garb, both expressing and negating an alternative gendered connection to the sacred:

- carrying water jugs on their heads;
- watching the church steps without access to the church itself;
- going into trance and being incorporated by an *orixá*;
- fulfilling a personal pledge to their own guardian saint or spirit;
- publicly reaffirming the Afro-Brazilian leadership of the Candomblé "cult houses," which succeed, in spite of increasing hardship and expense, to celebrate their god, Oxalá.

Whereas the above lists emphasize the distinctiveness of the two religious traditions unfolding in an overlapping time/space continuum, there is also a third agenda present, that of the recognition of the city of Salvador as a unique backdrop for this diversity of religious expression. Thus, Bahia's identification with the local traditions of various religions is also reaffirmed, traditions which, under the guise of syncretism, appear not conflictive but conciliatory. Yet, as I have shown in this analysis of the structure of the Festival of Our Lord of the Good End, the state's recognition of religious diversity should not be interpreted as a historical shift that marks Catholicism and Candomblé as equals on a level religious playing field. Rather, I would stress the differences between the Catholic and African traditions and the continued hierarchical relationship between them.

On the Catholic side, the washing of the steps is organized by upper-class Bahian men who are generally white and whose position has been traditionally reinforced and strengthened by the official church. In the past, the church worked to protect and further the ends of the rich and powerful, but now its hegemony is being challenged by the theology of liberation. The presence of the Bahian State governor, the mayor of the city of Salvador, and the Cardinal, indicate a commingling of politicoreligious power which has characterized Brazilian church-state relations for centuries. Although it is true that during the reading of the decree that "liberated the cults" two Afro-Brazilian priestesses flanked the governor, it is not insignificant that the mayor and the Cardinal were joined together on one side, and the priestesses were on the other side.

In contrast, we have seen Candomblé groups unite in public worship of Oxalá as Bonfim, the supreme deity of many of Bahia's African descendants. Within this perspective, it is the female sacerdotes who have preserved the African cultural traditions, and their religion is associated with neither male control nor the overt power of the state. Instead, Candomblé worship looks to a long by-gone period and celebrates a mythical homeland where female power and African culture is revered and respected.

Thus, the ceremony of the washing of the steps of Bonfim is an apparent affirmation of the myth of Brazilian "racial democracy," that is, the myth that in Brazil there is no racism and that instead there is a harmonious mingling of the races. The ceremony appears to confirm that myth because it visibly tolerates Afro-Brazilian religious expressions at this sacred church site. Yet, perhaps ironically, this festival also reinforces rather traditional relations of race and gender. Is it not also possible to see these powerful Bahianas as symbols of previously oppressed and disempowered traditions? Two generations earlier other mothers were wet nurses and slaves, forced to clean the church as an extension of the duties they performed in their masters' homes. This ambiguous, public ritualized inversion of black female sacerdotal power contrasts with the dominant white, male state and church. Yet, those same state and church powers have now elevated the once illegal, despised, and scorned cults. A popular symbol of the people has now been gentrified for national tourist consumption and positioned to attract international Afro/diasporic root seekers. Taking their place in a much larger national or international drama, these shifting, cultural symbols represent a multilayered struggle for cultural authenticity.

Endnotes

1. For theoretical support and inspiration I drawn on situation-analysis as developed by the Manchester School and exemplified by Cohen (1974), Gluckman (1958), Mitchell (1969), and Turner (1974). I draw on their work to unravel the complex relationship between the use of symbols and political processes. I am interested in the politics of culture from various points of view, including the instrumental value of symbols in the distribution, maintenance, and exercise of power.

2. Data from the Fundação Instituto Brasileiro de Geografia e Estatística (IBGE) from the 1970 census.

3. See Yvone Maggie's dissertation (1988) for a reflection on Afro-Brazilian religious repression during the period 1890–1945.

4. There are many works on popular Catholicism, especially in Portuguese. For a theoretical discussion of this concept, see, for example, Pedro Ribeiro de Oliveira (1976). For a bibliography on these topics as well as his research report on a survey, see Oliveira (1970). Briefly, for his research Oliveria adopted three operational instruments or "constellations," which could indicate the relation of man to the sacred: the sacramental, devotional, and protection. He also claimed that the individual could relate to the sacred through an evangelical constellation (reading the Bible and the gospels) and through a magical constellation, which is defined as a nonreligious activity.

5. The *Jornal da Bahia* estimated the presence of five million people, about 61 carts, and more than 600 Bahianas that year (January 2, 1976).

References

Cohen, Abner
    1974 *Two Dimensional Man.* Berkeley: University of California Press.
Gluckman, Max
    1958 *An Analysis of a Social Situation in Modern Zululand.* Manchester, U.K.:
    Rhodes-Livingstone Institute, Manchester University Press.
Groetelaars, Martin M.
    1983 *Quém é o Senhor do Bonfim?* Bahia.

Maggie, Yvonne
1988 "Medo do Feitiço: Relações Entre Magia e Poder no Brasil." Ph.D. dissertation, Museu Nacional, Universidade Federal do Rio de Janeiro.

Mitchell, Clyde (ed.)
1969 *Social Networks in Urban Situations.* Manchester: Manchester University Press.

Oliveira, Pedro Ribeiro de
1970 "Catolicismo Popular no Brasil." *CERES* No. 9. Rio de Janeiro: CERES.
1976 "Catolicismo Popular no Brasil—Bibliografia." *Revista Eclesiástica Brasileira* 36 (March 1976): 272–80.

Silverstein, Leni
1994 "Candomblé Authenticity Struggles and the Brazilian National Project: Gender, Race, Religion, and Power in Brazil." Ph.D. dissertation, New School for Social Research.

Turner, Victor
1974 *Dramas, Fields, and Metaphors.* Ithaca: Cornell University Press.

Three

Ideologies and Cultures
on an
International Stage

⊠

This section moves from social relations and social structure to ideology, which will mean ideas as they are linked to social structure and cultural values. Thus, ideology in this section will include music, religion, and even a therapeutic system such as Alcoholics Anonymous. In addition to this commonality, the three essays share a concern with ideas and ideologies that originate outside Brazil and how those ideas get Brazilianized.

Carvalho's wide-ranging essay focuses on music, and it considers the history of Brazilian music from its origins to the present day. What is remarkable about this essay, in addition to its breadth, is how it situates Brazilian music in terms of ethnic and class relations. Carvalho begins with the classic triangle of Brazilian race relations: the music of Europeans, Africans, and Native Americans. Whereas most Brazilians willingly acknowledge that much of their music has African roots, Carvalho tacks in a slightly different direction to argue that the Native American concept of "anthropophagy" (cannibalism) may also be helpful for understanding Brazilian music. She argues that Brazilians enjoy cannibalizing the music of other nations and traditions.

Carvalho's argument brings us back to the concept of encompassment as described in the Introduction. To review, two terms may be in opposition, but at another level one of the terms can stand for or absorb the whole. Thus, I have both a head and hand, but my head comes to stand for me as a whole person. In this sense, the head "encompasses" the hand. In a similar way, Carvalho argues that Brazilians tend to "swallow" other musical traditions, thus adopting them but at the same time Brazilianizing them. A case in point would be bossa nova (the example almost everyone knows is "The Girl from Ipanema"), a Brazilian musical style that adopts international jazz but at the same time changes it and encompasses it with modified versions of the rhythms of samba.

The processes of anthropophagy can work in complicated ways. Brazilian popular music (MPB), an elite musical movement that drew extensively on folk music, can be said to cannibalize folk material and to swallow it up in sophisticated lyrics and musical forms. At the same time, the nationalist sentiment of MPB represents the Brazilian elite's cannibalizing of foreign cultural theories that honored folk traditions. In this and other ways, the Brazilian elite tends to swallow up theories and musical forms from abroad. At the same time, the lower classes and rural poor look to the urban elites for music to digest. (On the idea of eating and encompassment, see the essay on Dona Flor in DaMatta 1982.)

My essay looks at relationships of hierarchy and encompassment among ideas and practices associated with religion. Here, I consider four major religions of southern Brazil, three of which emerged outside Brazil: Catholicism, Pentecostalism, and Spiritism. Only the fourth, Umbanda, is Brazilian. I show how intellectuals representing each of the four religions view the other three religions and construct a world in which their own religion is at the top of a hierarchy of religions. In this sense, each religion views the religious system in a way that encompasses the other religions.

At the same time, I also bring in the concepts of hegemony, the theory that ideas of the dominant group tend to shape the entire system, and heterodoxy, the idea that some religions are less acceptable than others. Thus, I argue that the dominant religion, Catholicism, tends to view the religious system in an exclusionary manner, in which other religious views are rejected. At the bottom of the system, Umbanda tends to look at the system in an eclectic and ecumenical manner. Whereas both Catholicism and Umbanda seem to participate more in a hierarchical world based on exclusion or inclusion, in between them Spiritism and Protestantism see the religious system as more pluralistic. Implicitly the ideas of Spiritism and Pentecostalism about the religious system are closer to the modern value of religious equality and even to the idea of a marketplace of religious alternatives.

Jarrad's careful comparative study examines how Alcoholics Anonymous was Brazilianized (or encompassed by Brazilian cultural styles and values). Rooted in the evangelical Protestantism of the United States, AA is based on belief in a higher spiritual power. Because everyone has an equal relationship to this higher power, the members of the AA group are implicitly equal. The AA group also focuses on the principle of anonymity, or "principles above personalities." Jarrad draws on fieldwork to show how one group in Brazil reworked AA along lines that were more consistent with Brazilian culture. Thus, a charismatic leader emerged, and his words and actions came to overtake the importance of the literature and even the principle of anonymity. The buddy system of sponsorship also became reinterpreted according to the principles of patron–client ties. Likewise, the emphasis on written doctrine gave way to the personal relations of an oral culture. In short, in fundamental ways AA was reworked in its Brazilian setting. Yet, the new Brazilianized (or, to use Carvalho's metaphor, anthropophagized) form is also successful.

Jarrad's paper works with concepts that have interesting connections with some of the other papers. One area of convergence involves a practice that, to my knowledge, has never been discussed from a cultural perspective: the "relay." Jarrad notes that in American Alcoholics Anonymous, there is a "chaining" style of discussion that disappears in the Brazilian groups, where discussion revolves around the commentary of the coordinator. The chaining form of discourse is reminiscent of Kottak's discussion of relay races, which he found to be less prominent in Brazilian competitive swimming. Kottak argues that relays make more sense in American culture, where that type of race dramatizes the values of teamwork and efficiency that are found in the business culture. Comparing Kottak's discussion with that of Jarrad leads to the suggestion that the relay may be related not only to teamwork and efficiency but also to the idea of egalitarian individualism that specialization and teamwork presuppose.

Another area of convergence is the condition of anonymity, whose meaning Jarrad argues is transformed in the personalistic style of the Brazilian AA meetings. Prado also discussed anonymity, which she associated with the freedom of the large cities, and Coelho noted that the poor in large cities are anonymous with respect to media reporting. As Prado and Coelho demonstrate (following DaMatta 1991), the concept of the anonymity of large cities is useful to help clarify what it means to be an individual in Brazil. In contrast, Brazilian AA meetings are more like the Brazilian house: AA is a place where one is a person, not an individual, and therefore it is not a space for anonymity. I would argue that in the United States the concept of anonymity may be more associated with the community than the individual. The phrases "anonymous donor" or "anonymous police tip" come to mind, as does the practice of anonymity associated with voting. In the United States, an individual is more closely associated with "uniqueness," as in the phrase "Be an individual!" or the name of the famous clothing store of New York City: Unique.

References

DaMatta, Roberto

1982 *"Dona Flor e Seus Dois Maridos*: A Relational Novel." *Social Science Information* 21(1): 19–46.

1991 *Carnivals, Rogues, and Heroes.* Notre Dame, Ind.: University of Notre Dame Press.

Chapter Seven

Tupi or Not Tupi MPB:
Popular Music and Identity in Brazil

⊠

Martha de Ulhôa Carvalho

The phrase "Tupi or not Tupi, that is the question" was coined in the 1920s by the then avant-garde intellectual Oswald de Andrade in the "Manifesto Antropofágico" (1972 [1928]). The title is a pun referring to "to be" as in identity and "tupi" as in Tupinambá, the first native people encountered in Brazil. "Tupi" in this case implies cultural identity. Oswald de Andrade was a major representative of the Brazilian modernist movement, which aimed at modernizing Brazilian culture by denying academicism and finding a national language in the arts. Andrade and the modernists claimed an identity with the first inhabitants of Brazil, not in the romanticized sense of the nineteenth-century version of nationalism, but in the modern sense of a quest for a barbaric innocence.

Antropofagia, or cultural cannibalism ("anthropophagy"), is a modernist concept that legitimated the incorporation of foreign elements into Brazilian art. Oswald de Andrade claimed that Brazilians should practice *antropofagia*, absorbing from everywhere whatever fitted the Brazilian ethos. The concept of *antropofagia* itself goes back to sixteenth-century native South American religious cannibalism. For the Native Brazilian Tupinambá, the physical and spiritual worlds were intermingled, and it was possible to "eat" what came from both worlds. In the Tupinambá practice of *antropofagia*, people died in revenge for an ancestor, but at the same time their death meant the birth of another self in the cannibal, who added body scarifications and a new name after the human sacrifice.

In this paper I will argue that Brazilian musicians ritualistically capture other people's musical traits and incorporate them into their own music.

Brazilian music is thus revitalized, and its identity and survival is reinvigorated. To demonstrate this point, I will examine several types of Brazilian music leading up to the *MPB*, the acronym for *música popular brasileira* (Brazilian popular music). The name appeared in the 1960s in discussions centering on the controversy over the "internationalization" of Brazilian popular music and its "selling out" to jazz (bossa nova) and rock (*jovem guarda*, or "young guard"). There were also the famous MPB festivals (*festivais*, or *festival* in the singular), in which university students and others performed their compositions. Some of the music of the time, especially songs composed specifically for the festival competitions, was called MMPB (modern Brazilian popular music).

The rationale for using the term *MPB* to define certain kinds of Brazilian popular music is based on a search for identity in the origins of Brazilian culture. In the conventional formulation, Brazilian folk and popular music derives from the encounter of mainly three cultures: the Native Brazilian, the Luso-European, and the African. Apparently the indigenous portion of Brazilian music is minimal except for the use of a few instruments and dance formations (Alvarenga 1982). European-originated forms and scales, together with African-influenced rhythms and style of instrument interaction, are what one can readily perceive when trying to understand Brazilian popular music. However, as I shall demonstrate, what we cannot hear is the process by which Brazilian music is created—the fascination with prestigious foreign music, the embracing of foreign musical forms, and their incorporation and transformation into something original—and that was inherited from the Tupinambá.

Learning How to Create Music: A Brief History of Brazilian Popular Music

The native peoples of Brazil did not have an abstract term for music. The musical practices of the Tupinambá tribes who lived in the coastal areas of Brazil at the time of the discovery took the form of ritual song-dance-playing-and-drinking (Léry 1967; Staden 1974). These practices were part of the purification rituals for cannibalism (*antropofagia*), or they were performed in connection with the cults of the ancestors who needed to be praised and revenged.

The Tupinambá seemed not to care for transcendental life as it is praised in Christian civilization. They had an animistic vision of the world and did not distinguish between themselves and nature. For example, one would not eat a slow-moving animal because one's ability to run could be jeopardized. By the same token, vital energy was absorbed through cannibalistic practices. The aim of the raids was to revenge the ancestors who had been caught and eaten by the enemy. Each time an enemy was sacrificed in an act of revenge, a new name and body scarifications were added to the man who had killed the victim. Cannibalism linked the physical and the spiritual, the past with the future, and life with death. Catholic indoctrination substituted spiritual communion for cannibalism, undermining the efficacy of the native ceremonies by the implementation of a symbolic act with no concrete equivalence.

The method of catechization in Brazil incorporated into Christian life selected pagan elements. In the indoctrination of the Brazilian Indians, missionaries used the tradition of the Medieval miracle plays or *autos*—that is, sketches with Christian plots and with the Indian actors speaking Tupi, the native language. While the words were in Tupi, the music was in Gregorian chant style. The missionaries took advantage of the surface similarity between the native music language and the Gregorian chant modal structure in the religious indoctrination process.[1]

Similar affinities characterized the articulation of slave religion and music with that of the Portuguese. The African slaves disguised their religion with each African deity receiving a Catholic name.[2] They formed brotherhoods in the manner of the whites, and on days of religious processions, especially those in homage to Our Lady of the Rosary, the black communities reenacted the African kingdoms and courts. The brotherhoods were responsible for church music.

Very little is known about secular musical activity in colonial Brazil except that most of the musicians were mulattoes. The slave musicians were called *choromeleiros* or *charamela* players. Wind instruments were also played in military bands. Civil or military bands, which even today remain responsible for most of the musical training of professional wind instrumentalists, maintained the preference for the *charamela*. There is some documentation on the activity, in the mid-nineteenth century, of groups directed by barbers (Marcondes 1977). Those groups were probably forerunners of the *chorões*, that is, groups of urban musicians who developed (or maintained) a peculiarly Afro-Brazilian style of playing music in which the melody, either sung or played by wind instruments (*charamela*), was accompanied by a guitar that improvised bass lines. In my opinion the style is a remnant of African drum playing in which a multilayered ensemble performs polyrhythms. The *chorões* held serenades in which they helped popularize the song genre *modinha* ("little song"), a type of love song to be discussed below.

With increasing urbanization and the rise of a middle class, several new musical forms appeared. Dance forms adapted to the aesthetics and ethos of the emerging society, and some of the body postures in African-derived dances were censored according to Iberian moral standards. Thus, the "lascivious" African-derived *lundú* dance turned into the mestizo *maxixe*, while Brazilian musicians were playing the European-derived polka. As Béhague (1966) mentions, urban popular music in Brazil emerged through the association of folk songs and dances with imported urban dances. Brazilian popular composers such as Joaquim Callado, Chiquinha Gonzaga, and Ernesto Nazareth supported the nationalization of European dances such as the polka. At the same time, they helped accommodate to a wider audience more traditional forms such as the *lundú*, as well as to bring together new forms such as the Brazilian tango, the *maxixe*, and the early urban samba (see Béhague 1966).

In my opinion, Brazilian popular music today can be traced to two forms that emerged in the urban centers in the eighteenth century: the African-influenced dance (and later song) *lundú*; and the Portuguese (or Brazilian, according to some) *modinha*. In the nineteenth century, European rhythms such as the polka and the waltz were incorporated into the Brazilian popular music idiom. Another rhythm to have enormous influence was the Cuban *habanera*. Mixed with Brazilian genres mentioned above, they formed the forerunners of what today is called MPB (connected with the urban *samba* and the *lundú*), and what I call *música romântica* (romantic music, connected with the urban serenades and *modinhas*).[3]

Investing Music with Social Meaning

Popular musical genres in Brazil can be distinguished according to rhythmic structure, instrumentation, vocal quality, and also the styles of individual singers. Thus, the music of Amado Batista, Roberto Carlos, or Chitãozinho e Xororó is classified as a different category from that of Mílton Nascimento, Chico Buarque, or Caetano Veloso, who are known as MPB artists. The subtleties of the categorization are related to social class, but class in the sense of intellectual tendency and sophistication more than economic level. Artists such as Caetano Veloso and Mílton Nascimento may be referred to as "popular" or *popular brasileiro*, whereas artists such as Amado Batista may be referred to as "sub-popular" or *brega*.[4] However, when the term "popular" is used for artists such as Amado Batista, the term "MPB" is used for artists such as Caetano Veloso.

Composers of Brazilian popular music come from diverse social class segments, and its performers are professional or semiprofessional musicians. Its production for commercial consumption is independent of the original intent of its composer; the authors and performers seldom control the dissemination of their music in the media and other markets. The aesthetic value attached to their music sometimes is not based on musical criteria alone; rather, the meaning of each genre of popular music depends greatly on the social origins of the genre and its constituency. The relationship between popular music and social status in Brazil therefore depends on who makes the music, for whom it is made, by whom it is performed, and in what style the music is composed and performed.

Social class is then the major, but not the only, defining element for assessing the function and meaning of Brazilian popular music. In both MPB and "regular" popular music, class is crosscut by other social hierarchies, such as gender, age, and race. For example, for more than twenty years Roberto Carlos (romantic music) has sold millions of records per year. His public ranges from those who can listen to him only on the radio to members of the "high society." Therefore, cultural elitism has less to do with economic means than with factors such as educational background, age, and preferences.[5]

National identity was constructed by an intellectual elite that created an ideal image of "the people" and decided which kinds of traits were worth emphasizing and which ones were to be dismissed as decadent or unauthentic. As Renato Ortiz mentions in his study of Brazilian culture and cultural identity, all nationalistic debates in Brazil have been centered on the identification of the uniqueness of Brazilian identity vis-à-vis the dominant philosophies in Europe and the United States (1985:7). The folklore issue, for instance, was developed under the aegis of American cultural anthropology, which searched for the purer roots of Brazilianness that were to be found among social groups "uncontaminated" by progress and civilization. The urban middle class was thought to be without an identity of its own, and consequently its musical manifestations were dismissed in favor of more "authentic," "uncontaminated" manifestations (see Carvalho 1991).

Brazilian intellectuals followed the modernist approach to nationalism, in which the "true" Brazilian identity was to be found in folklore (see Andrade

1962 [1928]). Folk music meant rural music, but more than that it meant the music of isolated and marginalized social groups. The upper classes and intellectual elite were preoccupied with producing an image of ideal Brazilian culture. These people, who dominated the national image-making of Brazil, traditionally associated themselves with an erudite aesthetics that meant, in terms of music, the European classical music canon. In this canon, prestige was ascribed both to classical music, seen as a source of techniques and artistic erudition, and to folk music, viewed as a source of raw material. Urban popular music would be either watered down classical music or degenerated folk music. Thus, urban popular music was evaluated in terms of its degree of proximity either to folk music or to classical erudition. MPB, for instance, has high intellectual prestige because it employs sophisticated lyrics and arrangements and because it simultaneously uses folk material. However, the nationalist sentiment expressed in MPB is ambiguous because the songs deal, in upper-class and art music style, with a Brazilian identity that is rooted in rural and folk traditions. The struggle of common people is told by a narrator who stays outside the portrayed reality.[6]

In addition to following or responding to dominant European and North American cultural theories, the Brazilian cultural elite also responded to different foreign influences. In selecting among foreign popular musics, the Brazilian elite tended to choose dominant and prestigious musics. For example, in the late 1950s a generation of upper middle-class youth became interested in jazz, which they then linked to samba to create bossa nova.

The urban middle and lower-middle classes are less concerned with the cultural origin of the musics they use. They do not care if their music comes from Cuba, Mexico, Paraguay, or the United States, as long as the foreign music has characteristics that they can understand and use for their own expressive purposes. An example is the *lambada*. Brazilians of the middle and lower strata merrily danced *lambada* without caring whether it had a strong Caribbean influence or whether it was launched as a commercial product in France. Still, even for the urban middle and lower-middle classes, the fact that the music came from the "exterior" enhanced its prestige.

In a typical, middle-sized Brazilian town, the prestige connected to outside or "exterior" things meant, and to a certain degree still means, not only international influences but also what comes from Rio, such as Radio Nacional in the 1930s–1950s or TV Globo today (Carvalho 1991). For example, in the same way that something coming from Rio de Janeiro is more prestigious than something coming from the Northeast or of a rural origin, a genre coming from Europe or the United States has potentially more value than musics imported from Latin America.[7] Thus, on the one hand there is the relationship inwards, with who "we" are, and on the other hand there is the relationship with "them," with the Other. Latin America is "we," and Latin American musical elements, like every "household" member (women, African traits, native traditions), are ascribed a lower status.

Thus, Brazilians of all social levels—from the cultural elite to the middle and lower classes—look outward: rural to urban, urban to cosmopolitan, national to international. Rural people listen to urban music, and urban people prefer music from Rio, São Paulo, or abroad. The preferences are always for the music of a class of people at least a notch higher in the social hierarchy: urban music for rural people and "better quality" music for those who already live in town (Carvalho 1991). What is considered popular stands on a different level than what is officially considered national. The national is invoked by the elites, who see themselves looking up to the "exterior," but only to certain kinds of "exterior." At the same time, these higher social groups attempt to marginalize the lower groups. What might be a perfectly viable dance music to the middle class (the bolero, for instance) might be considered just a "commercial" music by the so-called opinion makers (critics, disc jockeys, teachers, journalists).[8]

After World War II there was an influx of Latin American music in Brazil. It was the heyday of rumbas, mambos, chá-chá-chá, and especially the bolero.[9] By the 1950s the bolero and the slower lyric samba known as the *samba-canção* begin to merge. The *samba-canção*, like the samba, stresses the second beat of the measure. This movement forward, an impulse away from the first beat, is also implicit in bossa nova. Bossa nova has a highly varied rhythmic structure, but it still has as its backbone a series of two "Afro-American" cells, with an accentuation in the second one. Again, there is the impulse forward, although this "Latin" connection is de-emphasized in bossa nova, whose followers tend to identify with jazz harmonies and ignore its relationship and derivations from the tradition of *samba-canção* and bolero.

Bossa nova also represents another aspect of the relationship between social class and popular music. It is music for listening and as such it is closer to art music, which emphasizes "aesthetic pleasure," than to dance music, which emphasizes sensual pleasure. This emphasis on listening, as well as the preference for more prestigious connections, is part of a traditionally aristocratic orientation.

Young Guard & Bossa Nova

As I mentioned before, an important development of popular music in Brazil in the 1960s was the appearance of Brazilian rock, at the time known as *jovem guarda* or "young guard" music. Young guard musicians performed versions of pop rock songs such as "Polkadot Bikini" by Beckriss and Vanze, and they also composed original songs in the same vein. Their constituency was the newly formed middle class, and they sang about modern and industrialized urban life. This middle class supported the military dictatorship, which repressed the intellectual elite who in turn supported MPB.[10] At the same time, the dictatorship favored the spread of mass media—and consequently the power of the culture industry which backed up young guard musicians such as Roberto Carlos—as part of a campaign to centralize communications and expand the internal consumer market. This expansion of cultural space plus the repression of MPB musicians opened room for young guard as well as other new forms of popular music to emerge, such as the modern *música sertaneja* (backlands music).[11] As a movement, young guard did not last long; its composers turned to composing what I call "romantic music"—music with a personal and sentimental thematic.

Bossa nova's thematic is also personal, although not as sentimental-erotic as the thematic of romantic music. The main difference is in terms of aesthetics: bossa nova is erudite and stems from the European classical music canon, whereas romantic music is popular and related to Latin American aesthetic values. Since the late 1960s romantic music has been a commercial success in Brazil; in contrast, bossa nova musicians were less aggressive and, like the classical composer Villa-Lobos, became more interested in the international market. Bossa nova musicians felt that they were closer to an international musical idiom than to traditional Brazilian music.

Both bossa nova and young guard musicians represented segments of Brazilian society that were undergoing the process of modernization that began in the 1930s. Bossa nova started out as the music of upper middle-class youth in Rio's South Zone, whereas young guard began as the music of a group that met in Rio's North Zone. The geographical localization alone sheds light on the social status of the two groups; the division of space mirrors one in social structure. The prestige associated with certain neighborhoods refers to a relationship between center and periphery rather than a mere difference between north and south. As in many Brazilian traditional cities, in Rio de Janeiro suburban neighborhoods are less prestigious than urban ones.[12] Tijuca, the North Zone neighborhood where the young guard musician Roberto Carlos and his partner Erasmo Carlos met, is suburban and therefore less prestigious than the South Zone neighborhood Ipanema, where the bossa nova musicians Tom Jobim and Vinícius de Moraes lived.

Both the bossa nova and young guard movements had as their leaders migrant musicians: bossa nova style was practically "invented" by the Bahian João Gilberto, whereas young guard "King" Roberto Carlos was a native of the state of Espírito Santo. Roberto Carlos began in Rio de Janeiro by singing in bossa nova style, but he was not successful with his connections in the North Zone of Rio. Neither Roberto Carlos nor Carlos Imperial, his first show host, had the sophistication and education of their South Zone counterparts. Thus, Roberto Carlos accepted the suggestion of CBS record producers to compose and sing music "for youth," which meant at the time (the early 1960s) music with rock'n'roll rhythms. Several young guard songs were composed by Roberto Carlos and Erasmo Carlos. Another part of their repertoire consisted of Portuguese versions of international rock.

If one analyzes closely bossa nova and young guard styles, certain similarities emerge, especially in terms of vocal timbre and melodic contour. Like bossa nova, young guard was also influenced by the bolero and *samba-canção* (see Marcondes 1977). The differences, crucial in terms of meaning, have to do with the kind of foreign musical connection, the class of people making and consuming the music, and the kinds of historical tendencies represented by those groups. The connection to jazz in the case of bossa nova, and rock in the case of young guard, meant a subsequent change of sound: subtle in the case of jazz because it was connected with instruments commonly used in Brazilian urban music; and more drastic in the case of rock, which introduced the completely different sound of the electric guitar. At its inception, young guard seemed to many to be very novel, but now, listening back and especially comparing it to its supposed model, I can say that young guard is nothing more than a romantic song with rock rhythms. Young guard represented the emergence of lower-middle-class youth culture, with all its related elements, including clothing, rebellion against the older generation, and a rudimentary sexual revolution. As young guard performers and composers matured, their themes and lifestyles changed. Although young guard as a movement did not last long, its successful trajectory toward modernization and upward mobility remains a model to musicians representing rural migrants and urban, lower-class ideals.

As in bossa nova, the timbre of young guard's performers was "soft" and smooth, and the lyrics also dealt with love, but the tone and content of the songs were very different. For example, in Tom Jobim's famous bossa nova song "Garota de Ipanmena" ("The Girl from Ipanema"), the woman is praised but kept at a distance from the poet. In young guard songs such as the classic "Que tudo mais vá pro inferno" ("That Everything Else Goes to Hell") by Roberto Carlos and Erasmo Carlos, the poet wants the woman to be much closer to him; he wants her to "warm him in the winter," i.e., to participate in a much more direct way in his life. The type of Brazilians and Brazil sung about in bossa nova has values that stem from the traditionally patriarchic and hierarchical Brazilian ideology, whereas young guard refers to a new group of people emerging in urban centers. This new subgroup of the middle class grew up while the country was being industrialized, and it took advantage of the new possibilities for upward social mobility created by the diversification of work. Young guard is modern in its use of modern instrumentation and technology, marketing strategies, and appeal to a large group of people.

Whereas young guard represented and expressed the desires and ideals of a new Brazilian subclass, bossa nova represented a Brazilian conservative tendency in aesthetics and ideology, even though it was "basically a reaction against the limits and prejudices of the more traditional samba" (Behague 1973: 219). There were several "progressive" elements that contributed to the bossa nova style, among them the incorporation of "dissonant" jazz harmonies. Other elements also central to the style, such as vocal timbre and lyric content, come from different historical and ecological circumstances. First, its timbre—half spoken and soft—comes not only from the fact that the music emerged in apartments, but also from the fact that the style of big voices was already being superceded by the crooning style of the small night clubs after the casinos, the place for big shows, were closed down in 1946. Second, the lyric content—sentimental love songs—follows the tradition of romantic music that can be traced to the *modinha* and serenades.

Except for a few masterpieces like "Desafinado," a beautiful match of content and form, bossa nova lyrics are unpretentious—one could say even commonplace and shallow. The "Garota de Ipanema," for instance, is a colloquial commentary about a beautiful woman who passes by the poet seated at a sidewalk table in a corner bar at Ipanema Beach (Rio de Janeiro's South Zone). The melodic line and prosody comes directly from spoken Brazilian Portuguese. Also the subject of the lyrics—praising the "charms" of a Brazilian woman—is part of a tradition of making loud commentary on passing women by men who are standing on the sidewalk or seated in a bar.[13] The function is the same as a whistle or a commentary made by any man to a women in the street, except that now it is made by a poet-diplomat, and therefore it passes as being in very "good taste."

Romantic Music

Young guard musicians such as Roberto Carlos drew on a popular musical tradition known as "romantic music" (*música romântica*), a tradition that dates back to the nineteenth-century *modinha* (little song). After undergoing transformations, the *modinha* became one of the main elements of the *serestas* of the first quarter of the twentieth-century, that is, a group of serenaders who sang and played in the moonlit streets. Men, dressed in white linen suits and Panama hats, serenaded their beloved well into the night with *modinhas* and other love songs, accompanied by groups of instrumentalists who usually played guitars, mandolin, flute, and violin.

Many consider the *modinha* to be folk music, although several *modinhas* are by known composers. A famous example is "Tão longe, de mim distante" ("So far away, distant from me") by the nineteenth-century (Italian style) Brazilian opera composer, Carlos Gomes. Like many *modinhas* of the last century, it is written in a *bel canto* style, especially the refrain which employs large skips in its melody. The lyrics of "Tão longe" ask: "Where are your thoughts that seem so distant from me?" The melody epitomizes the *modinha* pattern (undulating phrases, overall descending direction of phrases, and occasional chromatic ornamentation).

The tradition of love songs of the *modinhas* was followed up in the *samba-canção* genre for which "Vingança" (Revenge) by Lupicínio Rodrigues is a classic example. In "Vingança," a song of contemptuous jealousy for a lost lover, the author describes his joy when he hears that his ex-lover was crying and drinking heavily because she missed him. By then it is too late, since she has already "dishonored" him. The woman in Lupicínio's song "falls" because of her infidelity and her subsequent drinking. The author wishes to have her banned from society, "left to wander without a place to rest."

Bossa nova musicians did not approve of the tone of songs like "Vingança." It was too vulgar and realistic for the controlled and sophisticated goal of delayed pleasure held by intellectual artists like Tom Jobim and Vinícius de Moraes.[14] Women in bossa nova lyrics are kept at a polite distance, the same attitude found in traditional *modinhas*.

Lupicínio Rodrigues represented an image of gender relations in the 1950s, and therefore "Vingança" should be compared to an example of romantic music in Brazilian society during its period of "modernization" in the 1970s. In the song "Detalhes" ("Details"), Roberto Carlos also talks about a romance that is over. He is sorry that he lost the woman, and he wishes that the little everyday things of their life together will continue to remind her of himself. He hopes that the woman realizes how much he loved her. Although the rejected male in this song reveals resentment, he neither deifies the beloved (as in the traditional *modinhas*) nor degrades her (as in "Vingança"). In "Detalhes" the woman, though still looked down upon, is brought closer to the subject. This more proximate relationship is enhanced by musical gestures, such as the declamatory melody with its economy of notes and its insistence by means of shakes on certain tonal degrees. These musical features give the song a conversational quality, unlike the lyrical but distancing aspects of the *modinha*.

Ever since Roberto Carlos' successful 1966 young guard song "Quero que tudo mais vá pro inferno" ("Let everything else go to hell"), he has been the "king" of romantic music. Although Roberto Carlos (b. 1943) and his most constant partner, Erasmo Carlos (b. 1941), have a hybrid rhythmic style (rock, funk, bolero, *balada*, samba), they are more consistent in melodic and formal structure. In a typical Roberto Carlos song, the melody frequently contains fragments that use small intervals directly derived from spoken speech. As I mentioned before, this helps give Carlos' style a character of colloquial intimacy. Often the musical and poetic phrases are interrupted by pauses that, again, remind us of speech. Roberto Carlos' nasal vocal timbre is usually soft, with a sometimes breathy, sometimes pleading quality. Using very little vocal ornamentation except for occasional vibrato, his vocal style enhances his tone of romantic sincerity and vulnerability. Economy of means also applies to his compositional style, which often uses the AAA pattern both in rhyme scheme and melodic design. Frequently, two small melodic fragments repeated or in sequence are followed by a longer melodic phrase completing the musical period. In spite of the frequent repetitions, he achieves variety by gradually adding instruments to the orchestration, quoting music from older pieces when key words are mentioned in the song, and frequently modulating by ascending conjunct degrees. The language in Roberto Carlos' songs often describes everyday romantic situations (i.e., the pass, the anticipation of future lovemaking, self-pity, and jealousy). Women in Carlos' songs either eagerly await the poet's return home, or the romance is over, and they are remembered for the good times.

MPB

Although romantic music is the most popular musical genre in Brazil in terms of the number of people who consume it and its social class crossover, it is not considered authentic Brazilian popular music. Although what is considered authentic has changed over time, this status is now ascribed to MPB.[15] The roots of MPB are the 1930s sambas that were performed by Radio Nacional. The 1930s and part of the next decade were a golden age for Radio Nacional, which at the time was an instrument of propaganda for the populist centralized government. Samba then embodied the national identity.

In the 1950s samba absorbed the influence of the bolero and became slower and more songlike (*samba-canção*). As a reaction against the "stagnation" of Brazilian popular music, a group of middle-class artists started to gather in Rio's South Zone apartments to find a new way of playing samba, which became known as bossa nova. Some of these people (like Nara Leão) went to the poor quarters of the city, made contact with old samba players such as Nelson Cavaquinho, invited them to shows, and recorded their songs.

Other bossa nova artists (such as Edu Lobo) emphasized northeastern modes and rhythms in their compositions, and this tendency prevailed when the festivals appeared in the 1960s. Eventually the concept of "true" Brazilian music was broadened to include ingredients characteristic of music from the Northeast. Consequently, by the 1960s, "authentic" Brazilian popular music meant the samba as well as northeast-influenced music. Composers of *música-de-festival* (festival music) did not recreate the forms that existed in the Northeast (for instance, the *baião*, which enjoyed some success in the 1950s, or other northeastern forms such as *embolada* or *desafios*). Rather, they used some of the characteristically northeastern musical ingredients (e.g., some medieval scales that originated with the colonial missionaries) and applied them to their compositions. They also had a fixation on the theme of the hardships of the men from the northeast. These composers were idealistic students who felt they had a mission to produce a "truly" popular art.[16]

The nucleus of composers considered to be the great MPB artists today emerged from the festival era: Chico Buarque de Hollanda, Mílton Nascimento, Caetano Veloso, and Gilberto Gil. From 1964 to 1968, the last two were the main composers of *tropicalismo* (a deliberate carnivalization and musical bricolage).[17] Mílton Nascimento began composing regional-based music (from Minas Gerais), while Chico Buarque de Hollanda directed his efforts to the Brazilian "new song" movement.

All members of this generation, each in their own way, wanted to create a Brazilian music that was also a vehicle for social criticism. They used Brazilian folk and urban popular music in similar ways to the model advocated by the modernist Mário de Andrade back in the 1920s: to construct a nationalist art, the musician should transform raw folk materials into art. Mário de Andrade had also proposed that this kind of music should be "immediately disinterested." He was referring to the thought of his time, which classified folk music as "functional" and art music as providing "aesthetic pleasure" only. As I mentioned above, MPB aesthetics emulate the Western art music canon, which means that MPB music is considered "art" or erudite. Yet, MPB composers did not subscribe to the "dysfunctionality" of music. For them, popular music should be of the highest artistic quality, but its content, instead of being just a "purification" of folk music, should also have the function of social criticism and reinforcement of their idea of national identity.

By the 1970s MPB had become synonymous with authentic Brazilian popular music.[18] In a country as hierarchically structured as Brazil, MPB aesthetics stood at the top, against which all genres and artists were compared. In my research on middle-class popular music aesthetics, MPB artists and composers are cherished as the most important and best Brazilian composers. Brazilians enjoy MPB for many different reasons: Elis Regina for her interpretations of songs, Mílton Nascimento for his communication of emotion, Caetano Veloso for his vocal suavity and wit, and Chico Buarque de Hollanda for his perceptive and clever critique of Brazilian politics. MPB is made for listening rather than dancing. Consequently, people pay attention to its lyrics, its instrumentation, its arrangement and texture, the timbre of the singer, and the virtuosity of the singer and instrumentalists. A good MPB song should be in contemporary Portuguese, including the current foreign terms and slang. Like Brazilians in general, who are fond of puns and word play, MPB lyrics tend to avoid the commonplace: they can communicate on several planes at once on matters of social critique or existential meditation.

MPB artists aim at the creative communication of emotion by means of an elaborate language understandable to persons of "culture" and "good taste." This erudition permeates not only the composition and arranging process but also the performance style. For instance, it is rare that an MPB musician performs a folk tune as it has been collected. He or she (usually he) will elaborate on the tune by making a new arrangement, varying the performance style, or composing an altogether new tune in the folk style.

The song "Terezinha" is one such case in which Chico Buarque reinterprets folklore. The central figure in both the folk original and its popular/artistic variation is a woman in the process of meeting a male partner. In the nursery rhyme "Terezinha de Jesus," which is usually sung in rounds by groups of young girls, Terezinha de Jesus falls down and gets an offer of help from three courteous men. The first is her father, the second her brother, and the third is the one to whom she gives her hand. The rhythm is in three (a little waltz), and the melody has two phrases. Phrase "A" starts with two small repeated fragments of one measure each ("Terezinha/de Jesus") followed by a longer undulating fragment ("was so naughty that she fell down"), and phrase "B" answers the previous musical question with a single undulating, descending phrase: "Three men came to help her; the three took off their hats." The second verse tells about who came to help the little girl: her father, her brother, and a stranger.

In this song little girls are being taught about incest: they should not give their hand to their father or their brothers. The music enhances certain psychological aspects of the situation. The musical climax stresses the third phrase of each verse, highlighting both the cultural impasse of having to choose one male partner from many, and, most threateningly, having to accept a stranger as one's partner. The parallel to middle-class debutante balls is enlightening. It was, and in some towns still is, customary for teenage girls to be presented to society in collective balls. At the climax, the debutante dances a waltz with her father, her brother, and a third man who could be a boyfriend, a cousin, or an uncle. The debutante ball reinforced the nursery rhyme.

Folk songs are part of a repertoire that is usually seen as ageless, ahistorical, and permanent. People usually take folk songs for granted, and normally they do not pay too much attention to what the songs are saying; social knowledge is transmitted through folk songs almost unconsciously. Chico Buarque calls attention to the cultural context of the folk song by changing its voice and updating its language. He acts, then, as a revolutionary intellectual using mechanisms akin to those of Brecht. In his version of "Terezinha," Chico Buarque changes the poetic voice from a "she" to an "I," and the central role in the song is now played by a grown woman. In the first verse she refuses the man who treats her like a queen (the "father"); in the second verse she refuses the man who treats her like a slut (the "brother"); in the third she lets herself surrender to the man who treats her like a woman.

Unlike the bossa nova and romantic music musicians, Chico Buarque de Hollanda and other MPB musicians are worried about cultural liberation. Yet, MPB musicians share with their bossa nova colleagues the preoccupation with establishing a musical language that would stand on equal terms with other kinds of music in the international scene. Furthermore, like all kinds of Brazilian popular music, the MPB musicians incorporate foreign musical traits and emphasize the ones its constituency considers more prestigious.

Antropofagia

The mixture of heterogeneous musical elements is a trait of many popular musics in the world. The difference in the Brazilian case is how Brazilians see this mixture and give it meaning. The Brazilian cognitive framework is mestizo and, in my opinion, was taught to us in the process of catechization in the colony. At least in the case of music, we were taught to mix similar musical elements and to emphasize the most prestigious. This policy, which was carried out by the missionaries in their catechization of Native Brazilians, found resonance in the concept of the incorporation of physical and spiritual qualities through ritual cannibalism of the sixteenth-century Tupinambá.

The MPB artists who founded the tropicalism movement of the late 1960s revived the *antropofagia* concept. As for the Tupinambá in the 1500s, the modernists in the 1920s, and the bossa nova musicians in the early 1960s, the tropicalia artists believed that the absorption of some foreign musical elements would invigorate a "stagnant" Brazilian music. As an inspiration for their avant-garde experimentation, they deliberately absorbed "foreign" musical elements (such as electric guitar rock style) into the Brazilian musical "body." This same idea had been used before. In bossa nova, "foreign" elements (jazz harmonies) were ingested by composers, who used a "native" structure (samba) to produce a new genre (bossa nova). The incorporation of foreign elements worked in a two-way fashion. Bossa nova, which absorbed cool jazz, was later "eaten up" itself by jazz musicians elsewhere in the world.

I agree that Brazilians absorb and digest foreign musical ingredients to generate vital and varied Brazilian forms. I object, however, to the notion that this absorption of specific musical ingredients to reinvigorate music can be selective. Unlike the Tupinambá, who captured an enemy, fed him, gave him a spouse, made him a member of the tribe, and then sacrificed him, Brazilians cannot so consistently choose what musical influences they "swallow." Only certain musical borrowings are acknowledged by musicians and enthusiasts. For instance, bossa nova aficionados "forget" the borrowings from Latin American traditions in order to emphasize the use of jazz harmonies and the "coolness" of performance.

For many Brazilian intellectuals, only certain music qualifies as truly Brazilian; nonconforming examples are shunted into other categories. But is romantic music less Brazilian than MPB and bossa nova? All these genres use authentic Brazilian constants (like undulating and descending phrases, and speech-derived melodic contours and rhythms), but only the latter two are said to be Brazilian popular music. "Música Popular Brasileira" should include romantic music; the latter is just as much Brazilian popular music as MPB and bossa nova. Brazilian identity as expressed by musical style is connected more to how Brazilians see themselves in relation to foreign cultures than to the so-called roots of Brazilianness (their Iberian, African, and Amerindian past). As a result, the prestige of a musical genre is *not* assigned according to musical criteria; rather, it depends on the genre's connotations in terms of social class and hierarchy.

Acknowledgments

I wish to thank Charlotte Heth for her guidance on a 1987 independent study on the sixteenth-century Tupinambá, which introduced me to the concept of *antropofagia*, and Martin Hatch for urging that I should introduce my native understanding of how Brazilians identify themselves through music into my analysis. I also want to thank David Hess for editing the English, and Tom Turino and Charles Keil for their comments on another work which led me to expand the sociological aspect of my research.

Endnotes

1. Jean de Léry's examples of Tupinambá music, the only surviving specimens from the sixteenth century, are all syllabic (one syllable per note). Generally, they employed conjunct motion (notes following the order of the scale), elements also present in Gregorian chants (Léry 1967).

2. Candomblé (especially in Bahia), Tambor de Criola (Maranhão), and Macumba (Rio de Janeiro) are African-Brazilian religions in which spirit possession plays an integral role. Because of slavery and the prohibition of non-Catholic religious performances, the slaves were forced to disguise the African divinities as Catholic saints. African and Catholic religious ceremonies are performed in parallel even today. For example, the Tambor de Criola in the state of Maranhão is celebrated on a day dedicated to a Catholic saint, and it starts out with Catholic ceremonies such as the rosary. In a separate ceremony, the Tambor proper is performed. Thus, the ceremonies are parallel, rather than syncretized (according to Ferreti, communication of Glória Moura).

3. The two tendencies are not exclusive (i.e., a composer can and does compose music using both styles). In my opinion, the main difference between the *lundú* and *modinha* types is based on melodic contour and lyric content. *Lundú*-derived songs have a melodic contour closer to the intonation of spoken Portuguese; they tell a story using a melody with small intervals and a restricted vocal range. The lyric content of these songs is frequently realistic and sometimes ironic, and attention is focused on the subject of the song. An example is the "One Note Samba," where both the music and lyrics describe the love for the muse as something as inevitable as the movement of tonal chords in the song. In contrast to the *lundú*-derived songs, the *modinha*-derived songs have an undulating melodic contour, and frequently their lyric content is expressed in a contemplative and distant manner. An example is another song by Jobim entitled "Luíza." Because the *modinhas* have a more extended vocal range and use bigger intervals, they call attention to their melodic contour and away from the song's lyric content. In the *lundú*-derived songs, the emphasis is put on the lyric content; in the *modinha*-derived songs the emphasis is put on melody.

4. See Araujo (1988) for a definition of *brega*. The distinction between MPB and "brega" is similar to the distinction made by Adorno (1941) between "serious" and popular music, with the latter accused of standardization and repetition.

5. See Bourdieu (1984) on the concept of *habitus* and the uneven distribution of cultural goods.

6. See DaMatta (1991), who writes on the "dilemma" of Brazilian society: to negotiate a democratic ideology of equality in relation to the law (the individual) in a hierarchical world ruled by personal relations and clientelism (the person).

7. This is true despite the fact that the town I worked in (Montes Carlos, Minas Gerais) has much more in common culturally with the Northeast than with Rio de Janeiro. In general, Brazilian music shares several characteristics with Latin American traditions, and in fact it has absorbed much from Spanish America, although this fact is not officially acknowledged.

8. In my study of A.M. radio, I noticed that although it is mostly used by the rural migrant segment of the town and by people in surrounding areas, its programming does not include music that is made in the rural areas.

9. The bolero originated in Cuba at the end of the nineteenth century and arrived in Brazil via Mexico. Boleros have a characteristic bongo rhythm pattern that accentuates the second beat in a 4/4 time signature.

10. In Chile this repression occurred after 1973 with the Pinochet dictatorship. The difference is that in Chile the government actively interfered in the production of music, favoring the usage of folk forms like the *cueca* and *tonada* as representatives of Chilean cultural identity. These forms were previously used by nationalist composers like Victor Jara and Violeta Parra, but then had to be put aside by composers aiming at a political positioning through music in Chile (Carvalho 1987).

11. In the 1980s the generational equivalent to MPB of the 1960s emerged: Brazilian rock. The "rock brasileiro" constituency is also a student population, but in the 1980s this segment of society did not occupy the same cultural space and have the same prestige that its 1960s counterparts had.

12. In reality, this prestige depends on social class. The hip South Zone of Rio formally referred to Copacabana, then it moved to Ipanema and Leblon, and now it is moving farther to Barra.

13. Much more could be said about the courtship patterns: women are to be "encaged" in the domestic domain; however, when in the streets, men are the ones that stay paralyzed, and women keep moving.

14. This tradition of love songs of contemptuous jealousy, as well as the tradition of serenading the beloved maiden who listens inside the house, highlights an important aspect of gender relations in Brazil and in Latin America in general: "machismo" and its female counterpart "marianismo."

15. For instance, bossa nova was not considered "true Brazilian music" among certain circles. Today, there is no doubt that bossa nova is Brazilian.

16. In the university circles of the time, especially the influential CPC (Centros Populares de Cultura), it was believed that "people's art" was different from "popular art." Art made "by the people" was alienated, whereas art made "for the people" was truer to Brazilian cultural identity. (See Chauí 1986 on the development of popular culture in Brazil.)

17. The concept of carnivalization was explored by Bakhtin (1988) in his study of the carnivalesque. *Bricolage* refers to a mixture of diverse elements (Lévi-Strauss 1963).

18. See Perrone (1985) for an analysis of MPB.

References

Adorno, Theodor W.
1941 "On Popular Music." *Studies in Philosophy and Social Science* 9: 17–48.
Alvarenga, Oneyda
1982 *Música Popular Brasileira*. São Paulo: Livraria Duas Cidades.

Andrade, Mário de
1962 *Ensaio sobre a Música Brasileira*. São Paulo: Livraria Martins Editôra (orig. 1928).

Andrade, Oswald de
1972 "Manifesto Antropofágico." In *Do Pau-Brasil à Antropofagia e às Utopias. Obras Completas No. 6*. Rio de Janeiro: Civilização Brasileira; INL (orig. 1928).

Araujo, Samuel
1988 "Brega: Music and Conflict in Urban Brazil." *Latin American Music Review* 9/1 (Spring–Summer):49–89.

Bakhtin, Mikhail
1988 *Rabelais and His World*. Translated by Helene Iswolsky. Cambridge, Mass.: MIT Press.

Béhague, Gerard
1966 "Popular Music Currents in the Art Music of the Early Nationalistic Period in Brazil, circa 1870–1920." Ph.D. dissertation, Tulane University.
1973 "Bossa and Bossas: Recent Changes in Brazilian Urban Popular Music." *Ethnomusicology* 17(2):209–233.

Bourdieu, Pierre
1984 *Distinction: A Social Critique of the Judgement of Taste*. Trans. by Richard Nice. Cambridge, Mass.: Harvard University Press.

Carvalho, Martha
1987 "Canto Nuevo." Paper presented at the Fourth Annual Meeting of The International Association for the Study of Popular Music, USA Chapter at the University of Pittsburgh, Pittsburgh, Pa. April 3–5,1987.
1990 "Canção da América—Style and Emotion in Brazilian Popular Song." *Popular Music* 9/3:321–349.
1991 "'Música Popular' in Montes Claros, Minas Gerais, Brazil: A Study on Middle-Class Popular Music Aesthetics in the 1980s." Ph.D. dissertation, Cornell University.

Chauí, Marilena
1986 *Conformismo e Resistência: Aspectos da Cultura Popular no Brasil*. São Paulo: Editora Brasiliense.

DaMatta, Roberto
1991 *Carnivals, Rogues, and Heroes*. Notre Dame, Ind.: University of Notre Dame Press.

Léry, Jean de
1967 *Viagem à Terra do Brasil*. 4th ed. Translated by Sérgio Milliet. São Paulo: Livraria Martins Editora.

Lévi-Strauss, Claude
1963 *Structural Anthropology*. New York: Basic Books.

Marcondes, Marco Antonio (ed.)
  1977 *Enciclopédia da Música Popular Brasileira: Erudita, Folclórica e Popular.* São Paulo: Art Editora.
Ortiz, Renato
  1985 *Cultura Brasileira e Identidade Cultural.* São Paulo: Brasiliense.
Perrone, Charles Andrew
  1985 "Lyric and Lyrics: The Poetry of Song in Brazil." Ph.D. dissertation, University of Texas at Austin.
Staden, Hans
  1974 *Duas Viagens ao Brasil.* Trans. Guiomar de Carvalho Franco. Belo Horizonte: Itatiaia Editora and São Paulo: Editora da Universidade de São Paulo.

Chapter Eight

Hierarchy, Heterodoxy, and the Construction of Brazilian Religious Therapies

⊠

David J. Hess

In many national societies, religion, medicine, science, politics, and other cultural domains take the form of pluralistic systems in which a variety of groups compete with each other for legitimacy, resources, and followers. However, actors usually do not build their systems and attempt to attract followers by competing on a level playing field, even if there are constitutional guarantees that would suggest otherwise. Some groups have a head start, and they may even get the state to sanction their practices as official or orthodox. Other groups start from disadvantaged positions; their practices have a nonorthodox or "heterodox" status. As a result, boundaries between orthodoxies and heterodoxies pervade what might at first seem to be a pluralistic field of open competition.

Brazil has long been recognized as a laboratory of religious complexity. The Brazilian constitution protects religious freedom, and in theory Brazilians may belong to the religion of their choice. However, the various religions are not by any means equal competitors. Rather, the religious arena in many parts of Brazil has two major poles—one represented by the Catholic church and the other by the popular religions of African origin—with a number of other positions in between. The two poles are the product of Brazil's colonial legacy of racism and slavery, and in this sense the religious playing field is already structured by a more general and historically rooted hegemony.[1] As I have argued in *Samba in the Night*, the general hegemony of a privileged class of predominantly European descent, crosscut by the gender hegemony that empowers heterosexual men, conditions the general structures of orthodoxy and heterodoxy in the religious domain. In an almost textbook example of the distinction between orthodoxy and hetero-doxy, the Catholic church was for many years the official religion in Brazil, and likewise for many years the African religions were banned and/or per-secuted, as discussed in more detail in Silverstein's essay in this volume. Fur-thermore, as Silverstein also discusses, the Catholic/African polarities also align with another major dimension of social hierarchy: gender, given that the Catholic church orders and hierarchy are still limited to men, and many of the African religions grant a privileged place to the "mothers-of-the-saints."

In this essay, I will consider how boundaries between orthodoxy and het-erodoxy are maintained even in today's situation of modern legal structures that sanction freedom of religion and religious pluralism. Although the var-ious groups in the religious arena could be described as competing for a seg-ment of an apparently modern religious marketplace, I will argue that even as they go about competing for a piece of the market the actors end up reconstructing relations of hegemony that are their cultural legacy. To make this argument, I will engage in a detailed analysis of the work of four promi-nent intellectuals from four of the main religious positions in southern and southeastern Brazil: a Jesuit priest and parapsychologist (as a representative of the Catholic church), a Pentecostalist minister, a Spiritist intellectual, and an Umbanda medium, writer, and intellectual. I will argue that the social position of the four religions is evident in the way the intellectuals represent their religion with respect to their competitors.[2]

More specifically, I argue that although all four intellectuals provide a map of the whole religious system in which their own religion "encompasses" the other ones, the strategy of encompassment varies in a way that corre-sponds to their social position. To review the discussion in the introduction to this volume, the term "encompassment" refers to the way in which two categories may be constructed as opposites at one level, but at another level one of the terms stands for the opposition as a whole (Dumont 1980: 239). In the case of religion in Brazil, each group will draw a picture of the reli-gious system that constructs itself in the encompassing position. That picture is what one would expect in a system of religious pluralism: each group mar-kets itself as the best option with the one true way. However, I will show that something else is also going on: the *ways* of encompassing the other groups proceeds differently in each of the four cases. In turn, the way in which the other groups are encompassed reflects, as I shall argue, the relationship to the social structure and broader structures of hegemony in society. In this way, I hope to show how a perspective that examines the construction of heterodoxy, hierarchy, and hegemony can lead to a deeper analysis of religious systems than one which assumes a level playing field and a competitive model.[3]

Methodological Background

In Brazil, relations among religious groups are often clearly articulated in debates over who has the best exorcism rituals or therapies for spirit attack and possession. Therefore, this essay focuses on an amalgam of medico-religious-scientific ideas which defies easy compartmentalization as medical anthropology, the anthropology of religion, or the social studies of knowledge. The four positions considered here emerge from a set of choices that Brazilians from the urban South and Southeast often have available for "treatment" of cases of nonceremonial, domestic spirit possession and spirit "infestation" (i.e., ghost or poltergeist attacks).[4] Of the religious specialists available, four of the most salient are Catholic priests, who generally shy away from exorcisms and often recommend the psychotherapeutic approach of Jesuit parapsychologists; Spiritist (Kardecist) mediums, who practice a kind of talking exorcism known as "disobsession," which is directed mainly at spirits of deceased humans; Pentecostalist ministers, who perform prayer-based exorcisms directed at the devil; and Umbandist mediums (sacerdotes of a spirit mediumship religion with Christian, African, and Native or Amerindian elements), who will tend to view cases of spirit attack as due to sorcery and therefore may, in these cases, perform antisorcery rituals.

The research presented here grows out of fieldwork among the Spiritist movement in Brazil from late 1984 to early 1986, and the materials presented here are based on interviews conducted during a summer trip to Brazil in 1988. Three leading representatives of the religions were interviewed—the Jesuit Father Edvino Friderichs, the Pentecostalist Reverend Nasser Bandeira, and the Spiritist Hernani Guimarães Andrade. The fourth—the Umbandist Antônio Alves Teixeira—died shortly before my visit, but because of the wide diffusion of his publications, I decided to base this section on his published books rather than substitute an interview with other, lesser known Umbandist mediums.[5] The interpretation of his texts is complemented by an interview with a family who had recourse to an Umbandist healer in 1988, just as it is made possible by my own observations of Umbanda rituals and the general ethnographic literature on Umbanda.

Before proceeding to a discussion of the rhetoric of encompassment, I want to emphasize what is *not* being claimed or attempted in this essay. While the question of historical dynamics and development is an important one (and one which I have pursued elsewhere, e.g., 1987a), this essay is restricted to the narrower problem of describing a structure of representations at a given historical moment, specifically the mid-to-late 1980s. Furthermore, although the study is ethnographically based, I have not hesitated to use written texts. The level and type of problem being addressed here is more or less constant between texts and interviews: my experience is that a Jesuit view of the religious system, for example, is not likely to change dramatically depending on whether one asks the Jesuit directly or reads it in a book which he gives to me at the end of the interview.

There is also the question of the representativeness of the four religious healers/intellectuals whom I discuss. Certainly in a country as large and divided as Brazil it would be foolish to deny the tremendous regional diversity. I could multiply the number of positions discussed here from four to forty and still not achieve "representativeness." There is likewise a tremendous variation within, for example, the Spiritist movement or among Catholic intellectuals, not to mention within the broader Catholic church itself. Although each of the four persons discussed occupy or occupied leadership positions, I do not claim that the ideas of, for example, Padre Friderichs are in some sense modal for the Jesuit community, nor that those of Teixeira are representative of Umbanda as a whole. Not only would the answer to such a question require an extremely expensive and time-consuming survey, but it would also be beside the point. Instead, by taking one exemplar of each of these positions and interrogating his discourse, I will show, for example, what is "Jesuit" about a given Jesuit's construction of exorcism, healing, spirit attacks, and the others with whom he is in dialogue, rather than assess how representative a given Jesuit's discourse is of Jesuit intellectuals in general or, even more problematic, of the Catholic church as a whole. My concern here is with delineating certain representative *differences* among these four religions rather than with assessing how *representative* the differences are for each of the four religions.

A Jesuit

Padre Edvino Friderichs, S.J., is officially retired, but he maintains a busy schedule at the dormitory where he lives in the Anchieta High School

(Colégio Anchieta) in Porto Alegre, the capital city of the southernmost Brazilian state of Rio Grande do Sul. Although he is known in the press as an exorcist, he describes himself as a parapsychologist—that is, a student of the controversial scientific discipline dedicated to the study of what are believed to be paranormal phenomena—and as a parapsychologist he attracts a steady stream of clients. His work with haunted houses and ghosts has won him fame, but the mainstay of his work is relaxation treatment for cases of depression. I visited him in June 1988, and spent a few days with him while he treated a thirteen-year-old girl who was the focus of a poltergeist attack and a great deal of press coverage. During this time, I was able to talk with him at length and to watch him do his work as a healer.

Friderichs studied with Padre Oscar González Quevedo, S. J., a Spanish priest who lives in São Paulo and has taught his version of parapsychology to a generation of Latin American clergy members. In order to understand Friderich's theory and practice of healing, one must first examine some of Quevedo's key ideas. Quevedo believes that ghosts and haunted houses are not the work of spirits or demons; however, he deviates from official science by arguing that many of these cases cannot be reduced to naturalistic explanations such as fraud, hallucination, faulty wiring, childhood pranks, or overly active imaginations. Instead, he believes that haunted houses often involve "telergy," an unknown biological energy generated by the body of living persons, frequently adolescents.

The Jesuits back up this claim with a strong endorsement: their interpretation follows more or less the accepted theory of most American and Western European parapsychologists, except that the latter call this energy "recurrent spontaneous psychokinesis" and implicitly believe that it comes from the mind rather than the body. As a result, Jesuits in Brazil adopt and transform—or to use Martha Carvalho's term (this volume), "anthropophagize"—American and European parapsychology, a heterodox science with low prestige in the northern hemisphere. Because of the high prestige of almost anything North American or European in Latin America, parapsychology can paradoxically serve to legitimate the Catholic church with respect to Spiritism, Umbanda, Pentecostalism, and other religions and religious healing systems. Furthermore, the ways in which Jesuits have transformed international parapsychology suggests that the science has been encompassed by Catholic church dogmas. For example, Quevedo created a category of "supernormal" phenomena—Biblical prophecy, the miracles of Lourdes, the raising of the dead, and the cure of lepers—which are beyond the "extranormal" and "paranormal" phenomena of parapsychology and are instead the province of the theologian (1974: 100—103). As a result, the secular parapsychology of the northern hemisphere becomes part of a broader, Catholic framework.

At one point in Quevedo's scheme, however, northern hemisphere parapsychology encompasses Catholic dogma. The exception is important because it involves rejecting an alternative explanatory system, demonic infestation, which in Brazil has increasingly become the province of Pentecostalists. Quevedo refuses to accept the possibility that the devil might be the cause of at least some cases of spirit infestation and possession. In place of this explanation, he advocates a psychological interpretation. Quevedo's secular view of possession resulted in problems with the church hierarchy: during much of the 1980s, he was under prohibition to lecture or give interviews because he had published a book that questioned the reality of demonic infestation and that the church subsequently burned. Although officially sanctioned exorcism is now relatively rare within the Catholic church, the church hierarchy is apparently unwilling to give up its right to perform it. With this exception, Quevedo's parapsychology has nonetheless been extremely influential within the church. Even when he was under prohibition to lecture or give interviews, the church continued to advocate his type of parapsychology, altered, of course, with respect to the issue of demonic infestation.

Quevedo can be an extremely polemical writer, and as a debunker his rhetoric is somewhat akin to that of the American skeptical group, the Committee for the Scientific Investigation of Claims of the Paranormal. However, there is an interesting difference: in the U.S. atheistic skeptics debunk parapsychology, whereas in Brazil Jesuit parapsychologists debunk Spiritism and Umbanda, a "cultural shift" that corresponds to Latin Americans' higher level of belief in things spiritual. An example of Quevedo's debunking is his book *Curandeirismo: An Evil or a Good?* (1978), in which he argues that a group of medical doctors to whom Spiritists turned for endorsements of their beliefs in spirit surgery were already biased in favor of Spiritism. In general, Quevedo and the Jesuit parapsychologists view Spiritist and Umbandist healing mediums as *curandeiros*, which in Brazil is prohibited by law and subject to a fine and jail sentence.

Like Quevedo, Friderichs is more interested in the this-worldly telergic theory than the otherworldly demonic theory of ghosts, haunted houses, and poltergeists. "There are no haunted houses," he told me, "only haunted people." Basing his therapy on Quevedo's telergic theory, Friderichs focuses on helping the afflicted person to be more relaxed and therefore to stop emitting the energy that he bellieves causes poltergeist attacks. In general, he provides his clients with one or more half-hour sessions of guided relaxation. When he judges that his clients have achieved a suitable level of relaxation and hypnotic susceptibility, he suggests that they feel relaxed and happy, and, in the case of infestations, that they no longer produce the phenomena.

Friderichs' book on the topic *Haunted Houses* (1980) is written for a lay reader, and in it he surveys over fifty cases of haunted houses, some of which he was personally involved as a healer. The case histories often begin with the interpretations of the press or the afflicted—a demon, an evil spirit, or a spell—and end with his own interpretation, in the process marking a discursive shift from the popular to the "scientific," the traditional to the modern. Friderichs is highly critical of these other interpretations and their associated therapies, as one can see in the following case history, titled "Demons in Ipiranga":

> As I have already explained in other articles, the devil is not the cause of these alarming events [the Pentecostalist and popular Catholic explanations], nor is an *exú* [an Umbandist explanation] or the spirit of a dead person [the Spiritist explanation], but instead it is one or more of the residents of the house where these phenomena occurred. . . .
>
> People involved in such cases should not turn to Spiritism; that would be the worst of solutions. Nor should they turn to Umbanda or sorcerers. The exorcisms and blessings of the Protestant or Catholic church also will not resolve anything. Only a well-oriented parapsychology should intervene, because this is the speciality which studies and cures such pathologies. (Friderichs 1980: 52).

Friderichs supports these assertions with claims of efficacy. For example, in one case of a haunted house, the family had already called in Spiritists and Umbandists seven or eight times, who "applied their magical rites, without doing anything" (72). Only when Friderichs applied his therapy of relaxation did the spirit attack recede.

In short, Friderich's approach is to dismiss the etiologies of other religious healing systems as "popular" and "unscientific." He also warns that the alternative religious healing systems can heighten the suggestibility of the family and even exacerbate the telergic outbreak. Thus, alternative healing systems are rejected not only as inefficacious but also as potentially counterproductive. Nevertheless, perhaps in deference to the church hierarchy, Friderichs does present a few cases in which exorcism by a priest was successful. Furthermore, he does combine relaxation therapy with the Lord's Prayer, Ave Maria, Gloria, and sometimes his blessing. Although he by no means denies the importance of divine intervention and help, he also believes prayers and his priest's blessing as sanctioned by the Catholic church can be useful for their power of suggestion over people who generally believe in spirits, sorcery, and demons. Friderichs' parapsychological therapy therefore leaves room for conventional religious healing as understood by the Catholic church, but he also suggests that at least in some cases it can be translated into a psychological idiom and understood as efficacious due to the power of suggestion.

Jesuit parapsychology therefore inscribes in several ways its position as the discourse of an intellectual elite within a dominant religious institution. Despite the fact that parapsychology is considered a heterodox science, Jesuit parapsychology aligns itself with official science and modern psychotherapy against other religious healing systems, which are rejected as unscientific, popular, and at times even illegal and dangerous. Jesuit parapsychology also rejects the claims of efficacy of other religious healing systems and urges the afflicted not to have recourse to multiple healers. In turn, the elements of alternative religious healing systems—such as exorcism and prayer—are only accepted to the extent that they are encompassed within the framework of the parapsychological cure.

A Spiritist

Like Jesuit parapsychologists, Spiritists also believe that their religious healing system has a scientific basis, and no Spiritist in Brazil has been more important in describing and defending the scientific nature of Spiritism than Hernani Guimarães Andrade. A retired engineer and a native of Minas Gerais, the interior state known for its clever political leaders and conservative Catholic traditions, Andrade has lived since the 1920s in the state of São Paulo, where he has gained a reputation as a leading figure among Spiritist intellectuals. I got to know him during my previous fieldwork among the Spiritist movement in Brazil, and in 1988 I met with him again and spent an afternoon discussing several topics, including his theory of poltergeists.

As a "Spiritist" (or "Kardecist," as outsiders call them), Andrade is a student of Allan Kardec, a nineteenth-century French educator who developed a systematized doctrine on spirit mediumship and the spirit world. As Spiritists describe it, Kardec's doctrine is a philosophy rooted in scientific knowledge that has moral implications; hence, for Spiritists it is a synthesis of philosophical principles, scientific research, and religious morality. Spiritists tend to be whites from the middle class, but there is a tremendous variation in ethnic and class membership among Spiritist centers, and frequently some overlap with Umbanda. Like Umbandists, Spiritists believe in the existence of a spiritual body (called the "perispirit"), communication with the dead via spirit mediums, and spiritual progression and purification according to the law of karma, which governs reincarnation.

Andrade—or "Doctor Hernani," as he is known within the Spiritist movement—is dedicated more to the research and scientific side of Spiritism than to its numerous charitable activities, and his work has set a standard of empirical psychical research which few of his colleagues have emulated. Among his projects Andrade has completed a book of case histories of anomalous childhood memories of past lives which he believes are suggestive of reincarnation (1988b), and he has also completed two detailed case studies of poltergeists (1982, 1984), subsequently published as a book (1988a). Examination of the two case studies of poltergeists provides an example of how a Spiritist intellectual encompasses Jesuit, Pentecostalist, and Umbandist frameworks within that of Spiritism.

Beginning with the Jesuit/Spiritist relationship, like the Jesuits Andrade finds support for his ideas in North American and European parapsychology. Just as Jesuit parapsychologists such as Padre Edvino select and cite North American and European parapsychologists as authorities to legitimate their position that the poltergeist is only an expression of the psychic energy of the living, so Andrade has found a few North American and European parapsychologists who believe that poltergeists may, in some cases, be explained not by the psychic energy of the living but by the intervention of a spirit. Andrade therefore embraces parapsychology and defends a heterodox position within this already heterodox science: the "survival theory," a position that holds there is empirical evidence in favor of postmortem survival. As a result, Andrade's ideas are placed on an equal footing with those of the Jesuit parapsychologists. In other words, his spirit-intervention theory and the Jesuits' psychic (telergic) energy theory represent two alternative explanations within parapsychology which may now be considered as two theories that are in principle equal and that will stand or fall depending on who has the best evidence.

One way in which Andrade's viewpoint appears as more scientific than that of the Jesuits has to do with the format of his texts. Whereas Padre Edvino's work is written at a popular level for a layperson, Andrade's research adopts the detailed, erudite, case-history approach similar to that of some North American and European parapsychologists. Unlike the Jesuit texts, Andrade's case histories are written for other well-educated laypersons and other researchers, both within the Spiritist movement and outside it. By assuming an erudite implied reader, Andrade's texts contrast with most Catholic parapsychology texts as well as with those of Umbanda, both of which assume a popular reader. As a result, the Spiritist's discourse is in this sense more "scientific," even though his adoption of the survival hypothesis is considered less "scientific" by most parapsychologists.

In the Suzano case, Hernani describes how a Jesuit priest provided psychological counseling for a family afflicted by a poltergeist. Because I have already discussed the case in detail elsewhere (1991b), I will only summarize its relevant aspects here. In the Jesuit's account (Fitzpatrick 1983 [1970]: 21), the family came to the priest and asked him to bless the house. After he refused they sought the aid of Protestant pastors and "some of the local Spiritist leaders, including a famous *macumbeiro*" (22). (The latter is a derogatory term that Spiritists sometimes use for an Umbandist medium, just as Catholics sometimes use the term "Spiritist" to refer to both Spiritists and Umbandists.) Later, the family approached the Jesuit again, and he persuaded them that a more appropriate action was a psychotherapeutic session between him and the family's oldest daughter, who was the focus of the ghostly attack. During a session of counseling, the Jesuit discovered that the girl harbored profound resentment toward her father, and in the book about the case he claims that he convinced her to adopt a more accepting attitude toward her father.

Fitzpatrick argues that his session of psychotherapeutic counseling ended the poltergeist attack, but Andrade claims that there is a discrepancy in the Jesuit's chronology. According to Andrade's interviews with the family, the therapy session probably occurred after the poltergeist had already ended, and it therefore could not have been responsible for ending the spiritic invasion. He claims that the extinction of the poltergeist instead corresponded to a Spiritist "*desobsessão*" (exorcism) ritual, the effectiveness of which confirms the Spiritist interpretation. In disobsession sessions mediums receive earthbound spirits that plague humans, and they convince these spirits to accept the help of "spirits of light," who then take the earthbound spirits onto higher planes.

Andrade therefore concludes that the interpretation of the Jesuits and most North American and European parapsychologists fits the facts of the case less convincingly than his own, spirit-intervention interpretation. He places the Spiritist and Jesuit interpretations on equal ground as two opposing theories, one of which matches the empirical evidence better. In this sense, the Spiritist interpretation ends up encompassing the Jesuit explanatory system and therapy.

A more complicated example of encompassment is Andrade's treatment of the family's interpretation, which provides an encounter between the Spiritist framework and that of Umbanda. Although the family was Catholic, they believed that the spirit attack was probably caused by black magic performed by the father's ex-lover, who was also an Umbanda medium. According to the Spiritist mediums whose disobsession treatment was, in Andrade's view, the probable reason for the end of the spirit attack, the spirits involved were indeed "elementals," that is, "virgin entities, entities that were never incorporated in a human body" (1982: 77). Andrade's interpretation therefore appears to agree with the Umbandist interpretation to the extent that both perspectives recognize that evil spirits might have been sent to perturb the house. However, his interpretation also encompasses that of Umbanda by showing how the attack was resolved via a Spiritist ritual and not an Umbandist one.

The second case that Andrade discusses involves a comparison between Spiritism and Pentecostalism. In the Guarulhos case the Pentecostalist family believed that the devil had infested their house. Given their beliefs, the family only used prayer sessions and other techniques of remediation consistent with their religion. However, unlike the Suzano case, where the disobsession was successful, the Guarulhos case dragged on for years and did not have a clear resolution. At times, members of the family saw apparitions of the evil spirits which attacked them, but to the family the apparitions represented manifestations of the demon. Andrade argues that these spirits were more likely "the metamorphosis of very backwards spirits, such as `umuluns' or `exús,' " both spirits recognized by Umbanda (Andrade 1984: 65).[6]

Unlike the Jesuit, who openly rejects other explanatory systems and therapies, Andrade is more suggestive and tentative. For example, he rarely dismisses Pentecostalist, Umbanda, or folk Catholic exorcism rituals as lacking in efficacy; instead, he notes how they may provide some relief to the victimized families. Although Andrade defends a Spiritist version of parapsychology in his published writings, in personal correspondence he has noted to me that Spiritist therapies do not always work, and in some cases the remediation techniques of other religions do work. For example, he has told me that in other cases he believes Umbanda or Candomblé rituals may have successfully extinguished the poltergeist, although not necessarily for the reasons given by the practitioners. Still, he believes that poltergeists generally involve a spirit of some sort. For example, in the Guarulhos case he translates the Pentecostalists' demon into a kind of spirit that is recognized in the Umbanda pantheon, although he does this in a way that transforms the Umbandists' *exú* from a playful trickster into something more nefarious. He even recognizes the important effects that the psychic energy of the living has on poltergeists. Thus, he recognizes the role of a force akin to the Jesuits' telergy, which he believes the invading spirits draw on in order to have enough energy to accomplish their poltergeist antics. In short, opposing viewpoints are incorporated into his own framework as pieces of the puzzle rather than as unscientific superstitions.

Although Andrade's interpretations situate Spiritism as the discourse of encompassment, he avoids rash claims about the lack of efficacy or potential danger of other systems. He does not pretend to have any answers; he believes that different healing strategies work in different contexts, depending in part on the family's belief system. In his book Andrade lets readers draw their own conclusions on the question of whether the spirit-intervention or psychokinetic theory (roughly equivalent to the Jesuits' telergic theory)—or some combination—is the correct one (1988a: 225–-227). Likewise, in a letter to me written in May 1989, Andrade even stated that he thinks many poltergeists "extinguish themselves" of their own accord, with or without intervention. Nevertheless, his own viewpoint is clear: spirit infestation is due to spirits. Although to Andrade the Spiritist theory and healing strategy is just one approach among many, it is also first among the alternatives: "hegemonic" in the conventional sense of the term.

A Pentecostalist

Reverend Nasser Bandeira is a minister in the Four-Square Evangelical Church (Igreja Evangélica Quadrangular), a Pentecostalist denomination which originated in the United States. In addition to his work as a minister in Porto Alegre, Bandeira works for a radio station and is actively involved in local party politics. He is well-known as a preacher and exorcist both in his native state of Rio Grande do Sul and throughout southern Brazil, as his scrapbook of newspaper clippings attests. He travels throughout southern

Brazil giving sermons and exorcizing demons, and his services have at times been so large that they have been held in a soccer stadium.

When he asked me how I had heard of him, I showed him a clipping from the Rio newspaper *Jornal do Brasil* (May 5, 1988). He explained how that case, as for many others, was an example of "sensationalism." In other words, people were faking poltergeist or demonic attacks for purposes of financial gain. However, he also believed that "negative forces" were involved even in cases of sensationalism. By "negative forces" he did not mean evil spirits; he believed only in manifestations of the devil. His source of authority was the scripture, and he described to me the story of the fallen angel who became the devil, which he referred to as "the Spirit." He went on to say how the devil frequently preys on nonpracticing Catholics, who are legion in Brazil and frequently seek out Bandeira's services for exorcism rituals.

Bandeira explained his method of exorcism in a typical case. He generally likes to have two assistants anoint the house with oil, and frequently they put oil over the whole house, including the windows. He then tells the Spirit to leave "in the name of Jesus Christ." Nothing else is needed, he explained, just the word of the Lord. "If it is the Spirit," he said, "then it works. If it doesn't, then there's some other cause."

Although for him the only justification for this healing system is belief in the good book itself and faith in Jesus, Bandeira is quite conscious of opposing perspectives. In the stories that he told me about his experiences as an exorcist, the Pentecostalist minister proved not only to be a master story-teller (obviously one reason why he was able to build and maintain such a large following) but also the adept constructor of narratives in which the Pentecostalist framework encompasses the other religious healing systems.

Clearly, Bandeira is capable of recognizing alternative, secular approaches to spirit possession and infestation. Although sometimes his naturalistic explanations fall under the category of "sensationalism," sometimes when his exorcism does not work he explores more psychological interpretations. In general, he is well aware of the ways in which the idiom of demonic infestation can serve as a way to express some of the social problems that currently plague Brazil, such as child abuse or poverty. By recognizing that in some cases his clients may express psychological or social problems in the spirit idiom, he carves out a place for a secular, psychosocial discourse within his own framework. A secular, psychotherapeutic or sociological perspective therefore is seen not as an opposing, alternative framework, but as a useful interpretive strategy on which he sometimes draws. It therefore has an important place within his own framework.

In other anecdotes, Bandeira recognized yet another perspective on spirit possession, that of the Jesuits. He told me how he had been planning to go to a town in the interior of the state of Rio Grande do Sul where there was a case of spirit infestation, but he decided not to go after a Padre Edvino Friderichs had gone there and apparently had healed the girl. Despite the Jesuit's success, Bandeira still believed that the cause of the infestation was the demon, not the paranormal forces of the girl. He knew about the Jesuit theories, but he did not accept them. The pastor explained that while he believed in "mind over matter," he did not think it could be a very significant force. He had once seen a film of a famous Russian psychic who exerted a tremendous effort just to make a ping-pong ball move around on a table top. Referring to the girl whom the Jesuit priest had successfully treated, he asked me, "If it took so much effort for a mind of a gifted psychic to move a ping-pong ball around on a table top, how could you expect the mind of a little girl to make her mattress fly up and to toss pots and pans around?"

While he rejected the opposing theory of the Jesuits, he still recognized that the Jesuit's treatment had been—from all accounts—successful. He explained Friderich's success as follows: the Jesuit's treatment worked not because his relaxation therapy had calmed the telergic energies of the girl's body, but because he had also appealed to God for help, and his prayers were answered. Likewise, he acknowledged that even the Spiritists, who also use prayer in their disobsession sessions, had helped a little in this case. Thus, just as Friderichs believes that other healers may be unwittingly successful due to the psychological power of suggestion, so Bandeira believes that other healers may be successful to the extent that they appeal to God for help and their prayers are answered.

Regarding the question of spirits as an explanatory system, however, Bandeira said that the only spirits he believed in were liquid ones, that is, alcohol-induced. However, he admitted that in other cases the devil might cause phenomena that people misinterpret as spirits. For example, a woman claimed to be able to communicate with the spirit of Getúlio Vargas, the famous dictator of Brazil during the World War II years and also a native of the state of Rio Grande do Sul, and her family called on Bandeira to help. According to the woman's mother, she had actually met Getúlio when, as a child, she had worked on his ranch for a few weeks. This fact made the Spiritist interpretation, that she was indeed communicating with the spirit of the famous dictator, all the more plausible to the family. However, Bandeira did not accept the Spiritist interpretation; instead, he told the woman that she saw only the devil in the form of Getúlio. They argued for a while about whether or not the spirit was really Getúlio, and then Bandeira commanded the Spirit to leave, and it left.

Thus, Bandeira encompasses opposing perspectives either by translating them as true demonic possession or as the result of some kind of naturalistic cause which in turn may also be the effect of indirect demonic influence. Like the Spiritist Doctor Hernani, Reverend Nasser accommodates other explanatory systems as elements in his own framework. For Bandeira, spirits are translated as one manifestation of the devil or as indications of social problems, and telergy or psychokinesis is accepted as a possibility but one not very relevant to cases of poltergeists, possession, and other forms of demonic attack. Also like the Spiritist, Bandeira acknowledges the potential efficacy of other religious healing techniques, as one saw in the case of the girl from the interior of the state of Rio Grande do Sul.

However, Bandeira also reserves a category of cases that are phenomenologically the most impressive and in which the devil also openly represents himself. This category of genuine, direct, undisguised demonic possession is at the heart of his framework; without these cases, his reinterpretations of the other cases would be much less convincing. Bandeira gave me two examples of his most impressive cases, the first of which he said was the most impressive of his career. It occurred when he was very young and was just at the beginning of his ministry. He had heard of the woman possessed by a thousand demons, but he had not volunteered his services, perhaps because he was somewhat afraid. Nevertheless, when he was called, he went. The woman's face was completely changed, and at one point the devil left her and entered her dog. After a long and strenuous battle that was nearly as dramatic as the movie *The Exorcist*, he eventually succeeded in exorcizing the woman (see Hess 1994 for more details).

Thus, some cases represent genuine, direct, and undisguised demonic possession. Presence of the demon is recognized by the signs of abnormality and even, to him, paranormality—the woman's changed physiognomy— whereas those signs are missing in the cases of ersatz infestation or possession. The signs add to Bandeira's framework an empirical basis that is similar to the empirical grounding which the Jesuit parapsychologist and Spiritist intellectual also give to their theories. When the signs of paranormality are present, the only healing technique that will work is faith in the Bible and an appeal to Jesus Christ. To the extent that other religious healers may experience success with their techniques, it is because they, too, call on Jesus or God to help them. Thus, other systems may be successful, but only because they unwittingly incorporate the Pentecostalist approach. By explaining how its own discourse is unwittingly incorporated in the other, the Pentecostalist perspective encompasses the other frameworks of religious healing.

An Umbandist

Umbanda emerged in the early to mid-twentieth century in Rio de Janeiro, São Paulo, and a few other cities, principally in southern Brazil (Brown 1986). Unlike Catholicism, Spiritism, and Pentecostalism—all of which originated in Europe or North America—Umbanda is an indigenous Brazilian religion. It is sometimes characterized as a Spiritist/Afro-Brazilian syncretism, but it also borrows from Amerindian, Catholic, and occultist doctrines and practices, and the exact mixture of religious traditions is a subject of both geographical variation and ideological controversy. Umbandists recognize the Yoruba *orixá* divinities, the Catholic saints, and the Spiritist spirit guides, but the mediums of a typical Umbanda temple will receive the spirits of *caboclos* (Amerindians), *pretos velhos* (old black slaves), *exús* (Yoruba trickster spirits sometimes syncretized with the devil), and *pomba giras* (female counterparts of the *exús*).

Umbanda is sometimes contrasted with Quimbanda, or black magic. This opposition is a slippery one because Umbandist mediums may practice "Quimbanda" magic to undo other Quimbanda spells (therefore, they consider their work to be "on the side of good"). Likewise, the term "session of Quimbanda" may be used to refer to ordinary Umbanda sessions where the mediums receive *exú* spirits and give consultations to their clients. Antônio Alves Teixeira is one example of an Umbandist who does not view Quimbanda negatively, although he uses a pseudonym (Antônio de Alva) for his books on Quimbanda. He was also a prolific author whose writings on Umbanda and Quimbanda could be found in bookstores throughout Rio and São Paulo, and whose text *Impressive Cases of Black Magic* will serve as the principle source of evidence for this section of the essay.

Teixeira was born in 1914 in what was then the frontier state of Mato Grosso. When he was twelve, he moved with his family to the state of Rio de Janeiro, where he studied in the military school in Rio, became a teacher, and later founded and directed a high school in the Rio area. In 1953, he worked in the Travelers of Truth Spiritist Center, where he founded and directed "the Xangô Phalanx, as well as experimental and transcendental study sessions" (8). Xangô is the Yoruba *orixá* of thunder, associated in Brazil with justice, and the term "phalanx" (*falange*) refers to a group or "line" of spirits organized in a hierarchy under one guiding spirit or *orixá*. At this time, Teixeira began to publish, and by the early seventies he was sometimes appearing on the radio, where he had a program on palmistry.

Like many Umbanda mediums, Teixeira is a kind of walking syncretism, and his self-description is a good example of the ecumenism of Umbanda, which is how I would also describe its style of encompassment. In a chapter on his personality, Teixeira writes the following:

> Being, as I am, born under the sign of Capricorn, I have as the spiritual leader (*chefe*) of my head, Oxalá, who, as is known, is assimilated with Our Lord Jesus Christ.
>
> Beyond Oxalá, I also have Xangô, Oxum, Iansã, Abaluaê, Caboclo Guaicuru (de Oxóssi), "Sir" Lucifer, and Old Black João Quizumba.
>
> In Kardecism [Spiritism], at the table, I have Dr. Carlos Chagas. (15)

Teixeira then describes how each of the entities is related to his personality. As a son of Oxalá, he is "in general, a creature of peace, although I have, to tell the truth, a very violent nature that, however, only comes out when, in fact, there is a good cause or reason" (16). Following Xangô he attempts to do justice; like Oxum he is very emotional and sensitive; like Iansã he is vain; from Abaluaê he derives his humility and resignation; and like "Exú, Lucifer, I am sometimes argumentative and stormy; however, I don't harbor anger or rancor against anything or anyone" (16).

From this self-description, one gets a sense of Teixeira's ecumenical outlook, which is typical of Umbanda mediums whom I have met. The same outlook is also expressed in his book *Impressive Cases of Black Magic*, an autobiographical account of his experiences of helping victims of sorcery which he describes in a short, case history format. Because of the similarity of this narrative format to the cases discussed by Friderichs, Andrade, and Bandeira, the text is a particularly appropriate one for purposes of comparison.

Teixeira's discourse differs from the other three figures in that he directs no explicit comments against the opposing religious healing systems; instead, he focuses on how he solved the problems of the people who came to him for help. Furthermore, unlike the other religiotherapeutic practices, his treats much more the syndromes of this world—lover's quarrels, impotent husbands, long strings of financial setbacks, and disease—in short, bad luck. His diagnosis is always the same—sorcery—and his rituals of countersorcery—at least the ones he chose to write about—are highly successful.

In one case history, "A Strange Case of Madness," some of the diacritics of the broader arena of conflicting and competing positions come out. A woman named Dona Elza came to Teixeira to seek help for her son, who had been placed in a mental hospital where, "despite everything that the attending doctors had tried, he had not gotten any better, and several days had already gone by" (37). Teixeira diagnosed the problem: "There was a disagreement between [Dona Elza] and a certain woman and, as vengeance, this woman had done some black magic [*trabalhado*] so that [Dona Elza's] son would go crazy" (37). Teixeira then took Dona Elza and her husband to a medium who "incorporated" (that is, let her body be taken over by) the evil spirit which in turn confessed to everything it had done. They were able to take the boy home from the hospital that same day.

This case history shows first the limitations of official medical discourse and the effectiveness of spiritual healing. One might argue that it also appears to legitimate Spiritism rather than Umbanda, because the healing ritual is closer to a typical Spiritist disobsession session than an Umbandist countersorcery ritual. However, Teixeira goes on to say that the mediumistic session was not enough to protect the boy; the family also had to return to their farm, where they followed the medium's instructions: "On arriving, they went to the entry gate of the farm and, truthfully, from there they removed (buried in the dirt, near the entry gate) the 'material' that had been put there, which is to say a cross and a doll with its legs cut off" (40).

Teixeira's case history therefore moves from the discourse and treatment of orthodox medicine to a version of Spiritist disobsession to the deepest level: sorcery and the countersorcery ritual of digging up the planted objects. The last level represents the system of etiology and practice that distinguishes Umbanda/Quimbanda from the other religious healing systems considered. Although Umbandists accept the spirit obsession theory of the Spiritists, they are distinguished by their discourse of sorcery and antisorcery rituals. The nature of the antisorcery ritual varies widely. In this case, it involved digging up the planted materials and destroying them. In another case that I investigated, an Umbanda medium received an *exú* spirit, who explained that a neighbor had performed a work of black magic against the family. The *exú* agreed to leave in exchange for some *cachaça* (Brazilian rum), cigars, and seven white candles. The *exú* also demanded a black chicken, and he then killed the chicken with its teeth and drank its blood.[7]

Although Umbandists accept a wide variety of natural and supernatural explanations and healing systems, they do tend to privilege sorcery and anti-sorcery, especially in cases of apparent spirit infestation or possession. Teixeira, for example, implicitly gives the sorcery explanation primacy by placing it last in his narrative of the case. Still, he refrains from making bold negative statements about the other systems of healing, statements of the type made by Edvino Friderichs or Nasser Bandeira. In general, Umbanda mediums whom I have met have tended to be much more accepting of other religious healing systems than the others are of Umbanda. As religious healers of lower status than Spiritists, Jesuits, or Pentecostalists, Umbandists are more aware of the oppressive arm of the state. They know that it is probably to their advantage not to incite other healers to criticize them, and their ecumenical position is therefore in part a plea for tolerance of their own practices.

One might therefore argue that the only way in which Umbanda encompasses the other healing systems is through a rhetoric of tolerance and ecumenism. On this point, it is relevant to note that some Umbandists claim that the term "Umbanda" means "all of us," and it is sometimes represented as a uniquely Brazilian religion that brings together and mediates the European, African, and Amerindian cultural traditions in a complex harmony that represents an ideal of contemporary Brazilian society.

However, there is another way in which Umbanda encompasses other religious healing traditions. This way does not involve explicit written or spoken discourse; instead, it occurs through the implicit symbolism of the rituals which Teixeira, like other Umbandists, sometimes employs to "undo" (*desmanchar*) black magic. These rituals are extremely complicated (see Hess 1992c), and this essay will therefore be restricted to a few comments on a part of a series of rituals which he performed to help a woman with marital problems. In a part of the ritual dedicated to the *orixá* Abaluaê, Teixeira began by going to a cemetery, where he arranged an offering of nine white dahlias in the form of a cross at the foot of a cross; a brand new, white, smooth cup of mineral water; and a cross of nine white candles.

Then, in a low voice, he chanted (three times) the following song: "He runs crazy, crazy without end; he runs crazy, for his children to help!" He described his subsequent action as follows: "I put a small piece of paper on which I had written, in the form of a cross, the names of Dona Cecília and her husband, by the seventh gravestone to the left and toward the back side of the cemetery . . . burying it in the earth that surrounded it" (35). Finally, Dona Cecília made her request to Sir Abaluaê, namely "that her husband became the man she dreamed of," etc. The ritual was so effective that some time later Dona Cecília came to Teixeira to ask him "to make her husband a little more distant, so much had he changed, so much had he turned into what she wanted, in truth" (36).

The strong claim of efficacy helps legitimate the Umbanda ritual and reveals its strength in comparison to other systems, but this Umbanda ritual also encompasses alternative religious healing systems through its ritual symbolism. In other words, like the Umbandists' ecumenical discourse, the ritual itself is ecumenical. It borrows the cross from orthodox Christianity (including both Protestantism and Catholicism), the candles and the request from the votive offerings of popular Catholicism, the white cup of mineral water from Spiritism, and the sung *ponto* and the *orixá* of dedication from the African religions. The other positions appear as pieces of a whole which only Umbanda brings together.

In addition to encompassment through ritual symbolism, there is a suggestion of a second kind of encompassment: Umbanda brings the elements of other religious and healing traditions together by translating an explicit, written or verbal language into a language of bodily ritual action. Spiritist disobsession, Jesuit relaxation treatment and counseling, and Pentecostalist exorcism and prayer are all techniques that emphasize speech and even dialogue, just as the three religions are anchored in a written doctrine (Kardec's writings, Catholic church doctrine, and the Bible). They are, in a sense, religions of the book and the tongue(s), just as their intervention strategies render the bodily actions of ritual supplementary to the act of speaking.

In contrast, while there is a undoubtedly a role for speech in the antisorcery rituals of Umbanda, those rituals place a relatively greater emphasis on bodily action: sacrificing an animal, uncovering a buried work of black magic, or placing objects in the proper location for an offering to one of the *orixás* or spirit guides. Even where speaking occurs in these antisorcery rituals, it tends to occur less in the form of dialogue, and more in the form of a formulaic language, as in Teixeira's sung chant and Dona Cecília's magical use of writing.[8] Thus, the Umbanda antisorcery rituals, at least the ones discussed here, suggest an inversion of the hierarchy of the other three religions through the encompassment of the act of speaking and writing by another language: the language of ritual action.

An Anthropologist (Concluding Comments)

To summarize my argument, the Jesuit's pattern of encompassment of the other groups is the most exclusionary: Friderichs warns the Brazilian people about the harmful possibilities of using the intervention techniques of their religious rivals, and Quevedo actively debunks Spiritism and Umbanda.[9] At the opposite extreme, the Umbandist's rhetoric is much more ecumenical: Teixeira is much too much the "cordial man" to engage in the blunt rhetoric that one finds in Friderichs and Quevedo. If one is to find encompassment in Teixeira's rhetoric, it is in the more implicit, "silent" forms of the rhetoric of ritual arrangements and the relationship between the bodily action of Umbanda ritual and the speech of talking therapies. Finally, the Pentecostalist and Spiritist are somewhere in between: Bandeira and Andrade see the other perspectives almost as alternative theories that they may accept as partial explanations or reject as erroneous patterns of reasoning rather than useless superstitions.

Thus, each of the four positions constructs a framework that encompasses the other three positions, but the structures and strategies of encompassment vary from one position to the next. Is this variety in the strategies and rhetoric of encompassment simply a random outcome of individual thinkers? I would argue instead that it is rooted in their positions in the social structure, and here is where I return to the general questions of hierarchy, hegemony, and heterodoxy. Friderichs, for example, is not merely a Jesuit intellectual, but a Jesuit intellectual in Brazil, the largest Catholic country in the world, where in the 1980s 80 to 90 percent of the population was at least nominally Catholic. Although lay support is soft—as the well-known expression "Catholic by day, *espírita* [Umbandist, Kardecist, etc.] by night" indicates—the Catholic church is still the hegemonic religion in Brazilian society. Catholicism was the official religion until the end of the nineteenth century, and its hegemony in the religious arena has continued into this century.

For example, in the 1930s under the dictatorship of Getúlio Vargas, the Catholic church joined with the state and medical profession to close Spiritist and Umbanda centers (see Hess 1987a). Subsequently, the Jesuits have attacked the spirit mediumship religions less through the state, which now enshrines freedom of religion, than through science (their parapsychology courses and texts), which can still be used to show that their competitors are engaging in silly superstitions even if those practices are no longer illegal.

Still, both through the strategy of state suppression and the more recent strategy of scientific debunking, the actions of the Jesuit debunkers continue the coalition between parts of the Catholic church and other leading groups in society: the medical profession, science, and the state apparatus, in turn controlled, for most of the 1960s through 1980s, by the alliance of the military and capitalist class. In other words, as the Jesuits go about constructing spirit infestations and techniques for intervention, they are also reproducing the general hierarchies and hegemonies of Brazilian society.

The other religions are positioned at various levels of heterodoxy with respect to the Catholic church. Although today there is greater tolerance for spirit mediumship religions, old timers whom I met still remember the Vargas years as well as numerous cases of prosecution for illegal practice of medicine, and the more pessimistic see the return to "democracy" in the 1980s and 1990s as just another phase in the cycle of oscillating periods of repression and tolerance. Because Spiritism is a predominantly white, working- to middle-class movement with its own highly educated and well-placed intellectual elite, Spiritists have been better able than Umbandists to defend themselves against state repression and to reply to Jesuit criticism. In fact, their scientific discourse plays a key role in positioning themselves above Umbanda and the Afro-Brazilian religions.

Pentecostalists also position themselves above Umbanda and the Afro-Brazilian religions, but through their status as a Christian religion. Although Pentecostalism has a large following among the lower classes, that religion does not openly violate as many of the central dogmas of the Catholic church as do Spiritism and Umbanda, and as a result the relations between Pentecostalism and the Catholic church and state have been somewhat more harmonious. In recent years the Catholic church has even adapted to changing times by letting a Catholic Pentecostalist movement develop within the church. Pentecostalism is, furthermore, a type of Protestantism, which is the religion of the English, Americans, German descendants, and other more or less privileged ethnic groups.

Although, as Brown (1986) has shown, middle-class participation is significant in Umbanda, the religion has a greater following among the working class and people of color, and it is often thought of as a poor people's Spiritism. Umbandists also suffered disproportionately more than Spiritists during the period of police repression. Furthermore, Umbanda lacks the large number of intellectuals that characterizes Spiritism, and the religion does not have an elaborate doctrine. Instead, Umbanda has often been described as a pragmatic religion, almost to the extent of being more magic than religion. People go to Umbanda centers for consultations with the spirit guides or for sorcery/antisorcery rituals, not to study written doctrine.

Umbanda's orientation toward action has sometimes been explained as an empty market niche that has wide appeal in the lower classes with their higher magical beliefs. However, given the nonhegemonic position of Umbanda in the religious system, it makes sense also to explore the way in which Umbanda discourse reflects its position as a "muted group." Women and underrepresented ethnic groups have sometimes been described as "muted groups" because they are often forced to speak the language of the dominant groups or else to fall silent (Ardner 1975; cf. Gal 1991). In this sense, Umbandists speak of Christian humility and Spiritist principles because those are the languages of the higher status groups. However, by focusing on action—ritual practices of sorcery and countersorcery—Umbandists also encompass the other religions by showing that what people say is less important than who they are or what they do. In this way, the muted quality of their religion as a nonbook religion is transformed from a negative to a positive attribute.

The various strategies of encompassment of all four groups make sense when one considers that the religious actors are not playing on a level field. If one is a Catholic intellectual, an exclusionary strategy can help preserve an increasingly fragile position of hegemony, much as do the exclusionary pronouncements of the American Medical Association in the United States against alternative cancer treatments. Likewise, if one is an Umbandist (for whom police persecution is still a living memory among old timers), ecumenism and eclecticism may be seen as strategies for winning the tolerance of other groups. In between, Spiritists and Pentecostalists operate in a more modern and pluralistic world in which they are less heterodox than Umbanda and the African religions, so their rhetoric corresponds to a more sectlike view of the religious arena—more like a North American-style religious marketplace—in which the other groups are relatively equal in a competitive field.

From this perspective, the Jesuit and Umbandist have something in common with each other in contrast to the Spiritist and Pentecostalist. The former live in a world of traditional Brazilian hierarchy and personalism. The Jesuit provides an interpretation that urges exclusion and hierarchy: do not try the other techniques of intervention because they will harm you. In a parallel but inverted way, the Umbandist urges inclusion and personalism: he is a walking syncretism who creates linkages among all groups through his stories and practices that suggest religious ecumenism or eclecticism. By urging ecumenism, the Umbandist mediates his position at the bottom of the hierarchy.

In contrast, the Spiritist and Pentecostalist have a much more empirical approach. They observe other practices and admit that they may work in some cases. They tell stories that show how other groups may achieve some success, but their stories incorporate the other theories and practices into their own, broader framework and sometimes claim that the other groups' techniques work for reasons that their practitioners do not understand. The Spiritist and Pentecostalist constructions of religious techniques neither reject nor embrace the other groups, but instead carefully sort out what they find acceptable and what they find unacceptable. In short, their logic is rooted in a more pluralistic and egalitarian rather than hierarchical vision of the religious arena. That makes some sense when one considers the historical roots of Spiritism and Pentecostalism as offshoots of the Protestant Reformation and the world of religious sects that it created.

The differing strategies of encompassment discussed here provide a way of elaborating the problem which DaMatta (1982, 1991) has made central to his anthropology of Brazilian society: the clash between the modern and traditional, individual and person, equality and hierarchy. From this perspective, I am inclined to see the Jesuit and Umbandist vision as traditional, and the Spiritist and Pentecostalist as modern. Yet, as DaMatta also emphasizes, this clash occurs on "many levels." To analyze the clash in any other way means falling into a very rigid sort of analysis that misses the complexities and contradictions of Brazilian culture. Thus, on another level it is possible to think of the Jesuit as the leading modernizing force in this religious dialogue. At least he is analyzing the cases in terms of secular psychology rooted in a concept of individual and interpersonal psychodynamics. In contrast, the other three intellectuals are all constructing the cases in terms of a hierarchical world of spirits that has long been recognized as a reproduction of the traditional social relations of patron-client ties.

Another, perhaps more complicated alternative is to see in Umbanda a democratizing and modernizing tendency because its mediums admit all spirits and magical practices as equals. Thus, on the one hand Umbanda reproduces a traditional world of hierarchy and personalism through its diagnoses of sorcery and countersorcery and its appeal to spirit guides as otherworldly patrons. On the other hand, Umbanda inscribes religious modernity through the pluralism of the types of spirit guides who are allowed in and the types of ritual actions that are acceptable. Many have recognized the democratic spirit of Umbanda in its recognition of African slave and Native Amerindian spirits, and in its openness to mediums regardless of class, gender, race, or sexual preference. Umbanda is, perhaps more than any other religion in Brazil, an equal opportunity employer, both for mediums and for spirits.

I would therefore hesitate to see any one religion as the modernizing force. Locating a democraticizing, modernizing tendency is a complicated business because it cannot easily be operationalized through concepts such as sectarian pluralism, appeals to science, ethnic/gender equality, or ecumenical spirit. What seems clear is that as the various religious intellectuals go about constructing their world, they end up reproducing the deep tension in Brazilian culture that all the essays in this book explore in different ways. In this ideological arena that involves the meeting and mingling of secular and sacred, scientific and magical, and Christian and non-Western religions, the clash between the modern and the traditional constantly shifts both within and among religious perspectives. By sorting out the complexities, social scientists can help locate sites of democratization that extend well beyond new constitutions, parties, and elections.

Acknowledgments

The summer 1988 field trip to Brazil was made possible by a Faculty Major Grant from Colgate University. I wish to thank Roberto DaMatta, Alan Harwood, and Jeffrey Jarrad for comments on an earlier version of this essay, and James A. Boon and David Holmberg, who introduced me to theories of religious complexity. The essay has circulated and been cited as "Religious Pluralism and the Rhetoric of Encompassment."

Endnotes

1. Antonio Gramsci's concept of hegemony has been defined and refined in several ways (see, for example, Bocock 1986; Elling 1981: 92; Frankenberg 1988; Gramsci 1980: 87–91). One common thread is that hegemony involves the problem of how coalitions or networks of ruling groups and classes rule, not merely by controlling the state, but also by exerting ideological influence through the various institutions and cultural domains, including religion, the press, voluntary associations, and what we would today call the culture industry.

2. My study of comparative mappings builds on an analysis presented by Carlos Rodrigues Brandão (1980) by showing how the different mappings reconstruct hierarchy and hegemony. Likewise, this essay builds on other, related

studies of Brazilian religion (for example, DaMatta 1982 and Greenfield 1987) on how Brazilian spirit mediumship religions articulate a hierarchical world view and social order, and my own discussions of how hierarchical and personalistic values often encompass those of individualism and equality in the thought of Spiritist intellectuals (1989, 1991b).

3. Although I have framed this discussion by referring to the question of "religious pluralism" (see also Hess 1992b), the case materials discussed here involve healing rituals that are sometimes conceptualized in a scientific idiom. Consequently my framework for interpreting religious pluralism may also contribute in a specific way to discussions of heterodoxy in science (e.g., Hess 1992a) and in medicine. Most previous discussions of medical pluralism focus on the relations between "modern" biomedicine and "traditional" or alternative medical systems (e.g., Leslie 1980; for Brazil, see Montero 1985). The framework developed here suggests one way in which studies of medical pluralism could include not only the relations between official and alternative medicine but also the relations among alternative healing systems. These relations may be relatively harmonious, as Baer argues in the case of the American frontier in the nineteenth-century, where "folk systems often liberally borrowed from one another and to some degree coalesced into a syncretic amalgam" (1989: 1104). However, in cases such as the arena of Brazilian religious therapies, class and status divisions may play themselves out as conflicts among the alternative healing systems. In this way I am extending discussions of medical hegemony from a focus on either internal divisions within professionalized medicine or between it and alternative medical systems.

4. A poltergeist, based on the German for "noisy ghost," is a kind of "haunted house" that is centered on one or more people and involves object movements, fires, water leakages, or other kinds of apparently anomalous physical disturbances. Sometimes poltergeists are distinguished from hauntings, which are place-centered, of longer duration, and with more visual and auditory effects rather than physical ones. I tend to refer to them both as "spirit infestation," in contrast to spirit possession, in which spirits or demons are believed to take control of someone's body.

5. Although the religious system is gendered at the level of sacerdotes—from the men-only Catholic priesthood to the women-only priestesses of the most traditional Candomblés—the four persons in this study are men. As I have discussed elsewhere (1994), even though women have a much greater role as mediums in Spiritism and Umbanda, the intellectuals and leading mediums tend to be men. Still, the rhetorical strategy of the male Umbanda medium discussed here seems to have some parallels with discursive strategies of women as a "muted group," a topic which will be discussed in more detail in the conclusion.

6. See Hess (1989, 1991b: ch. 5) for a more detailed discussion of the Guarulhos and Suzano the Guarulhos and Suzano cases.

7. I did not witness the ritual, which was described in a local newspaper report, but I did interview the family after it took place (again, more details are in Hess 1994), and I have seen animal sacrifice on other occasions. Nor is animal sacrifice the only form of countering sorcery. For example, when I talked to another Umbandist medium when he was incorporating an *exú* during a Quimbanda session, he told me that the best way to rid a house of haunting spirits was to spread a certain kind of herb around the house. The point, again, is not to determine whether a given strategy is in some way modal for Umbanda practice, but instead to show how the elements of the discourse contrast with those of the other three positions.

8. Again, Umbanda is so varied that it is important not to overgeneralize. As discussed above in the case regarding the boy in the mental hospital, one of the Umbandist healing strategies involved something like Spiritist disobsession, although that strategy had to be completed by finding the buried work of black magic. Certainly the more Spiritist-oriented side of Umbanda is likely to follow more the pattern of Spiritism and employ strategies akin to disobsession; however, Umbanda's difference from Spiritism and the other religions lies in its use of the antisorcery rituals, which is why I have focused on them here.

9. The title of this section reflexively flags my recognition that my interpretation of this arena of medical, religious, and scientific practices involves a fifth view, one which has in a sense already encompassed the other four views. By setting up the structure of this essay as a discussion of four of the major positions in the religious field in southeastern and southern Brazil, by attempting not to side with any one of the positions, and by showing how each position deconstructs the others as it constructs itself, my own anthropological discourse is implicitly caught up in the same structure as that of the religious discourses: the encompassment of other positions.

References

Andrade, Hernani Guimaraes
  1982 O *"Poltergeist" de Suzano*. São Paulo: Instituto Brasileiro de Pesquisas Psicobiofísicas.
  1984 O *Poltergeist de Guarulhos*. São Paulo: Instituto Brasileiro de Pesquisas Psicobiofísicas.
  1988a *Poltergeist. Algumas de suas Ocorrências no Brasil*. São Paulo: Pensamento.
  1988b *Reencarnação no Brasil: Oito Casos que Sugerem Renascimento*. São Paulo: Pensamento.
Ardner, Edward
  1975 "Belief and the Problem of Women," and "The Problem Revisited." In Shirley Arnder, ed. *Perceiving Women*. London: Dent.

Baer, Hans
1989 "The American Dominative Medical System as a Reflection of Social Relations in the Larger Society." *Social Science and Medicine* 28(11): 1103–1112.
Bocock, Robert
1986 *Hegemony*. London and New York: Tavistock.
Brandão, Carlos Rodrigues
1980 *Os Deuses do Povo*. São Paulo: Brasiliense.
Brown, Diana
1986 *Umbanda: Religion and Politics in an Urban Religious Movement*. Ann Arbor: University of Michigan Press.
DaMatta, Roberto
1982 "The Ethic of Umbanda and the Spirit of Messianism." In T. Bruneau and P. Faucher (eds.), *Authoritarian Capitalism: Brazil's Contemporary Economic and Political Development*. Boulder, Colo.: Westview.
1991 *Carnivals, Rogues, and Heroes*. Notre Dame, Ind.: University of Notre Dame Press.
Dumont, Louis
1980 [1966] "Postface: Toward a Theory of Hierarchy." In *Homo Hierarchicus*. Chicago: University of Chicago Press.
Elling, Ray
1981 "Political Economy, Cultural Hegemony, and Mixes of Traditional and Modern Medicine." *Social Science and Medicine* 15A: 89–100.
Fitzpatrick, John, S.J.
1983 *O Poder de Fé*. São Paulo: Pensamento. (Earlier edition. São Paulo: Milesi Editora, 1970.)
Frankenberg, Ronald
1988 "Gramsci, Culture, and Medical Anthropology: Kundry and Parsifal? or Rat's Tail to Sea Serpent." *Medical Anthropology Quarterly* 2(4): 324–337.
Friderichs, Edvino A., S.J.
1980 *Casas Mal-Assombradas. Fenômenos de Telergia*. São Paulo: Loyola.
Gal, Susan
1991 "Between Speech and Knowledge: the Problematics of Research on Language and Gender." In Micaela di Leonardo (ed.), *Gender at the Crossroads of Knowledge*. Berkeley and Los Angeles: University of California Press.
Gramsci, Antonio
1980 *The Modern Prince and Other Writings*. New York: International Publishers.
Greenfield, Sidney
1987 "The Return of Dr. Fritz: Spiritist Healing and Patronage Networks in Urban, Industrial Brazil." *Social Science and Medicine* 24(12): 1096–1108.
Hess, David J.
1987a "The Many Rooms of Spiritism in Brazil." *Luso-Brazilian Review* 24(2): 15–34.

1987b "Religion, Heterodox Science, and Brazilian Culture." *Social Studies of Science* 17: 465–477.

1989 "Psychical Research and Cultural Values: A Comparison of Two Theories of the Poltergeist." *Newsletter for the History and Sociology of Marginal Science* 1(2): 1–4.

1991a "Ghosts and Domestic Politics in Brazil: Some Parallels between Spirit Infestation and Spirit Possession." *Ethos* 18(4): 407-438.

1991b *Spirits and Scientists: Ideology, Spiritism, and Brazilian Culture.* University Park: Pennsylvania State University Press.

1992a "Disciplining Heterodoxy, Circumventing Discipline: Parapsychology, Anthropologically." In David Hess and Linda Layne (eds.), *Knowledge and Society.* Vol. 9, *The Anthropology of Science and Technology.* Greenwich, Conn.: JAI Press.

1992b "New Sciences, New Gods: Spiritism and Questions of Religious Pluralism in Latin America." *Occasional Papers of the Thomas J. Watson Institute for International Studies*, Conference on Competing Gods: Religious Pluralism in Latin America. Brown University.

1992c "Umbanda and Quimbanda Magic in Brazil: Rethinking Aspects of Bastide's Work." *Archives des Sciences Sociales des Religions.* 79: 139–153.

1994 *Samba in the Night: Spiritism in Brazil.* New York: Columbia University Press.

Leslie, Charles (ed.)
1980 "Special Issue: Medical Pluralism." *Social Science and Medicine* 14B: 191–289ff.

Montero, Paulo
1985 *Da Doença a Desordem. A Magia na Umbanda.* Rio de Janeiro: Edições Graal.

Quevedo, Oscar Gonzalez, S.J.
1974 *O Que é a Parapsicologia?* São Paulo: Loyola.
1978 *Curandeirismo: Um Mal ou Um Bem?* São Paulo: Loyola.

Teixeira (neto), Antônio Alves
ca. 1970 *Impressionantes Casos de Magia Negra.* Rio: Eco.

Chapter Nine

The Brazilianization of
Alcoholics Anonymous

⊠

Jeffrey Jarrad

Although in many ways Brazil is considered a modern nation that prides itself as having the eighth largest capitalist economy in the world, it is also a country in which the legacy of colonialism, latifundia agriculture, hierarchical social structures, and Mediterranean patron-client relationships remain powerful. Students and critics of Brazilian society often focus on how this struggle plays itself out in formal institutions, but this legacy is also reproduced in a myriad of ways in Brazil's informal institutions. The analysis of these relations is integral to the debate on the future of democracy in Brazil. Anthropology can contribute to this debate by developing a better understanding of how Brazil's informal institutions and day-to-day life work to reproduce a problematic social structure.

This essay focuses on one aspect of everyday life in Brazil: the voluntary organization known as Alcoholics Anonymous (AA). I analyze differences in the practice of AA in the United States and Brazil with particular reference to the central AA concept of "anonymity,"[1] which is employed at the personal level to safeguard the identities of individuals, and at the organizational level to maintain the survival of the group. Anonymity, as it evolved in AA in the United States, presupposes concepts of individual and community that become problematic when elaborated within the particularistic system of values that characterizes key aspects of Brazilian social interaction.

The central theme of this essay is that the core AA concept of "anonymity" is elaborated differently in Brazilian AA groups, despite overt references to the same literature, practices, and traditions as AA groups in the

United States. By contrasting one AA group in the United States with a group in Brazil, I will show how AA in Brazil has been transformed in ways that derived from its traditional hierarchical system of personalistic values.

Background: Alcoholics Anonymous in the United States and Brazil

AA is a voluntary association of alcoholics who help each other attain and maintain sobriety. The philosophy of AA reveals its deep roots in American culture (Kurtz 1979, Trice and Staudenmeier, Jr. 1989). Founded by two middle-class men, AA is grounded in the voluntary choices of individuals who desire to change their lives by freely associating with each other in an egalitarian, democratic setting. In addition to the social contract, it is rooted in Protestant beliefs about moral discipline and the personal relationship of the individual to God. Furthermore, the organization cloaks its members in anonymity in order to protect them from the stigmatizing outside world.[2]

The struggle by AA's American founders to find workable forms and practices that now constitute AA occurred in a specific historical context: post-Prohibition, middle-class, white America.[3] AA's democratic nature is widely admired but this aspect of AA emerged from the long debates on the ability of alcoholics to govern themselves, the successes and failures of past moralistic approaches of temperance societies, the founder's struggle with his own charisma and desire to lead in an organization based on anonymity, and the problems created and avoided by a loose structure of quasi-independent groups (Kurtz 1979, Maxwell 1950). This solution avoided the problems of earlier temperance groups and retained the essential values of consensus and grassroots control; someone who disagreed with the rest of a group could, and often did, form a new one.

Herb, an American businessman, brought AA to Brazil in 1948. He returned to the United States a few years later but left a small AA group composed of foreign businessmen. AA soon acquired Brazilian members but growth was very slow. Today, however, AA in Brazil reports thousands of groups.

The AA that was Brazilianized was therefore a representation in a Brazilian context of a moment in AA's historical development as it was interpreted by Herb. "Brazilianization" was, and is, also an historical process, an ongoing "conversation," to use Bellah's expression, in which different cultural strands enter in conflict, are selected and interpreted, but within a generally-recognized framework of what these strands are (Bellah et al. 1985). The goal of this paper is to examine the interpretation of certain elements of AA within this framework. The transfer of an apparently objective account of AA to a different location represents an appropriation of the written principles and acted practices as they were interpreted in a Brazilian context that includes a strong tradition of hierarchical and personalistic social relations.

My analysis is based on the comparison of an American and a Brazilian AA group on the dimensions of meeting structure and organization, the role of AA's written words, and the practice of a key AA institution, sponsorship. I also discuss the universe of AA groups from which these cases are taken to provide the appropriate context. Before proceeding to the comparative task of this essay, however, I first outline the origin of AA in the United States.

The Americanization of Alcoholics Anonymous

In 1935 two middle-class New Englanders—Bill W., a stockbroker on Wall Street, and Dr. Bob, a physician in Akron, Ohio—started a voluntary association of persons who shared a common desire: to stop drinking. Bill W. had attended the Oxford Group, a popular evangelical Protestant religious movement of the 1930s, whose members employed confession, prayer, charitable acts, and open discussion of emotional difficulties to further spiritual growth. His experiences in the group and his persistent failure to control his drinking culminated in a spiritual conversion experience, to which he attributed his first success at prolonged abstinence after years of fruitless attempts to stop drinking by force of his own will. Bill believed his conversion experience allowed him to give up his futile attempts to control his drinking and to hand this task to a "higher spiritual power," a concept central to AA's philosophy.

Religious drinking-reform movements based on abstinence from alcohol were popular throughout the nineteenth century in the United States. AA reshaped this evangelical Protestant moralism with the idea that alcoholism is a disease. Bill believed alcoholics were physically sick with a terminal and incurable condition. Bill also believed that in the face of these frightening medical facts, "alcoholics" might "surrender": relinquish their obsessive denial of their inability to control their drinking, accept a "Higher Power," and stop drinking.

These two principles—(1) the alcoholic was physically allergic to alcohol in a unique and peculiar way that fostered uncontrollable craving and would lead to death, and (2) the basis for sobriety lay in a spiritual experience—became the backbone of AA philosophy. The early AA founders followed the American temperance tradition in their belief that total abstinence was essential to recovery for alcoholics to counter the "allergy" that kept them drinking once they started. To help prevent alcoholics from taking the first drink, the object of their "mental obsession," Bill laid the groundwork for AA's concept of "sobriety," a new way of living that negated what Bill saw as the fatal egotistical delusion that alcoholics could solve their drinking problems alone. The AA group provided the forum in which members helped each other and followed their own "spiritual program," based on Bill's spiritual conversion, that fortified sobriety.

In 1939, Bill W. created and codified AA's philosophy in the form of the famous Twelve Steps, published in the book titled *Alcoholics Anonymous*, under the authorship of "Alcoholics Anonymous." The "Big Book," as it is called, contained stories of men and women who had accepted the fact that they were alcoholics: the first step in AA's program to recovery.[4] The Big Book facilitated AA's growth beyond the small cadre of early members by codifying their interactions and experiences into principles for personal recovery, referred to as the Twelve Steps, and the principles for group and organization management, the Twelve Traditions. The early founding members sought to maintain the voluntary interdependent relations upon which their sobriety depended while avoiding any hints of authoritarianism and hierarchical relations they thought would "turn off" newcomers. They also feared that members would place their faith in leaders who might "slip" (to return temporarily or permanently to drinking), and then slip themselves. The solution lay in the concept of "anonymity." Designed in part to avoid the stigma of the "alcoholic" label, anonymity means much more in AA.

Anonymity underlies AA's remarkable ability to survive where many similar organizations failed. The Twelfth Tradition states in full, "Anonymity is the spiritual foundation of our Traditions, ever reminding us to place principles above personalities." Anonymity means that AA members cannot speak for AA, nor should they seek personal gain from their membership. Bill W. feared that any alcoholic, including himself, who received personal attention by virtue of speaking for, or leading, AA would inevitably end up with an inflated ego, then slip and bring negative publicity to the organization and other members. According to the Twelve Traditions, AA's activities are basically limited to carrying "the AA message to any sick alcoholic who wants it" (Alcoholics Anonymous 1957: 294).

Anonymity, in Bill W.'s view, assured that AA's authority would rest in the common experience of the group rather than in a leader. This egalitarian structure also presents an unbroken path between the newcomer and the "highest ranking" member. The message is that each and every one arrives in the same condition and has an equal chance to achieve a sober life.

Comparison of AA in the United States and Brazil

Cultural analyses of AA have generally focused on the historical and philosophical roots of American AA in Protestant theology: the concept of surrender (akin to conversion), the confession and testimony of the saved, the personal relation to God, the individual's voluntary decision to seek help, the individual's responsibility for his or her recovery, and AA's egalitarian structure that rejects authority.[5] These elements are often discussed when they are encountered as problems for members of AA who are minorities in the United States. Madsen (1974: 156-57), for example, notes that AA's greatest foreign successes have occurred in Canada, Ireland, England, Scandinavia, New Zealand, and Australia. He believes the "core of Protestant middle-class values that unconsciously form the central philosophy of AA" is the major obstacle to the success of minorities in AA. He further argues that to be successful for Mexican-Americans, AA "would have to abandon the concept of anonymity and replace it with a public image of *recovered alcoholic* that the community must be conditioned to see as brave, commendable, and noble" (157).[6]

The following case material illustrates how AA in a city that will be called São Pedro, Brazil, retains an institutionalized concept of anonymity transformed in a cultural context that includes traditional patterns of social relations. The case material is drawn primarily from one American and one Brazilian group.[7] These groups both exist in a larger context of styles and types of groups in their respective AA universes. In both settings, groups stand in relation to each other in certain respects, such as meeting times, locations, and styles; thus I supplement the discussion with data from other groups as necessary. First, I outline the structure and flow of an American meeting and describe the different types of meeting structures. This is followed by a description of the key roles played by AA literature and sponsorship. Second, I present in more detail a Brazilian meeting and analyze the role of literature and sponsorship in the Brazilian context. These elements are compared between the American and Brazilian groups in the conclusion.

AA in Coastal City, U.S.A.

Meeting Structure

The Beacon Group of AA meets every Tuesday from 7 p.m. to 8 p.m. in the gymnasium of a church in Coastal City, U.S.A. Between the entrance and the meeting space is a long table with coffee, tea, and cookies in a "self-serve" layout. One walks the length of the table and circles behind it to enter the circle of about fifteen chairs at the front of the gym. More chairs in a long semicircle extend toward the back of the gym. The design permits a latecomer to settle in the back without disturbing the speaker in the circle. It also maintains the circle as the central structure of the meeting. There is no desk or table to mark the chairperson's spot; it is merely one seat like the others.

Approximately 60% of the members of Beacon Group are males. The Group's membership mirrors Coastal City's predominantly white, working- and middle-class population. Non-AA members are rarely encountered; the standard call for visitors to identify themselves may produce a non-AA spouse, but usually no one responds. Participation by the family of the alcoholic member is thus rare. Members in Coastal City, U.S.A., have a range of meeting types from which to choose: speaker, speaker-discussion, and various discussion-type meetings such as Step meetings, "Big Book" meetings, men's meetings, women's meetings, and gay and lesbian meetings. They follow three basic patterns: speaker-discussion (18% of meetings), discussion (67%), and speaker (15%).

A Speaker-Discussion Meeting   In Beacon Group's speaker-discussion meeting, there is no designated seat or desk for the chairperson, a typical format for not only this type of meeting but also for discussion-type meetings. The chairperson sits in the part of the circle facing the most chairs, thus spatially symbolizing the fundamental equality of the chairperson with the other members. The position rotates once a week or every other week. The assignments are made by a steering committee which meets every other week to attend to group business. Preference for chairpersons is given to members who have finished their Fourth and Fifth Steps of the Twelve Step Program for sobriety.[8] There is sometimes a "greeter" who chats with people coming in and identifies new faces. The job is not consistently filled—no one "greeted" me the first time I came in. It is just something that some of the members like to do now and then.

The speaker is usually introduced as a friend of the chairperson. The speaker has twenty minutes to speak. Following the speaker's talk, members raise their hands to "share." Everyone speaks from his or her seat; there is no real "front" of the room. In discussion groups, sharing is the main part of the meeting. The chairperson might select or request a topic, read a passage from the "Big Book" or choose one of the Twelve Steps as the theme for the meeting.

Discussion fills the remainder of the time. The term "discussion" may be misleading, because rather than entailing a give-and-take of opinions, it consists of a series of comments, vignettes, and stories by members based on the chosen topic, one of the Steps, a phrase from the "Big Book" or, in the Beacon group for example, the speaker's story. "Discussion" in the American AA meetings resembles a relay race in which one element from a member's story or contribution will be picked up by the next member, who will apply it to his or her life story, thoughts, or problems. The next one to speak will relate this same thought to his or her circumstances in a "chaining" mode of discussion. In general, the reference point of the speaker and the discussion is each member, "doing his or her own program," but speaking to the group. Denzin calls this form of discourse "dialogic": "The dialogic structure of the member's talk does not involve a reciprocated conversation with another member; rather, the member speaks to the group, as in a monologue. However, a monologue is not produced, for the collectivity is addressed" (1987: 115).

Discussion Meetings   There are two other types of meetings held in Beacon City: "discussion" meetings and "speaker" meetings. Discussion-type meetings do involve more intimate interaction than speaker-type meetings. Discussion meetings are sometimes "closed" meetings, restricted to those who are AA members, that is, excluding both nonalcoholics and newcomers. This provides greater anonymity, and consequently members feel more comfortable speaking about personal issues.

In most discussion meetings a small number of members sit around a table, or there may be a desk at the open end of a semicircle of chairs. In the Main Street Big Book Group, one person volunteers to choose a reading from the "Big Book" as the basis for discussion at the next meeting. This person will sit at the desk, chair the meeting, and begin the discussion with the reading. The discussion group chairpersons ensure a fair and equal distribution of time. Meetings are almost always scheduled for one hour, and they rarely run over. The chaining style of discourse is evident in discussion groups, despite much greater talk about current personal problems than in speaker-discussion meetings. Even in the discussion-type meeting, there is rarely a give-and-take discussion. Rather, the discussion passes from one person who wants to speak to another. Sharing in these groups thus involves confession but does not involve the exculpation of an intermediary nor the reciprocal exchange of intimacy with a friend.

Speaker Meetings   To complete the picture of styles of meetings in Beacon City, there is the speaker meeting. In speaker meetings the speaker stands in front of a table or podium to address the audience seated in rows of chairs who do not respond; thus, there is no "chaining." At the Easy Does It Group speaker meeting, the chairperson sits at the side of the room or near the front, starts the meeting, and introduces the speaker. There are two speakers per meeting, each with a twenty-five minute slot. Speakers, who are chosen in advance, will not go over or under that time. They do not use notes but frequently remark how much they had been thinking about the task for several days. The assignment of the speaker role is not based on length of sobriety or whether the member is the wisest one around. It is often used to "help along" someone who needs a boost.

Within the three styles—speaker-discussion, discussion, and speaker—the roles of the chairperson and the style of speaking are similar. The chairperson provides a lose structure, just enough to keep the meeting going. The speakers share because it helps them to "work their own programs." Rituals of humility reinforce this attitude. As one speaker said, "If you get benefit for your recovery from my words, that is great, but I do not really believe I have anything to teach anyone."

Sponsorship

Toward the end of the meeting in the Beacon Group, the chairperson asks a member to hand out the "anniversary chips," or poker chips that are given to members who have designated anniversaries in AA. One color is given upon acceptance of AA, a different color is given for thirty days, then sixty and ninety days. Annual anniversary chips are given every year from the date the member first accepted AA. Because records are not kept, members must claim their chips when the appropriate category is called out. The recipient accepts the chip and a handshake amidst hearty applause, and the event is the emotional highlight of the meeting.

The chairperson asks for any announcements. There are usually a few, often about an upcoming AA dance, social activity, or administration meeting. Next, the chairperson asks for people to volunteer as sponsors. About fifteen out of this group of fifty do so. The object is that a newcomer or someone without a sponsor can pick someone out and after the meeting make contact. It is not done during the meeting.

Sponsorship is derived, according to Kurtz (1979: 89), from "a profound awareness concerning sobriety that 'you keep it only by giving it away.'" The Big Book states, "Practical experience shows that nothing will so much insure immunity from drinking as work with other alcoholics" (AA 1976: 89). Sponsorship is one outgrowth of the Twelfth Step, which bases sobriety on helping others, as Bill W. helped himself by reaching out to Dr. Bob. Basically sponsorship means that a member with more experience in the program provides individual assistance and support to a newer member. It is a major means of communicating the AA wisdom to new members.

In Coastal City's Beacon Group, sponsorship is an important part of the program. Members report a wide range of relations with their sponsors, but what is important is that sponsees choose sponsors who are "right" for them, who will tell them "what they need to know." Some people need a tough, army-sergeant approach, whereas others are comfortable with a quiet confidant. Sponsees often discuss switching to a new sponsor with whom they can establish better rapport.

Members frequently mention that they benefit more from the sponsee than the sponsee could possibly benefit from then, another example of the humility that pervades these meetings. Another way in which they show humility is that the sponsor and the "sponsee" do not display their relationship. In fact, members rarely identify their sponsors in meetings, even when receiving chips at their anniversary dates. After one meeting in which a member celebrated three years in the Program, I asked about this and was told: "It's your Program, not your sponsor's. You earn the chips. Your sponsor is one part of your Program, but if you do not work it, your sponsor will not do you any good."

In summary, the AA community in Coastal City is loose, yet intimate. Someone is always available should members need to telephone in an emergency, to socialize, or to explore feelings about a spouse or a boss. "Greeters" may meet people at the door, introduce themselves, and give out their phone numbers. Potential sponsors are identified in the course of every meeting without revealing the identities of those who might need them. But if new attendees identify with the other members, decide to take the First Step, to accept that they have lost control over alcohol—in short, if they decide to become members of AA, then they will be welcomed as equals. They may be asked to speak, to chair a meeting, to serve AA. Any position is available and none is obligatory—they are offered as tools for each member's own recovery. New members will encounter people who believe all personal differences pale compared to the shared disease of alcoholism. They will describe in lurid detail the misery they experienced and caused while drinking, the new opportunity AA gave them, the difficulty of trying to change, and the price of failure to do so. Their style of discourse is intimate and confessional, but it does not create or identify obligations. The impersonal word of literature provides a common and stable reference point that will never let one down with a slip. Members stress the only choice that counts: show up or die, but no one will make that choice for anyone else.

The Group of Goodwill, São Pedro, Brazil

In the Brazilian group, there are many similar elements to those described above: references to the Steps, Traditions, sponsors, and the names of Bill W. and Dr. Bob, the anniversary and entrance "chips," and the stories of personal despair and hope regained. The differences reflect the development of AA in a different culture.

The Group of Goodwill is located in a working-class area of São Pedro, a large city in southern Brazil. There are no other groups in the immediate vicinity; the density of AA groups in Brazil, even urban areas, is considerably lower than in the United States. The public transport system is extensive, however, and connects this neighborhood with the rest of the city. Members of the Group of Goodwill come from the neighborhood and from other parts of the city, including the wealthiest sections.

The "coordinator" (*coordenador*)—the Brazilian name for whoever chairs the meeting—is Sérgio, a large, charismatic, powerful-looking engineer for the state rail company, who has held the position of coordinator for twelve years. This is Sérgio's "home group," the group he entered one Sunday afternoon fifteen years ago. The discussion of Sérgio's group begins with a description of a meeting at the Group of Goodwill, followed by descriptions of the role of the AA literature and sponsorship in the Group.

Meeting Structure

With a few exceptions, the Brazilian groups I attended adopt the "speaker" type of meeting. The group chooses the speaker in one of two different ways. The coordinator may pick people out of the "audience." He waits for one speaker to finish, then calls on another. The coordinator may maintain a list of speakers at his table.[9] As arriving members approach the coordinator's table to sign in, they can sign up to speak. Under this method, the coordinator will ask for volunteers or ask specific members to speak if not enough people sign up. The group described here follows the former method; Sérgio is the coordinator and he chooses the speakers.

Sérgio arrives early, he unlocks the gates to the church school and walks upstairs to the room reserved for the AA meetings of the Group of Goodwill. Next he sets out the ashtrays, puts up chairs, and, if it is a day to celebrate someone's "anniversary" in AA (which is frequently the case), he makes sure the refreshments are ready. Other members drift in and Sérgio gives them directions about what to do. Coffee is prepared by one or two members and served during and after the meeting. People straggle in, help out, chat. The room fills up as 5:30 p.m. approaches. The room holds about fifty people, not enough for this group. By the end of the two-hour meeting, there are usually people leaning in the windows to the hallway.

The room slowly fills. Parents, spouses, and relatives of AA members—or people who are not members but whose relatives are concerned about their drinking—are often in attendance, and Sérgio explicitly encourages their participation.

The room is arranged in "classroom" fashion with a desk at the front facing rows of chairs. There is a chair for the speaker at the side of the desk facing the "audience." Unlike the meeting room in Coastal City, pictures of Bill W. and Dr. Bob hang on a side wall, and the Twelve Steps and Twelve Traditions are printed on large posters on the opposite wall. These pictures and posters, reminders of AA's founders and principles, appear in almost every Brazilian group I observed, images of the founders that personalize the birth of AA.

Sérgio sits at the desk and attends to the paperwork, which consists of preparing the envelope for the portion of contributions that passes to the Regional AA Council and the sign-in book, a universal feature of Brazilian AA groups (one signs in with first name only, however), but one I have never encountered in American groups. Almost everyone greets Sérgio personally:

males with a handshake, females with the customary Brazilian greeting of a kiss on each cheek. The entrance to the room is beside Sérgio's desk, so it is impossible to slip in unobserved. People who arrive late detour to greet Sérgio whether or not someone is speaking to the group. Next to Sérgio sits the secretary Maria, a handsome woman whose flashy clothes contrast with Sérgio's modest appearance and bespeaks her residence in the wealthy district of the city.

Sérgio rings the bell and calls the meeting to order promptly at 5:30 p.m. The group recites the Serenity Prayer in unison.[10] Sérgio booms out, "Paulo! Come here!" Paulo, a member whom Sérgio has selected as the first of the evening's speakers, slowly gets up, walks to the front, and greets Sérgio with a handshake while the crowd titters. He stands next to the desk at Sérgio's side, faces the group, and waits. Sérgio is not ready for him just yet. He scans the group and points to Manoel. "Hey, my friend, how is the new job going? The job I got you?" The crowd chuckles. Manoel smiles and says it is going well, "Graças ao Deus" ("Thanks to God," a common phrase in Brazil that appears in nearly every conversation). Sérgio moves on and greets from his desk six or seven other people. Sometimes this goes on fifteen or twenty minutes in a light atmosphere peppered with jokes and laughter. The standard reply, "Tudo bem" (akin to "fine" or "OK"), is sometimes sufficient. Sérgio moves down the line and calls on me, as he often does, and asks, "How is it with our resident professor?" Next he questions the parents of a young alcoholic; the three sit together. The mother says that it's been rough lately, and her son nods. Next, Sérgio says: "Hey, rich girl—yeah, you there in the back. How are you? And my old friend there. Don't hide! How's the job going at that garage, the one I got you?" If he is satisfied that all really is "tudo bem," or if the person jokes back, he moves on.

Sometimes Sérgio is not satisfied and will push a bit more. Lack of humor, a flat response, or a downcast look appear to be signs that someone is in a difficult spot. These tight spots may or may not be related to specific negative events such as loss of a job. It may be an absent alcoholic's worried relative who expresses concern. Sometimes members hint they feel shaky, unsure about lasting another "twenty-four hours" without drinking.[11] On one occasion, for example, a visibly shaky young man leaves the meeting after only an hour. Sérgio quietly directs another more experienced member—one of several "assistants" who sit near him—to follow the young man. They return together later. He often arranges to meet with such a person personally after the meeting, or to go to his or her house.

Finished with his quick scan, Sérgio notes the newcomers who have indicated they are interested in joining AA. Often new people show up just to observe, to check it out. It is, however, impossible to be "just an observer"—either for someone with a drinking problem or an anthropologist, in contrast to groups in Coastal City. To attend the Group of Goodwill is to participate. A new face does not go unnoticed, and without fail Sérgio pays special heed to the new members and makes sure the patient speaker Paulo knows who they are so he can direct his remarks or relevant aspects of his story to them. Differences notwithstanding, attention to newcomers is part of AA practice in both Brazil and the U.S. Stories and conversations follow stylized patterns that focus on the speakers' drinking life and how they got into AA, or about current problems and how AA helps them to find solutions. This focus on the newcomers structures the narrative of stories to maximize the possibility that the newcomer will identify with the speaker's story.[12]

Finally, Sérgio finishes his scan of the room and motions to Paulo to start. Paulo walks to the front of the room and stands at the *cabeçeira da mesa*, literally, "the head of the table" but in Brazilian AA the side of the desk or table behind which the coordinator remains seated. A chair is placed next to the table but most speakers prefer to stand. In this group, the speaker faces the audience but cannot see the coordinator without turning partially around. This format is virtually universal in the groups I visited.

One exception to this format occurred in the meetings held three times a week at Group New Hope, the largest in the city and located in the wealthiest district.[13] This group holds "discussion" or "theme" meetings, in which the coordinator and the participants sit in a circle and the coordinator leads a discussion based on a theme chosen by the group the previous week, such as humility, love, sex, money, jealously, or, less often, one of the Steps. The coordinator comments frequently after members share, and he poses questions back to the group. There is considerably more give-and-take in this meeting, including interruptions, than in any other—American or Brazilian—I have seen, but the dialogue is always directed to and by the coordinator, who clarifies comments, refines the arguments, and states positions on the debate. Unlike the chairperson in the American groups, his role is much stronger than a mere moderator; he appears more as the resident expert. Thus, even the more democratic form of meeting in Brazil—itself a rare occurrence—differs considerably from the antiauthoritarian system of rotating and downplaying the role of chairperson in the American groups.

Even in small groups where an informal or discussion meeting seems "logical" by Beacon City, U.S.A., standards, one finds speaker meetings. For example, in the only AA group in Perí, a small city near São Pedro, members all know one another well. Meetings average six to ten persons, with a total membership of about ten regular members and another ten to fifteen who show up from time to time. Hernani, who has two years in AA, complained about boredom: "We know each others' stories so well...It's hard sometimes to come to a meeting though I know it's good for me." Hernani decided to learn to be a coordinator partially out of boredom. I asked why they did not try another format, like sitting around a table and talking informally, and he smiled and said: "We just don't...I suppose we would just talk about soccer or something...at least this way I know we will talk about alcohol. Also, old Roberto would get upset if we changed the style. He thinks AA should be done the way it has always been done. He's pretty conservative."

The Group of Goodwill meeting proceeds as follows: Sérgio loudly demands to see Paulo's chip. The chips are the size of poker chips and carry AA's emblem. The colors indicate the length of time a person has been in AA, and to all new members receive a chip upon joining. Sérgio requires nearly all members to show their chips to him and the crowd. In his view, it is a ticket to freedom, the first rung on a ladder from hell and a sign of commitment to AA. Paulo wrestles his out of his wallet to prove he still has it. He also shows his one-year chip and his three-year chip. Satisfied, Sérgio leans back and Paulo starts to talk about avoiding the first drink. AA members transmit the doctrine through various means, particularly homilies. "Avoid the first drink" is one of the most common. If one avoids the first drink, the second through the umpteenth are not an issue. Paulo discussed the changes he made when he was in situations where alcohol was used. He periodically directed his remarks to the two new members, identifying pitfalls and tactics for avoiding them. He told them simply to avoid parties and drinking friends, a task which, he admitted, was not easy at the beginning. If they found themselves in an alcohol-laden environment, they should fill a glass with a soft drink and keep it full the whole time.

Sérgio does paperwork while Paulo speaks. Sometimes he stops to look at Paulo, who is standing in front and to the side of him. Sérgio appears to be preoccupied at times but he misses little. He periodically prods Paulo and points out the newcomers in the group. On occasion he makes a comment during or after a speaker's story. Brazilian coordinators often commented on the speakers' stories.[14] Paulo finishes his talk and returns to his seat. Sérgio calls another name, then two more to follow the next speaker. Sometimes he insists that certain persons speak, especially, he told me, if he feels they are not pushing themselves in the group. Members with less than a year are particularly fragile, according to Sérgio. He watches them and calls on them to talk if they appear to be hesitant when he calls on them in his initial "scanning." He summons speakers and prompts them to address their wisdom to the new members. He calls the new members to speak in front of the group after a long string of speakers have built up the tension. The new members often cry; some can hardly speak. They almost always speak about their problems and how they hope to start a new life. If Sérgio feels they are running on too long or losing the audience, he will tap them or usher them to a closing. By the end of the meeting, Sérgio has spoken a few words to just about everyone in the room, and about ten out of the fifty people in attendance have spoken in front of the group. Sérgio's orchestration of stories, alternating humor and pathos, is very powerful and directs the whole meeting toward the newcomer. One member commented to me after a meeting, "He really knows his theater."

The show is not over. Sérgio calls on a young, rotund man who usually plays the fool ("bobo"). Sérgio smiles as he calls the fool's name, as do others in the group. This is the time for comic relief, and the "bobo" comes through. In response to Sérgio's questions about how things are going, the "bobo" tells a long tale about why he quit his last job. The manner of his speaking and the stories he tells have the crowd and Sérgio rolling with laughter. Humor is also important in American groups, particularly as a part of the rituals of humility—it is most often directed against oneself and one's foolish drinking lifestyle, self-delusions, and alcohol-related stupidity (see also Denzin 1987). Expressions of humility through self-directed humor are common in Brazil; however, this performance is quite different. There is no mention of alcohol, no self-deprecation.

Sérgio next calls upon the pastor to say the final words. I never knew if he really was a pastor and no one could tell me. A dark-skinned, shabbily dressed man with a gray beard and a slow, careful step, the pastor slowly walks to the front of the room. Again, the crowd and Sérgio smile in anticipation as the show continues. Sérgio jests but the pastor remains expressionless. The jests bring laughs to the other AA members. The pastor starts his talk at a whisper, quieting the room. His words are spiritual, prayer-like and gentle. Sérgio never ceases his teasing, smiling all the while, but he and the pastor appear to know this routine well. The pastor finishes his words of comfort about the loving grace of God, and he sits down. The audience is calmer and quieter. Sérgio asks for the secretary's report. Maria reads from the sign-in book to give the number of persons present and summarizes the financial report, how much money was collected by passing the hat and how much of that (a fixed percentage) will go to the central administration of AA in the state. Everyone recites the Serenity Prayer again and the meeting ends. People crowd around the initiates and around Sérgio. Every meeting ends with at least six or seven people gathered around Sérgio to talk to him. He takes time for them all.

The meeting lasted two hours, the Brazilian standard, that is, twice as long as the meetings in all the groups of Coastal City. My informant told me: "Brazilians could not possibly fit everyone in in one hour. We switched many years ago."

Oral Culture and Written Authority: AA Literature in Brazil

Sérgio does not mention the AA "literature" when he delivers his story, nor is it common to hear a specific reference to the "Big Book" or other AA works in the Group of Goodwill. I never saw anyone in São Pedro read from the "Big Book," a common sight in the United States. Literature-based meetings, referred to as "Step" or "Big Book" meetings, are common in the United States. About 15% of the meetings in Coastal City are specifically designated as "Big Book" meetings, and another 18% are "Step" meetings. In addition, other types of discussion meetings often involve "Steps" or "Big Book" readings as the theme for the discussion.

The literature is often praised in the Group of New Hope in the wealthy district. In other groups it is hardly mentioned. Still, even in the wealthy district the "Big Book" is often mentioned but, it would appear, rarely read. In my discussions with members from different groups in São Pedro, few members even from Group of New Hope demonstrated an intimate knowledge of the literature. There are some AA "intellectuals" in São Pedro who do know the literature well. For example, Maurício, one such AA member who had visited AA groups in the United States during business trips, lamented what he believed was a general disinterest by Brazilians in the AA literature and noted that this was a major difference between the American and Brazilian groups. He has struggled to get literature-based meetings going for years with moderate success, and only at the Group of New Hope.

AA literature is nonetheless usually displayed in Brazilian meetings and offered for sale. Sérgio, who has read the "Big Book" (based on references he has made to it in interviews with me), openly states that a new member should *avoid* reading the AA literature. He believes, and frequently declares in meetings, that alcoholics are confused and therefore reading the literature too soon would put misleading ideas in their heads that should only be dealt with much later, after at least a year or two. The important thing is to "avoid the first drink" and to "come to meetings."

It is true that in American groups it is also often repeated that the most important task for the newcomer is to come to meetings and to get a sponsor, but to leave the rest for later. The "rest" includes the literature, the discussion meetings, probing the more subtle psychological problems that are said in the Beacon Group of Coastal City only to come out after a few years of sobriety. These parts rarely appear in São Pedro. In Brazil, membership of AA is a social relationship of *persons*, whereas in the United States it is a moral commitment of *individuals*.

Sponsorship

If the literature is not a major part of Sérgio's interpretation of the AA "Program," sponsorship is. Sponsorship to Sérgio is a "sacred bond" between the sponsor and the sponsee. Newcomers are encouraged to choose sponsors as soon as possible, which most do on the day of their entry into AA.

Most Brazilian members of AA choose as sponsors the person who first introduced them to AA; or charismatic, well-respected, or higher-status members; or persons with whom they feel comfortable as friends. In most of the cases I witnessed, newcomers choose the person who brought them into AA.

Miguel, for example, wanted to choose me as his sponsor because in his mind it was through me that he got to AA. I knew his family, and Miguel and I had chatted a few times. His family was quite concerned about his drinking. He had given me a ride to an AA meeting one Sunday afternoon and decided to join AA on the spot. He chose someone else after I declined his request to be his sponsor based on my impending departure, but it is commonplace for newcomers, as a token of respect and gratitude, to name as sponsor their first AA contact, without regard for experience, length of sobriety, stability, or other qualities. In some cases, this led to one member choosing a sponsor who had only a few weeks of sobriety, a practice that Philip, an expatriated American who has been in AA in São Pedro five years, considers to be dangerous.

In Brazilian groups the newcomer receives a chip upon entry, a small plastic medallion signifying membership in the AA fellowship. It is the *padrinho* who gives the newcomer this chip and says a few words in a small ceremony in front of the group. Brazilians translate "sponsor" as *padrinho*, which is the same Portuguese word used for "godfather." *Padrinho* therefore carries the sense of protector or patron that "godfather" connotes. *Afilhado* is the Portuguese term for "sponsee." *Afilhado*, derived from *filho*, "son," connotes "godson."[15]

The *padrinho* gives chips at all the anniversary points: three months, six months, one year, and annually thereafter. For many members, this is the extent of their relation with their sponsor. Two years after Miguel entered AA, his only relationship with his *padrinho* was on the chip anniversary dates. He never discussed personal problems with his *padrinho* and mentioned him only in the course of his story when recounting the sequence of events that brought him into AA. When he did feel the need to talk to someone, he said he would talk to a few AA friends after a meeting.

AA members in São Pedro often choose charismatic or respected members as sponsors. Sérgio, a charismatic man with a forceful "presence," had more sponsees than he could name. Sérgio claimed to disapprove of the practice of choosing sponsors based on their higher class or strong personalities, but he recognized that many chose him "because I speak loudly and with authority." His reservations did not seem to prevent him from accepting new sponsees during the time I observed the group.

Sérgio expressed displeasure at this method of choosing a sponsor and clearly preferred the third method: seeking a sponsor with whom one has some affinity or spiritual bond. Several well-respected AA members who are often sought as sponsors—all but one with an older male—share this opinion. Maurício, for example, believes sponsorship in the United States is taken much more seriously than in Brazil: "Everyone here has a sponsor, but only to get their [anniversary] chips. We do have different styles . . . the army-sergeant style bothers me; we are based in love. Perhaps we have too much love . . . you have heard about the Brazilian *jeitinho*?"

The *jeitinho* is the Brazilian "under-the-table, off-the-record, between-you-and-me" personal favor or deal. If the logic of Protestant dyadism is either this or that, then the logic of the Catholic *jeitinho* is neither this nor that—there is always an in-between, a way around the absolute (see DaMatta 1991, Barbosa, this volume). To Martha, a Canadian who, with nearly twenty years experience with AA (in Brazil), her sponsees expect her to wink her eye more:

For some time it seemed to be rather fashionable to choose me as a sponsor. People I didn't even know in AA would come up and ask me. They're mostly men. Well, let's say I'm a little tough on my sponsees . . . like somebody comes to tell me something I know is an absolute lie. I say, "Why come to tell me lies? I didn't ask you anything. If you're going to tell me something, tell me the truth; it doesn't really make any difference to me." Most of them leave.[16]

Both Maurício and Martha believe that AA members cannot do the Fourth and Fifth Steps without honest soul-searching. They agree that confronting the lies the alcoholic lives is the path to recovery, but they feel that through the *jeitinho* Brazilian AA members avoid the painful process of self-examination. One example, mentioned above by Martha, is if the sponsor overlooks lies in the stories the sponsee is telling. Martha also provided another example:

When people are in this Macumba business, they are drinking *cachaça* [rum]. And then they tell me that it doesn't do any harm because it is the spirits who are drinking. So I tell them, "It's your blood that gets the *cachaça* and your head that goes batty and you better find another sponsor because that won't go down with me!" I'm not going to tell someone he shouldn't drink *cachaça*; if he's in AA, he knows he shouldn't.

Why would people go through the trouble to do a Fifth Step if they were not willing, in Martha's opinion, actually to do it? She believes it is *para inglês ver*—all for show, to be able to say Martha, a respected member of AA, is their sponsor. She has fewer sponsees now than in the past, which she believes is due to her reputation as an honest, i.e., difficult, sponsor. This is how her sponsor treated her and she—still—deplores the "insincerity" of people who seek her as a sponsor. This "insincerity" speaks to the different conceptions of the recovery process that Martha and her Brazilian sponsees hold. Antze's discussion of the homology between AA's model of alcoholism and recovery and the core Protestant drama of sin and salvation is instructive. Within AA ideology, the alcoholic has a fatal flaw—the disease of alcoholism—that will lead to death. Willpower alone is insufficient. Recovery involves a systematic self-examination involving confession, repentance, and restitution to allow one's Higher Power to remove one's "character defects" that lead to drinking (Antze 1987: 166). The "disease" of alcoholism is blind; it does not matter "who you are." All are the same and recovery involves the same process for all.

In Martha's view, there is no place in such a scheme for the *jeitinho*, for contradiction, style or mediation. Ambiguity is just a means to rationalize drinking, and that means death. There is, or should be, no escape from the self-examination involved in the Steps.

Padrinhos do serve other roles for some members. Sérgio still sees his original *padrinho* from time to time and credits him with having saved his life by showing up at Sérgio's apartment every day to take him to a meeting until Sérgio "got" the program. Sérgio says he still asks his *padrinho* for advice. Sérgio tries to implement this model of the *padrinho/afilhado* relationship: direct intervention, strong advice, and clear directives. This is why he arranges meetings with newcomers, visits groups with them, and takes them to or from hospitals, prisons, treatment clinics, and homes of relatives. People know which groups he visits on which nights, and I often saw the same people at the different meetings he attended around the city. When asked about his paternalistic behavior toward newcomers and his belief that one should choose a "spiritually compatible" sponsor, Sérgio reconciled the two this way:

When I first went to a meeting, this man, João, was there. I recognized him from the street. I said I would think about AA. He didn't let me. Day two he came to my door, "We're going to a meeting in the City." I went. Day three, four, five, six, seven—the same thing. After a while I started to tell my story. I was in. He watched me for quite a while, met me at meetings. Then he let me go on my own.

Arturo was a sponsee of Sérgio. He says that Sérgio was hard on him but he needed it: "He gave me structure. It's all theater. He has a heart of gold. I go back there now and then."

Hierarchy and Organizational Structure

Members of AA in São Pedro from different groups have differing opinions about their leaders.[17] Rui, for example, does not attend meetings at Group of Goodwill but knows Sérgio. He strongly denies that there are people who "own" AA groups, but he would not discuss Sérgio's behavior in relation to specific AA principles.[18] Maurício, an "AA intellectual," frequently travels to New York on business and attends AA meetings there. He is very familiar with the Steps, Traditions, and the literature in general, and he likes to compare AA meetings in the United States and Brazil. According to Maurício,

Sérgio does not really present a problem because there are other groups around the city people can go to. It would be different if his were the only one in town and you had to do it his way or not go at all...I have also never heard of him keeping anyone from attending meetings for any reason. That would be serious if it happened...a violation of the Third Tradition [which holds that anyone who wants to stop drinking may attend AA]. He probably does violate the Traditions, but he does not stretch the rules too far.

José, who has served on the regional AA Service Board, believes leaders like Sérgio emerge all too often in Brazilian AA. He attributed this to two causes. One is that AA in Brazil is younger than in the United States by fifteen important years of maturation. José believes the added years of experience for AA in the United States have taken it beyond the long struggle for the appropriate organizational form independent of personal ties. José thinks that AA in Brazil is just beginning to tighten up its organization to reduce the influence of individual personalities.

However, José is not certain if time will make a difference. He believes the tendency for individual influence to grow in a group is much more a part of life in Brazil: "You Americans have a profound sense of 'my rights.' You have more education in democracy. Here in Brazil this will happen in any group: the leadership will grow stronger. We like the idea of no authorities [a reference again to the Third Tradition] but we do not observe it."

José cannot decide whether this situation is good or bad. Perhaps, he speculates, because Brazilians accept a leader more readily than Americans do, this helps those Brazilians whose lives are chaotic and who need someone to tell them what to do, which coordinators often do. Sérgio does this in no uncertain terms. He peppers his talks with references to his past careers as a thief, assassin, and kidnapper. They may be exaggerations or they may be true, but they certainly enhance his image as a powerful man, a man from the streets. I encountered members in other groups who were genuinely afraid of Sérgio and would not attend the Group of Goodwill for fear of what he would do if they ever slipped. Few of the older members really believe the threat: it is part of the folklore of Sérgio.

Conclusion: The Meanings of Anonymity

In the language of AA, alcoholism is a "disease" that strikes people of all classes, races, and nationalities. The AA solution is to provide a safe zone in which the alcoholic who wishes to change may resocialize to a new lifestyle based on abstinence (Maxwell 1984, Rudy 1986). Anonymity for AA is the safeguard that permits the alcoholic to admit his powerlessness over alcohol, to identify with other AA members, and to accept the terms of a new life. Anonymity permits the alcoholic to avoid the stigma attached in many cultures to the label "alcoholic" and it permits the organization as a whole to avoid the pitfalls of charismatic leadership and public controversy that undermined previous attempts to help American alcoholics.

The cases described here suggest that "anonymity" has different meanings in Brazilian and American groups.[19] In Coastal City, U.S.A., structural, social, and symbolic elements reveal and reinforce a sense of anonymity at the personal level and define the group as a tool for the personal recovery of anonymous individuals. The frequent use of circular and semicircular formations structurally emphasizes, first, the equality of all in the face of the common disease and, second, the personal nature of the commitment to the recovery process. The group has no center; it is not organic. Anyone can arrive late or not at all without disturbing the group or evoking comment. The group follows a cafeteria model: members are free to take a bit of wisdom, leave a commented directed to all and no one in particular, and to come and go as is necessary for "working one's own program."

The patterns of interaction reinforce the undesirability of a strong central authority to whom one owes one's sobriety, allegiance, or respect. Hierarchical implications of the chairperson and speaker roles, for example, are denied through ritual displays of humility. The assignment and fulfillment of the chairperson role is carefully managed in the Beacon Group to assure equal access, to avoid personality conflicts, and to help other members along in their program. Chairperson roles rotate regularly, a process governed by the Group's own traditions, the Twelve Traditions of AA, and a committee that sets the schedules and assigns the roles. The chairperson in the Beacon Group does not seek to guide the discussion or provide comments. The meeting does not have a main goal, nor is there a clear direction to the discussion. Each individual contributes whatever he or she desires or needs without comment or regard for consistency or continuity. The "chaining" style of discourse reinforces the positive contribution of the speaker while positioning the discussant in a "one-way dialogue" with the group.

The use of the AA literature in the Coastal City Beacon Group extends this chaining style of discourse to a dialogue between the individual member and the "Big Book," one central and constant point amidst the flux of social relationships. People come and go at AA meetings: some stay once or twice or a month, then disappear forever; others remain for years; and still others attend a short while, leave the group and return years later.[20] Amidst this constant change of personalities, the "Big Book" represents a fixed reference point of wisdom accessible to everyone, a privately consumed map through a jungle of disorder attributed to alcohol.

If Beacon Group members consider anyone a guide, it is their sponsors. In this group, sponsorship is intimate, dyadic, and conducted outside the eyes and ears of the Group. The individual sponsor-sponsee relationship is not the subject of public celebration, but frequent references in the comments and stories describe how, when, and where one speaks with one's sponsor, what advice is given, and how much help the sponsor is. The *institution* of sponsorship is continually supported in public, but individual sponsors and their sponsees remain anonymous to the group.

In São Pedro, too, anonymity is a barrier against a hostile outside world in which alcoholics run the daily gauntlet of bars and drinking buddies on one hand and the threat of being discovered and stigmatized on the other. However, in contrast to the Beacon Group, Sérgio is the center of attention and the keystone in a network of personal relationships which define the limits of anonymity and create the possibilities for recovery. The spatial arrangement of the meeting room directs attention to Sérgio. There are no specific time limits for speaking; members speak until finished or until Sérgio prods them in the back. If Sérgio wants the meeting to continue past two hours, it will. The needs of the moment as Sérgio defines them, not the rights of the speakers and other members, dictate the length of the meeting.

Coordinators in São Pedro assume a much larger role in the conduct of the meeting, as the case of Sérgio demonstrates. Unlike the Beacon Group, the Group of Goodwill does not have an overseeing committee; Sérgio has been coordinator for sixteen years. Sérgio, and most coordinators I observed in São Pedro, use their role to provide continuity and order to the series of speakers' stories by giving comments frequently, sometimes after every speaker. In the rare discussion meetings, the coordinator kept the discussion on track with those comments, as a teacher might in a classroom discussion.

Some members say Sérgio is the *dono* of the Group; others say he is just a leader and does not violate AA traditions. All would agree that he helps people through direct action in their lives, through manipulating the resources of the Group, and by assuming a stable role in AA as coordinator of the Group of Goodwill, a fixed point in a chaotic world. AA members sometimes refer to newcomers as "babies," and Sérgio is their strong father who has clear ideas about what one should and should not do.

In sum, members of the Group of Goodwill place a greater emphasis on the group identity than members of Coastal City's Beacon Group. Sponsorship is publicly demonstrated at the anniversaries of the sponsee in the Group, in contrast to the private friendships of the Beacon Group sponsors and sponsees. Likewise, in the Brazilian group the speakers' stories are balanced by the coordinator to maximize their effect, in contrast to the chaining style in the Beacon Group, which carefully reinforces the individual autonomy and anonymity of its members. In Sérgio's group the literature takes a distant second place to Sérgio's advice, warnings, and commands and to the collective experience of its members. In the Beacon Group, the literature provides a private source of inspiration and a universal authority equally available to all.

If a member of Coastal City's Beacon Group moved to São Pedro, would he or she be uncomfortable at the Group of Goodwill? One expatriated American, Kevin, does attend the Group of Goodwill from time to time. He says he goes "to see new faces, to say 'hello,' for a change of pace—it's always a good meeting," but he adds, "I do not need a Sérgio breathing down my neck all the time. I can do my own Program, thank you." I speculate that over time most members of the Beacon Group would find constrictive the public nature of "working the Program" through this type of relationship with the leader and one's sponsor.

Sérgio's method of coordinating, or, some would say, "running his group" —his forceful words, threats of violence to assure abstinence, his charismatic presence—all evoke images of paternal authority and of a stable environment safe from the deadly temptation of the street. These images attract certain segments of the population, particularly the residents of the poor surrounding neighborhood and the young, wealthier residents of the city. For the members of the Group of Goodwill, the images define a space in which one can comfortably lose the anonymity of what DaMatta (1981) refers to as the domain of the "street," the cultural zone in which anonymity represents both opportunity and danger, a state devoid of the personal relations that confer identity and security. The Group of Goodwill is more than a refuge from the possibly fatal temptations of the omnipresent bars and drinking buddies; it is the cultural space of the *casa*, in DaMatta's terms, defined by Sérgio himself, by his orchestration of a predictable meeting, his late-night "rescue" missions, his sponsorship, his moral leadership in a confusing world.

Anthropologists and sociologists have contributed much to our understanding of how AA "works": learning a new way of thinking about one's past, revaluing the difficulties of the past through learning the ideology of alcoholism as a disease, socializing in and outside the meetings, identifying with a group of people suffering from the same affliction, and learning what that affliction is and how to interpret behavior in terms of it.[21] The program for recovery is always available from other members. Shared problems can be viewed in a new light through "working the Steps," which is demonstrated by sponsorship, serving, and helping other alcoholics.

These factors make AA "work" in São Pedro, but it "works" in different ways. The loose AA organization allows for the elaboration of different possibilities. One common possibility is the emergence of a strong central figure, generally male, whose behavior may be interpreted by others as violating the Traditions. He serves as a personal anchor, the center of a web of relations reminiscent of paternal authority, order, and stability. The existence of principles based on Calvinist theology, on egalitarian relations rooted in written traditions, on a private relationship of the individual to his or her sponsor and to a Higher Power through the literature—these aspects of the Program are based on individual anonymity and the collective relations of *individuals*. These elements are available and are applicable to some. But for many of the residents of São Pedro, their chaotic experiences are ameliorated through affiliation with Sérgio's group and his teachings about alcoholism.

Endnotes

1. AA has generated its own vocabulary, sometimes imparting words with its own meaning, such as "anonymity." I place such words in quotes to indicate that they have special meanings within AA.

2. For detailed descriptions of Alcoholics Anonymous, see Denzin (1987), Kurtz (1979), Madsen (1974), and Robinson (1979). On the Protestant theology of AA, see Antze (1987) and Bateson (1972).

3. This process largely excluded the voices of women and minorities. References to the "founders" of AA should be taken to mean the white, middle-class, Protestant males who predominated in its early history and membership until the last fifteen to twenty years.

4. "Recovery" refers to a life-long process, not a state. Since AA holds that alcoholism is incurable, it is impossible to escape it. One can only overcome it in a never-ending process.

5. See, for example, Antze (1987), Kurtz (1979), Rodin (1981); also Stein (1983).

6. On minorities and AA, see also Robinson (1983) and Sutro (1989).

7. Interview and observational data were obtained during fieldwork in AA groups in and around a medium-sized Brazilian city, "São Pedro," over a period of ten months. Data from American groups were obtained from ongoing research in and around a small American city on the East Coast, "Coastal City," and from the literature published by AA.

8. The Fourth Step is "We made a searching a fearless moral inventory of ourselves." The Fifth Step states, "We admitted to God, to ourselves, and to another human being the exact nature of our wrongs." Both appear in the "Big Book" (Alcoholics Anonymous 1976: 59), and they are conspicuously absent from the practice of AA in Brazil.

9. I use the masculine pronoun intentionally. In my visits to approximately twenty groups, I saw only one female coordinator, a Canadian who had lived for many years in Brazil with her European husband. "Secretaries" are usually women unless the groups have no regular female members. The secretary's job is to count the contributions of the day, summarize the log-in book, note the anniversaries, and complete any other paperwork that arises during the meeting.

10. In many groups in São Pedro, the first person plural pronoun is used instead of the singular pronoun, thus, "God, grant us . . . "

11. In AA, the goal is not to cease drinking forever, which may appear to the alcoholic to be impossible. It is, rather, to avoid a drink in the next twenty-four hours, hence the common AA expression, "One day at a time."

12. Denzin (1987), Maxwell (1984), Robinson (1979), and Rudy (1986).

13. A "group" refers to the permanent umbrella organization that rents the space for meetings. Many groups hold only one meeting a week. Group New Hope, the largest in São Pedro, held around thirty per week. On occasion, two different groups may hold meetings in the same space at different times (a room at a local church, for example), and merely change the name and the coordinator. Thirty-two groups in São Pedro hold 125 meetings per week, 75 of which are held in only three groups.

14. One new coordinator confided to me his nervousness at having to come up with a good comment after each speaker. Even in his particularly casual group, the discussion format was never used.

15. *Madrinha* or "godmother" is used for women, but they appear in this role less often, due in part to the low proportion of AA members who are female. The highest proportion of women occurs in the wealthiest districts of São Pedro, where women have been members of AA for longer periods of time as well.

16. The AA members who tell her lies are doing so in the context of the Fifth Step. They chose Martha as "the other human being" to whom they reveal the "nature of their wrongs."

17. To be "from" Group X usually means that one is a regular there. It may also mean that a member joined AA in that group, even if he or she rarely attends meetings there.

18. Maurício used the Portuguese word "dono," meaning "owner." "Dono" connotes a sense of authority, of one who presides over a house, plantation, business, or even a social group or regular gathering.

19. Because there are no national studies of variation in the practices of AA groups for either the U.S. or Brazil, generalizations to the level of national cultures must be tentative. In various meetings in New York City and in the Midwestern United States, I have seen little that differs from the structures and practices described for Coastal City in the Northeast. The same holds for the Group of Goodwill in São Pedro.

20. Robinson (1979), using survey data, found that 57% of AA members in England who had been with AA six years or longer had dropped out at least once, and the vast majority of these drank heavily while "out."

21. Denzin (1987), Madsen (1974, 1979), Maxwell (1984), Robinson (1979), and Ruby (1986).

References

Alcoholics Anonymous
1957 *Alcoholics Anonymous Comes of Age: A Brief History of AA.* New York: Alcoholics Anonymous World Services, Inc.
1976 *Alcoholics Anonymous.* 3d ed. New York: Alcoholics Anonymoous World Services, Inc.

Antze, Paul
1987 "Symbolic Action in Alcoholics Anonymous." In Mary Douglas (ed.), *Constructive Drinking: Perspectives on Drink from Anthropology.* Cambridge: Cambridge University Press.

Bateson, Gregory
1972 "The Cybernetics of `Self': A Theory of Alcoholism." In *Steps to an Ecology of Mind.* New York: Ballantine Press.

Bellah, Robert N., Richard Madsen, William Sullivan, Ann Swidler, and Steven Tipton
1985 *Habits of the Heart: Individualism and Commitments in American Life.* Berkeley: University of California Press.

DaMatta, Roberto
1981 "The Ethic of Umbanda and the Spirit of Messianism: Reflections on the Brazilian Model." In Thomas C. Bruneau and Phillippe Faucher (eds.), *Authoritarian Capitalism: Brazil's Contemporary Economic and Political Development.* Boulder, Colo.: Westview Press.
1991 *Carnivals, Rogues, and Heroes.* Notre Dame, Ind.: University of Notre Dame Press.

Denzin, Norman

1987 *Treating Alcoholism: The Alcoholics Anonymous Approach.* Newbury Park, Calif.: Sage Publications.

Kurtz, Ernest

1979 *Not God: A History of Alcoholics Anonymous.* Center City, Minn.: Hazeldon Educational Materials.

Madsen, William

1974 *The American Alcoholic: The Nature-Nurture Controversy in Alcohol Research and Therapy.* Springfield, Ill.: Charles C. Thomas.

1979 *"Alcoholics Anonymous as a Crisis Cult." In Mac Marshall (ed.), Beliefs, Behaviors, and Alcoholic Beverages: A Cross-Cultural Survey.* Ann Arbor: University of Michigan Press.

Maxwell, Milton A.

1950 "The Washington Movement." *Quarterly Journal of Studies in Alcohol* 11: 410–51.

1984 *The Alcoholics Anonymous Experience: A Close-Up View for Professionals.* New York: McGraw-Hill.

Robinson, Davis

1979 *Talking Out Alcoholism: The Self-Help Process of Alcoholics Anonymous.* Baltimore: University Park Press.

1983 "The Growth of Alcoholics Anonymous." *Alcohol and Alcoholism 18: 167–72.*

Rodin, Miriam B.

1981 "Alcoholism as a Folk Disease." Journal of Studies on Alcohol 42: 221–32.

Rudy, David

1986 *Becoming Alcoholic: Alcoholics Anonymous and the Reality of Alcoholism.* Carbondale and Edwardsville: Southern Illinois University Press.

Stein, Howard P.

1983 "Alcoholism as Metaphor in American Culture: Ritual Desecration as Social Integration." *Ethos* 13(3): 195–235.

Sutro, Livingston

1989 "Alcoholics Anonymous in a Mexican-Indian Village." *Human Organization* 48(2): 195–235.

Trice, Harrison M. and William J. Staudenmeir, Jr.

1989 "A Sociocultural History of Alcoholics Anonymous." In Marc Galanter (ed.), *Recent Developments in Alcoholism* Vol. 7. New York: Plenum Press.

Four

Brazilian Society:

Macrostructures in

Comparative Perspective

⊠

The final essays in this volume concentrate on Brazilian society as a whole and the question of macrostructures: the state and legal-judicial system. Among the most challenging and rewarding of the essays in the book, they show two accomplished anthropologists who are synthesizing a great deal of research.

Roberto Kant de Lima's essay grows out of years of fieldwork and archival research on university, police, and judicial practices in Brazil and the United States. He shows that the Brazilian state and constitution were borrowed explicitly from the United States, but the judicial system and police practices were not. Instead, the Brazilian legal system is codified as in France, not a common law system as in Britain and most of its former colonies. The common law system relies on custom and jury verdicts as a basis for building up legal precedent, and therefore it implicitly recognizes the different locales and regions as having parity with the formal legal tradition. In contrast, a codified system imposes a central structure on the entire system.

Furthermore, the Brazilian legal system is also hierarchical in the sense that it encodes a system of privileges. Much as in the Middle Ages, when certain ranks of society had their own special law, in Brazil there are special legal privileges for some groups, such as people who hold public office. There is also a legal tradition of defense for crimes committed to defend one's honor, and police procedures vary radically according to social position.

From the fact-finding procedures in criminal law to trial-by-jury procedures, the Brazilian system is quite different from that of the United States. Fact-finding procedures involve secrecy and inquisitorial practices, whereas trial-by-jury does not allow the jury members to discuss their opinions among themselves or in private. In general, Kant shows how in the Brazilian legal system there is an ambiguous boundary between public and private, two realms which are more sharply demarcated in the United States. He does not, however, fall into an evolutionary framework that would view Brazilian institutions as backward. Rather, he argues that the Brazilian legal institutions are products of Brazilian society and culture, and that they are deeply interwoven into the Brazilian way of life.

DaMatta also rejects evolutionary theories that see Brazil in terms of simplistic dichotomies such as traditional and modern, underdeveloped and developed. In this essay he develops a sustained critique of Western social science theories that would wish to reject Brazil as a chaos in which nothing makes sense. He states that those theories simply fail to understand Brazil on its own terms, as a decidedly mixed society in which modern and traditional institutions coexist in a complementary relationship.

In this essay, DaMatta reviews some of his most well-known interpretations of Brazilian national culture. He discusses the triangle of races and the Brazilian way of viewing difference as complementary relationships within a hierarchy. He also discusses the house and the street as physical representations of moral spaces, and he shows how personal relationships tend to encompass legal and economic ones. He reviews three of the major national rituals—a civic holiday, a religious holiday, and Carnival (Mardi Gras)—and he shows how they also form a triangle of relationships. Finally, he discusses the famous character from Brazilian fiction, Dona Flor, who has two husbands, one dead and the other alive. He argues that Dona Flor symbolizes Brazil, which refuses to choose between the traditional and the modern just as Dona Flor refuses to choose between her husbands.

Some theorists in the human sciences, such as Claude Lévi-Strauss, tend to work with pairs of oppositions. Others, such as Talcott Parsons and Carl Jung, worked with quaternities. DaMatta works with triads. He sees quaternities as reducible to dyads, and dyads as expressions of the dominant Western logic that reduces everything to an either/or logic. By choosing to discuss triads of cultural forms, DaMatta is self-consciously building an alternative, Brazilian way of looking at Brazil. He looks for mediating terms and ambiguous markers of the in-between. There, he argues, lies the solution to the Brazilian puzzle.

DaMatta's writing style is likely to be somewhat foreign to many readers. I read his essay as a very self-conscious and reflexive expression of his general theoretical position and stance as a Brazilian theorist and writer. Thus, he refuses to put in any section divisions or to divide up his essay into neat forms consistent with Anglo-Saxon writing conventions (see Kant de Lima 1992 for more on this point). Instead, he serves the reader an intellectual black bean stew (*feijoada*)—the national dish of Brazil—in which themes from many of his well-known essays are mixed together in a literate manner and spiced with many personal asides in the notes.

References

Kant de Lima, Roberto
　　1992　"The Anthropology of the Academy: When We Are the Indians." In David Hess and Linda Layne (eds.), *Knowledge and Society*. Vol. 9, *The Anthropology of Science and Technology*. Greenwich, Conn.: JAI Press. (Translation of *A Antropologia da Academia*. Niterói: UFF and Petrópolis: Vozes.)

Chapter Ten

Bureaucratic Rationality in Brazil and in the United States: Criminal Justice Systems in Comparative Perspective

⊠

Roberto Kant de Lima

Tradition and Modernity in Brazil

In the legal and political traditions of modern Western societies, democracy and citizenship are considered to be universal concepts. The necessary requirements for the existence of such political conditions in any given society are also considered to be universal. However, emphasis on the universal features of modern legal and political systems may have blurred the fact that there are important variations among these systems. In different social contexts, the same categories may have quite distinct, if not opposite, meanings; and such differences may seriously compromise, for instance, the effectiveness of public policies that fail to take into consideration cultural specificities. Therefore, more than we usually recognize, successful implementation of public policies may depend on emphasizing differences rather than on acknowledging similarities.

In this article, I present some of the results of ten years of research that I have completed on comparative truth-finding methods, both judicial and academic, in two different cultures, those of Brazil and the United States.[1] During this period I have done research in both countries, both archival and fieldwork, with the latter including the classical methods of anthropological research, such as participant-observation, structured and nonstructured interviews, and so on. Theoretically and methodologically, my hypothesis was inspired by the comparative perspective representative of current developments of social anthropology, such as in the comparative work of Louis Dumont (e.g., 1977, 1980, 1983) and Roberto DaMatta (1987, 1991) on hierarchy and egalitarianism, holism and individualism, and tradition and modernity in contemporary societies and cultures.

Contrasting the legal and political systems of Brazil and the United States is not always an easy task. On the one hand, Americans view Brazil as one among other homogeneously Latin American, "Hispanic" countries in contrast to the political frame of Anglophone North America.[2] On the other hand, Brazilians are accustomed to thinking of their country as a southern version of the United States, one which combines Anglo-American political institutions with continental European, but non-Hispanic, cultural traditions. From this point of view, Brazilians perceive Brazilian identity as very different from the surrounding South American Spanish-speaking countries.

This search for political identity has even resulted in Brazilians once naming the country after the United States: the "Republic of the United States of Brazil." Politically and legally, Brazil has a continental size and geographical diversity similar to that of the United States. Furthermore, like the United States Brazil is a federation, a union of semiautonomous states that have state representatives and state governments that are elected independently by the state population. Brazil also has a President and a Congress directly elected by the universal, popular vote of the whole country. It is true that in more than one hundred years of Brazilian history as a republic, some of these general features have been altered or even suppressed, but there is no doubt that the political system of the United States always remained as a point of reference for Brazilian political culture.

However, such is not the case for the judicial system. In Brazil there is a system of federal and state courts, as in the United States, but labor, civil, commercial, and criminal laws, as well as the laws regulating civil and criminal procedures, are federal. Brazil also has a Supreme Court (the *Supremo Tribunal Federal*), but this highest court has very different functions from the Supreme Court in the United States. The Brazilian Federal Supreme Court is much more of a superior court of appeals: a third, and sometimes fourth and last, degree appellate court for the state and federal courts, rather than a constitutional court as in the United States.

Moreover, the Brazilian judicial system follows the civil law tradition, where laws are codified and the legislature is the only legitimate source for making the law. This is quite different from the common law tradition of the United States, where precedents and jury verdicts actually make the law, together with the legislative state power, which makes laws, not codes. Brazil has, therefore, a mixed system, with a judiciary and a political organization

242

similar to that of the United States and a judicial system that resembles those of continental Europe. It is within this context that the universal requirements for the functioning of democratic systems and the rights of citizens must be identified and analyzed.

The Ambiguous Brazilian System of Conflict Resolution

A brief look at the Brazilian system of criminal justice, as it works today, will present us with a very complex and quite paradoxical legal reality. The Brazilian constitutional system seems to have been developed based on an awareness of the conquests of civil liberties that emerged after the French and American Revolutions. For example, after the proclamation of the Republic in 1889, Brazilian constitutional law granted due process of law to criminal defendants, who traditionally have the right to counsel and to a fair trial (*ampla defesa*), that is, to produce any possible evidence on equal standing with the prosecution. Constitutional law also guaranteed the presumption of innocence, and our latest (1989) constitution has even granted the right to nonself-incrimination equivalent to the Fifth Amendment of the U.S. Constitution.[3] The current Brazilian Constitution also includes a provision that any evidence proved to have been improperly produced will be excluded from the judicial process.

However, in contrast with those very modern, liberal, egalitarian, and individualistic rights stand traditional practices and conservative legal principles, including procedure laws and the articles of the Brazilian Code of Criminal Procedures. Probably resulting from the European continental legal tradition's emphasis on legal expertise, the Brazilian criminal justice system is based on codes that have been elaborated and defined by jurists and legal experts. This means that codes for criminal, civil, and commercial law, as well as for criminal and civil procedures, are not a mere collection of written laws, as in the legal tradition of the United States. Instead, the codes are organized into titles, chapters, and articles that successively enumerate and supposedly put coherently into practice logical principles and legal doctrines. Consequently, because the doctrines themselves vary and even among the followers of any doctrine there are frequent disagreements of interpretation, the jurists dispute among themselves for the "keys" to decipher such codes, in order to give the "true" interpretation to them. Obviously, the author or authors of these codes are considered to be their best interpreters, thus establishing a hierarchy of knowledge linked to the political circumstances that have determined the choice of certain jurists and the exclusion of others to elaborate these codes in a given period of time.

Codes, like constitutions, are from time to time reformed and rewritten in ways that reflect changes in the country's political conditions. However, because the interpretation of codes continues to be a matter of expertise, their reforms are not widely and openly discussed in Brazilian society or even in the Brazilian Congress—as occurred with those Brazilian constitutions that were written under democratic conditions. Codes thus remain an explicit testimony of many of the deeply rooted traditions of Brazilian legal culture, especially those related to inquisitorial fact-finding procedures, associated with pre-Republican hierarchical conceptions of society.

For example, despite the fact that the right to nonself-incrimination is guaranteed under the Constitution, the Code of Criminal Procedures states that the judge must repeat to defendants a legal formula that explains that if they do not answer a question formulated by the judge during the mandatory examination (*interrogatório*) by the judge, this fact may be used against them. In contrast to the Anglo-American system, defendants in Brazil are allowed to *lie* on their own behalf, and only the witnesses are held responsible for their statements in court. As a result, the defendant is not supposed to remain silent. There is even a legal saying that whoever remains silent agrees to the accusation ("quem cala, consente"), and a confession is expected from all defendants, who are gradually proven guilty.[4]

The judicial interrogation (*interrogatório*) is conducted exclusively by the judge, without the mandatory participation of prosecution or defense counsel. The judge asks questions based mostly on information provided from the police investigation (*inquérito policial*), which is officially defined as inquisitorial: a "state's proceeding against everything and everybody to find out the truth of the facts," to borrow the untranslatable expression of a *delegado* (a police officer in charge of a police precinct, known as a *delegacia*). That is, in contrast with the enlightenment and liberal legal tradition, secretly produced evidence has legal ramifications that can be used against the defendant.[5]

According to the opening statements (*exposição de motivos*) of the Criminal Procedure Code, criminal judges are supposed to find the *verdade real*, the judicial "real truth." (This contrasts with the *verdade formal*, the judicial "formal reality" that is reached at the civil proceedings, where only the plaintiffs are responsible for the production of evidence.) For this reason judges may bring up any facts they think are important to the proceedings, a practice that is consistent with the state's traditional role of "proceeding on its own accord," *ex-officio*, as in the old ecclesiastical and secular Portuguese criminal judicial proceedings. Most of the testimony of witnesses is given in an inter-rogation-like form, and thus witnesses are not heard in the form of exami-nation and cross-examination. Instead, it is possible to lead the witness as well as to ask questions that are not directly related to the facts at stake.

Likewise, jurors are not allowed to deliberate among themselves, and instead they must answer either yes or no to a formal list of questions (*quesi-tação*) that is prepared by the judge with the prior approval (or lack of approval) of the prosecution and counsel. The judge develops this list with the participation of the prosecution and defense, and s/he asks these ques-tions to the jurors in a secret room at the end of the trial. This proceeding takes the form of an *interrogatório* directed to evaluate the jurors' knowledge of the proceedings and/or of the law. Here, the judge asks very technical *per-guntas* (questions) on legal subjects, not questions on facts. In other words, the judge asks many things that the jurors do not know, instead of asking things they must know, as in the American examination and cross-examina-tion of witnesses. Finally, criminal judges are supposed to try according to their free judgment (their *livre convencimento*), and they are only limited by what is written in the records (the *autos*). The resulting inquisitorial-like police records (*inquéritos policias*) are literally sewn into the *autos*, becoming part of them and of their numbering sequence (*entranhados*). As such, according to the law their contents may influence the judge's decision.

Other judicial proceedings support the hypothesis that the inquisitorial legal principles found in the Brazilian criminal justice system are linked to the necessity of serving justice in a hierarchical society. For instance, the institution of a special prison (*prisão especial*) grants special conditions for those who are considered to have superior status—such as college graduates, members of the military, and even members of the boards of directors of unions—who have these privileges even when they are associated with com-mon people in the same case and accused of having committed a common crime. The Code also allocates jurisdictional and court privileges (*competên-cia por privilégio de função*) to people who are or were holding public office when they are accused of having committed a crime. They are granted these privileges even if they are accused of having committed common crimes that did not take place while or because they were performing their official duties.[6] Following the Mediterranean tradition (Peristiany 1965), criminal law also includes crimes against honor (*crimes contra a honra*) characteristic of hierarchical societies. In these societies, different laws rule relationships among distinct layers of citizens, and they are not enforced between the distinct classes but only internally, among peers. Thus, these rules are not, as in the legal tradition of the United States, universally applied to all citizens, even in theory.[7]

In addition to a hierarchical and nonuniversal system of laws, police procedures also play into a system of privileges. For example, because police procedures are officially inquisitorial, torture becomes a legitimate—even if unofficial—means of obtaining information or a confession. As a fact-finding technique, the Brazilian police's use of torture is not seen as simply police brutality, as would be the case in the United States, nor can it be explained merely as punishment of criminals and/or as deviance from ordinary police behavior. In addition to torture, the police, also unofficially, try cases and even purposely distort police records to avoid proper judicial trials. Sometimes these records are illegally retained by the police, on the request of lawyers and/or defendants (called *acautelamento do inquérito*), an action that consequently prevents the case from going on to the next step of judicial proceedings. This is all part of informal negotiations that may or may not include money and that are mediated by lawyers or by existing family, friendship, or police networks. The police are then blamed and accused of corruption and bribery; however, they officially have no discretionary powers, and therefore in a sense all the negotiations that ordinary police work involves are performed against the law.

In such circumstances, practically everything that the police and the judiciary have to do is not legal, and the criminal justice system's identity becomes ambiguous. Labelling illegal—or at the best unofficial—the criminal justice system's necessary negotiations, the Brazilian legal model encourages systematic suspicion, especially of negotiation and discretionary practices, in contrast to the model of systematic negotiation and the use of discretion in the United States. For the functioning of the system, it is always necessary to apply extremely general laws, usually federal ones, to the particular conditions of localities. Consequently, the application of the law is always particularized, personalized, and negotiated with respect to special social circumstances, in contrast with the system of universal application of the local laws to particular individuals and cases in the United States. It is obvious that responsibilities are very difficult to define in the Brazilian case, where the regular and gradual pattern of negotiation is imposed upon a gradual system of corruption: if every negotiation can be suspected as corrupt, then the question emerges, how does one sort out negotiations that are necessary for the functioning of the system from those that are made just for personal profit?

The Anglo-American Tradition of Negotiation and Trial-by-Jury

Legal traditions, both Brazilian and Anglo-American, have as a starting point in their contemporary history a common justification of the origins of the state judicial system. In fact, they agree that at the origins of the state institution there must be rational fact-finding methods that oppose facts to power. However, as was mentioned above, when it comes to the point of defining which judicial system the state must improve, there is no agreement between these different legal traditions.[8]

In the Anglo-American legal tradition, society is conceived to be in a state of turmoil where different individuals pursue distinct and frequently opposed interests. If those interests are left uncontrolled, social disorder and/or sheer oppression will be the consequences. The existence of a state judicial system is therefore justifiable as the very foundation of public order, a "necessary evil" or burden to be tolerated. The judicial system relies on general rules that are enforced and applied under a rational system of conflict resolution. However, the very existence of a public order and of state-controlled mechanisms of law enforcement is a permanent threat to the freedom of individuals and the community: the sovereign, who has imposed his justice over the barons' and the ecclesiastics' courts, must be controlled to prevent his abusing power.[9]

For this system, the means of controlling this uncomfortable but necessary centralized power is to decentralize the system of justice: the due process of law and the right to a fair trial is the right to a trial by the defendant's peers, according to the laws of the land. Here, the right to be tried by members of the defendant's community and according to the local laws assures that the individual's civil liberties, in any particular case, will not be suppressed by the sovereign.

In addition to this creative legal solution to the paradox of ensuring the individual's freedom in a state-controlled society, it is also interesting to note how this system deals with equality and hierarchy in society. In an aristocratic society, equality means similarity of social status. Thus, the peers who are supposed to try the accused and to serve justice are always, at least ideally, the defendant's peers: freemen try freemen, nobles try nobles, and so on. Initially, this fact-finding judicial system took an inquest-like form in which a group of peers who had previous knowledge of the facts tried the accused and had the mandatory task of answering the king's question on the defendant's guilt or innocence. The verdict was supposed to "state the truth" (*veredictum*). In this case, the evidence was not necessarily produced during the trial, because the facts already known by the judges could be an important part of the judicial decision-making. Furthermore, the verdict was not final, and an unsatisfied defendant could challenge the judges to a duel in order to prove his/her opinion and disprove the verdict.

In the Anglo-American tradition, this inquest system is said to have been gradually changed into the general judicial model of trial by jury. However, here the judges cannot know anything previously about the issues at stake, and all the evidence has to be produced before the court. The system also relies, on the one hand, on the presumption that everything that is said before the court is true, therefore holding responsible for perjury anyone who is proven to be lying. Everything that is said publicly is, thus, a fact. On the other hand, certain types of statements cannot be made publicly before the court, and consequently they are excluded from the trial according to exclusionary rules. The defendant is presumed innocent until proven guilty. The prosecution and counsel for the defense have theoretically equal opportunities to make their cases and give their arguments. This is why the system is called adversarial, and ultimately the judge is held responsible for compliance with these rules, which form the basis of a fair trial.

Both in Britain and in the United States the jury trial has been considered one of the most important guarantees of the citizen's civil liberties. However, there are significant differences between the forms of the institution in each society. In Britain, the concept of the "peer" evolved into a nonaristocratic but still elitist model in which the ideal jurors are currently supposed to be representative of a middle section of society, sharing the most common prejudices and values of their community. British judges are also said to interfere substantially with trial proceedings and outcomes, in contrast with the traditional role of American judges as referees. For instance, British judges may clearly disagree with the jurors' verdict (Devlin 1966).

In the United States, the jury trial puts into practice a different concept of equality: jurors are ideally supposed to be unbiased, without any prejudice concerning the issues at stake in a given case. Also, the judge is considered to be just a referee to what is sometimes figured as a "duel" between the prosecution and the defense counsel. As a result, in this tradition equality is associated with individualism; equality here means difference, not similarity. Defendants are not supposed to be tried according to the average moral prejudices of an ideal community, but by the unbiased decisions that are made individually by their fellow citizens. Unanimity requirements, for example, are sometimes not necessary for achieving verdicts, which can be reached through a majority vote (Murphy and Pritchett 1979; Rae 1981; Simon 1975).

However, the more important point is that while in the American judicial system trial by jury is the ideal model for adjudication, adjudication is *not* the ideal model for conflict resolution. In accordance with political and legal traditions that do not treat state rulings as trustworthy for private matters, negotiation is instead the ideal model. Actually, there is some evidence that points to private prosecution, not to trial by jury, as the most popular form of conflict resolution in American system until the beginning of this century, when public prosecution finally became mandatory (Steinberg 1984, 1989).[10] Still, whatever the legal tradition has been historically in the United States, the association of police discretion with the judicial discretion to prosecute and try has made police bargaining and judicial plea-bargaining the most common model for conflict resolution.

My observations of the system at work leave no doubt that the system encourages disciplinary over repressive techniques of social control,[11] and systematic negotiation instead of impartial adjudication: the general feeling is that a good deal will serve justice better than a reasonably fair trial, not only from the point of view of the defendant, but also from those of the state and victim. Moreover, negotiation is very cost effective for the community. Of course, a good deal presupposes a theoretically fair and explicit deal, with defendants being on a equal level with the public prosecutors and having clear knowledge of their rights, including the right to be tried by a jury, a condition that does not occur very often. In this system, then, adjudication is a kind of forced solution that may be unsatisfactory not only to the parties involved in the conflict but also to the taxpayers.

The consequence of this legal and cultural formula is that public order, in the most general cultural conception, is represented as the result of a consensus achieved through negotiation. Negotiation involves making explicit the contradictory interests at stake and the necessity of bargaining: everybody gives up something in order to get something out of the deal. It should be noticed that this legal principle also pervades jury trial proceedings: first, because through the exclusionary rules the facts that are made public to the jurors and to the audience are negotiated between the judge and the plaintiffs; second, because the verdict is a negotiated public decision among the jurors, inside the secret room.

A corollary is that on the one hand the system gives a general cultural emphasis to what can and cannot be done—or said—in public. In this realm the individual is never alone, s/he is always among peers who also have to pay attention to what they say or do, because everything publicly expressed may be used against the individual agent. On the other hand, only what is publicly said or done can be used legally against the individual. The police and the prosecution have to take this into consideration when they make their decisions to prosecute or try. What cannot be publicly produced, according to the rules of the game, whatever they were at a particular place or time, cannot become evidence and may not be taken into consideration by the jury. Police brutality may punish criminals but seldom convict them; thus, it has just the opposite effect as police torture in Brazil.

Finally, it should be clearly understood that the tradition of conflict resolution in the United States is deeply connected to that country's constitutional tradition. Constitutional law and criminal procedures are conceived of as two sides to the same coin: in the United States, the paradox of "having a government in a country of free citizens"—as the liberal Anglo-American legal scholars used to say—is placed in the hands of the judicial system. Verdicts in that system become precedents, and as a result jurisprudence becomes a way of making laws that is as effective and legitimate as legislation enacted by the legislature and enforced by the executive. The American legal tradition, on the one hand, emphasizes negotiation; on the other hand, it emphasizes an adjudication system that is also a realm where individuals, the community, and state interests have to get together and arrive at a decision—the verdict—in order to make the law for particular cases. The general law of the government is thus always universally applied through procedures of negotiation.

The Civil Law Tradition in Northern and Southern Continental Europe

As I mentioned above, legal traditions have in common as the justification for the existence of the modern state the necessity to implement a system of rational and impartial conflict resolution under a general system of law. However, institutional organization of social and public life has not developed the same way in the continental European culture as in the Anglo-

American culture. Especially after the French Revolution, countries on the continent consistently adopted Montesquieu's theory of strict separation of powers as the basis of their legal and political systems. The primary consequence was that for these systems legislative power was the only source of law. The executive function was to execute the law, and the judiciary function was to apply the law. The legislature was the only legitimate representative of the people's will, the only power which could legitimately make the law. The people's control over oppressive use of power, therefore, was conceived in terms of controlling the executive and judiciary state powers.[12]

For example, in the continental system judges were traditionally suspected of being "friends of the king"; therefore, laws must be as prospective, general, clear, and as detailed as possible in order to predict in every possible way any situation in which they would be applied. Ideally, detailed legislation of this type would prevent the judges from making biased interpretations when they applied the law. Consequently, legal expertise is the very foundation of the system, and knowledge of legal doctrines that inspired the codes (*direito*) is critical for the fairness of the application of the law. As the laws are generally codified, competition for better interpretations includes knowledge of the "keys" for the code, and it involves authors, nonauthors, and their respective followers in endless disputes, even when the law is not codified. The application of the law can only be evaluated and eventually criticized by experts: everything becomes a matter of authorized interpretation. This was how the civil law tradition developed into its present form, codified and written, and quite distinct from the Anglo-American common law tradition.

Legal procedures also developed quite differently. The inquest in continental Europe is said to have changed not into trial by jury, but instead into the *enquête* or *esquissa*. This system consists of the formulation of a public accusation which is then publicly investigated by the judiciary. After investigation, if evidence is found that a crime has been committed, and if there is evidence about who committed the crime, then a public accusation is made and adjudication becomes mandatory. There are only very few exceptions where judicial discretion can lead to avoiding a trial. The system does not encourage negotiation and the exercise of discretion through formally explicit proceedings, either administrative or judicial (for example, plea bargaining). On the contrary, from the outset negotiation is considered to be biased and partial, a form of avoiding proper judgment and therefore against the explicit goals of the administration of justice: trial becomes mandatory for the defendant, who apparently is merely the accused but actually at that point is already half convicted by the judicial investigators and legal experts. In this system, taking a conflict (be it civil or criminal) to the judiciary is undesirable because it is subject to the unofficial punishment of delays. On this perspective, asking for judicial remedies corresponds to asking for an outsider's intervention in private matters, a confession of lack of competence for solving one's own conflicts. Judicial intervention will be associated informally with punishment of the involved parties, who have renounced their negotiation privileges and must be subjected to every sort of punishment, which includes the judicial delay for attending their plea. As they have given up their own "time," they must be subjected to the "state time." Negotiations are legitimate in some cases, such as civil cases, but they should occur before the judicial proceedings have been initiated. After that, everybody (plaintiffs, defendants, and prosecutors) stands to lose, as occurred during the colonial judicial proceedings that were sent to Portugal for resolution (Schwartz 1973; Ana Miranda 1989).

Finding the truth in the civil law tradition is a matter of investigation, detection and interrogation, conducted by the judiciary, not by the community. Impartiality is associated with professional competence and legal expertise in the application of the law. The correct interpretation and application of the general law in any particular case is the main goal of the administration of justice. The judges' impartiality in this system is considered inherent in their status as public tenured civil service officials, and as such they are supposedly free from any bias that would result from pressures either from the government or from economic interests.[13]

In contrast to civil proceedings, where some adversarial principles are applied, criminal proceedings are mostly inquisitorially based, because they are supposed to find out not only what happened beyond a reasonable doubt, but what has happened beyond any doubt. This leads to a system where confession is the "queen of the proofs." Some legal scholars state that the fairness of the sentence is not linked to finding out what really happened because judicially it is only possible to have legal certainty. However, they add that confession is actually the only means of proof that ensures the fairness of the judge's sentence. If the judge has no available confession, uncomfortable probabilities and doubts that justice has been properly served will remain (see, e.g., Barandier 1985; Malatesta 1971).

The inquest, however, was not the only criminal fact-finding proceeding at work in continental Europe. According to Portuguese and Brazilian legal scholars, another kind of traditional proceeding was employed in Portugal (Mendes de Almeida 1973; Mendes de Almeida Júnior 1920). Called the *inquirição-devassa*, it was the main reference model for criminal fact-finding proceedings in Portugal and its colonies until 1821. The *inquirição-devassa*, or just *devassa*, developed first to find out the facts in cases of murder. Later, it became the main instrument of the Portuguese state for law enforcement and conflict adjudication. The main difference between the *devassa* and the inquest (also called *esquissa, enquête,* and *inquérito*) was that the *devassa* was a state proceeding held against the defendants without the previous knowledge of the defendant or defendants. It also could be started by the state of its own accord, *ex-officio*; that is, there was no necessity of either public or private charges or complaints.

The legal justification for this kind of judicial fact-finding proceeding was the existence of an explicit hierarchy in society. On the one hand, if public complaints or charges were necessary to start criminal proceedings, the lower classes would be afraid to accuse the powerful because they might take action against the accusers; on the other hand, if public accusations proved false against the high classes of society, their reputation would already be hurt. Serving justice therefore becomes equivalent to preserving and maintaining the *status quo ante*, the harmony of the already existing order as it was, with absence of conflict assumed to be the goal of public social life. For this reason, the state should take initial action through preliminary and secretive fact-finding proceedings. Only if enough evidence is collected beforehand would a formal criminal proceeding take place, starting with the defendant's interrogation and followed by the repetition of all the proceedings previously performed without the defendant's knowledge, but now performed in the defendant's presence. Only then could the defendant finally begin a defense against the public accusations. Adjudication, trial, and sentencing were mandatory at this point.

These *inquirições-devassas* did not even have to be triggered by a particular event. For instance, the Portuguese judicial system has a schedule for annual *devassas*, which were held during certain periods of the year, such as the *janeirinhas*, held every January. These were general *devassas*—such as the bishop's "visits" (*visitações*)—when judges came to towns to hear whatever the inhabitants would like to tell them. From the outset, the fact that those judges were from outside the village worked as a presumption of their unbiased behavior and judgment. The existence in the Portuguese judicial system of out-of-town judges (*juízes de fora*) also confirms the presumed positive correlation between disinterested parties and the impartiality of judicial decisions. This contrasts sharply with the Anglo-American legal tradition of trial by jury, where the best judgment is that of the local community and the solution for conflicts among hierarchically different individuals rested on a trial by known peers according to local laws, with evidence produced before the jurors in public proceedings that were accusatory and adversarial. The Portuguese legal tradition, in contrast, was based on preliminary inquisitorial state-produced evidence that was presented before judges brought from outside the community to ensure their impartiality. This colonial model was efficiently used by Portugal to control part of the Western world for quite a long period of time.

It is also evident that the Anglo-American system created another kind of public space: the preference for a negotiated settlement of disputes or even of a mandatory negotiated decision for conflict resolution imposed on the necessity of formal, and officially legitimated, negotiations. In order to settle the case, the implied parties had to state their interests explicitly and in public; however, if everything that is made explicit counted toward the decision, not everything must or could be said in public. In contrast, in the Portuguese system, which followed the ecclesiastical legal tradition, negotiations were always suspect and unofficial, notwithstanding their obviously necessary existence in order to apply the very general and distant law.[14] Any secret information could be used against individuals without their knowledge of their sources or of the methods employed to produce them. The confession as the final statement of the real truth was also the ultimate sign of the defendant's submission to the system. Relationships and borderlines between the public and the private realms are always blurred in the Portuguese tradition: the interpretation of intentionality of the facts is more important than the facts themselves.

Fact-Finding and Adjudicative Criminal Proceedings in Brazil

Brazilian criminal fact-finding proceedings are still said to have evolved gradually from the trial by jury to the French and Italian model of *inquéritos*, where preliminary inquisitorial-like proceedings, conducted by a specialized judge, were mixed with mandatory public accusation and defense. In fact, in Brazil after its independence in 1822 from Portugal, the 1831 Code of Criminal Procedures adopted the English model of trial by jury for the criminal justice system. Soon after that, however, in 1841, changes were made in the law to adapt the system to what the jurists called the Brazilian social reality. They argued that the jury system could not function because the low cultural level of the Brazilian people made them unable to understand the system.[15] Likewise, although colonial, pre-French Revolution, inquisitorial-like fact-finding proceedings were officially banned in 1821 from Portuguese and Brazilian law, comments and complaints against the remaining and current use of those proceedings constituted enough evidence that they were still in practice, and the complaints resulted in laws and resolutions against judicial and police officers, who were accused of still applying those methods, now against the law.[16]

By 1871—that is, shortly before the proclamation of the Republic in 1889—a mixed system was officially recognized and introduced into Brazil. At that time, in contrast to both the English and French systems, Brazilian law institutionalized a preliminary inquisitorial proceeding conducted not by a judge but by the judge's delegate, a police officer known as the *delegado*.[17] This proceeding could be, officially, purely inquisitorial, because it was not judicial: it was said to be merely auxiliary to the judiciary, an administrative action executed by the police, who are part of the state executive power.

After this preliminary police proceeding, a mixed judicial proceeding would be initiated if there was enough evidence for the prosecution to make a case. After the Republic was inaugurated, each state enacted its own code, but in 1941 the criminal procedures were again centralized and a federal code of criminal procedures was enacted. This code maintained the police inquiry (*inquérito policial*) as a preliminary administrative proceeding, inquisitorially conducted by the police *delegado*, a graduate civil police officer who is supposed to hold a law degree.[18]

After this preliminary proceeding, if the prosecution believes that a crime has been committed and if there is a probable perpetrator, the district attorney (*promotor*) files the charges (*denúncia*). The defendant is then called to be interrogated by the judge. If s/he is not found, the proceedings move on without the defendant's participation, and a defense counsel is appointed to represent him/her. The judge then hears witnesses for the prosecution and the defense in court, and finally the judge delivers the sentence, even if the defendant does not appear in court (*à revelia*). However, if the crime is an intentional crime against human life, the judge will deliver a sentence (*pronúncia*) which merely mandates a jury trial for the defendant, who then must appear in court in order for the trial to take place.

Jury trials begin by drawing the names of seven jurors from a set of twenty-one. The names of these twenty-one are drawn monthly from a list of two-to-five hundred names of individuals known or recommended by the judge and reviewed annually by the judge.[19] During the trial, proceedings held on the previous *inquérito* will be repeated: the defendant will be again interrogated by a judge, who usually is not the same individual who presided over the previous judicial proceedings. The judge then reads to the jurors the written records of the previous proceeding, including the written police records. Then, the prosecution and defense make final oral statements (*debates*) for two hours, with each side allotted a half hour to reply to the arguments of the other side, and with the defense always having the last word.[20] Jurors, who are not allowed to communicate either among themselves or with others during the trial, are taken to the jury room, together with the judge, the prosecutor, the defense lawyer, and the bailiff. A set of connected and correlated questions is asked of them, and they are required to answer yes or no, but still without any kind of discussion or communication among themselves. As they are seven in number, the verdict is reached by a majority vote, and counted after each of the judge's questions.

Brazilian criminal proceedings are consequently organized to show a gradual, step-by-step ritual of progressive incrimination and humiliation, the outcome of which must be either conviction or acquittal. The proceedings are represented as a punishment in themselves and must be performed even when the defendants confess their guilt. As a consequence, the courts are always behind schedule and overloaded, which seems to be one of the aims of the Brazilian judicial system, an important part of the punishment ritual for being involved, voluntarily or not, with state adjudication. This contrasts with the ideology of a "speedy trial" of the American legal tradition of trial by jury.[21]

Brazil and the United States: Public and Private Realms and the System of Conflict Resolution

When I first started looking into similarities and differences of truth-finding methods in Brazil and the United States, I learned that the general perspective which oriented most of the work done on this subject matter usually led to a comparison oriented mostly toward similarities rather than differences, that is, a method that proceeded in a way that the anthropologist Edmund Leach once said was characteristic of a "butterfly collection." Consequently, scholars usually concluded that comparison is impossible, or they ranked cultural differences according to a strong reductionist tendency that adopted as a point of reference those institutions for which the development is taken for granted and is well-known and predictable (e.g., the Anglo-American judicial system).

My purpose here, however, is different. I am not solely interested in challenging generally accepted views that affirm certain known trends toward progress, evolution, or social and economic development. Furthermore, as far as I can see, these are solidly established landmarks of our academic, legal, and political culture, and as such they have won a legitimate place in our theoretical sociological interpretations. What I am suggesting is that in order to enlarge our understanding of societies and cultures—and, especially, of Brazilian society and culture—emphasizing the differences may be better than ranking similarities found in distinct versions of Western culture.

On the one hand, explaining Brazilian society and culture with arguments that appeal only to supposedly backward characteristics not only may be a reductionist practice but also may prevent any real understanding of what is going on "down there," not only in Brazil but in South America as a whole. On the other hand, to suppose that the American system of conflict resolution is definitely protected against formal hierarchical, inquisitorial, and holistic elements means refusing to analyze the meaning of the practices actually performed by the social agents involved in the proceedings.

As we know, when it comes to the issue of the Brazilian and Latin American process of democratization, recent developments show, surprisingly, that the unintended effects of public policies and government action are more evident than the intended, highly predictable results. For instance, analysis conducted from the traditional perspective, which emphasizes legislative and constitutional practices and proceedings as general starting points for the process of democratization as a whole, are not able to identify and convincingly explain widely recognized "distortions" of the application of democratically elaborated and fully legitimated law. I suggest that these so-called distortions would be better understood if we were to look at the legislative and judiciary traditions of Brazilian culture.

Legitimate association of secrecy and inquisitoriality to hierarchy, made explicit in the legal justification for the *inquirição-devassa* proceedings, points to some very interesting characteristics of the contemporary societies of Brazil and the United States. The first is the particular definition and place of public and private realms. As I mentioned above, Brazil has inherited the

Portuguese colonial system of social control, which was not grounded on a clear separation between these realms: on the one hand, the judiciary and the police, and, on the other hand, the notaries (*cartórios*) were as two faces of a system of public/private transformations. The judiciary and the police decided when and what to negotiate, and in the process they decided to hide or make explicit conflicts, which in turn ended up being decided according to their own criteria.[22] The system of notaries decided which facts were the ones to be brought legitimately into the public realm. These facts are usually related to the legitimation of individuals' public identities (*registro civil*) and of transmission of property rights (*registros públicos*). As such, notaries become extremely important in the reproduction of Brazilian society, ultimately defining which individuals are legally part of each group.

Unlike this indefinite pattern of public/private relationships, the United States imposes a definite border between the two realms. As the system evolved, everything that is made public is supposed to express univocal meanings, from T-shirts to statements before the courts. On the opposite side of this public literality, individual privacy must be respected, and legal limits were imposed on state fact-finding procedures. However, this explicit model for conflict resolution is combined with a negotiation model, which must conform to the rules set for the judicial model. Of course, because the system emphasizes negotiation, bargaining is ultimately influenced by the actual status of the parties, and substantive differences related to their economic and political rank may enter into consideration, introducing hierarchy into the system.

Recent developments in the United States in official and unofficial fact-finding procedures point to increasing legitimation of secretive and inquisitorial-like means of producing evidence. Specifically, in the case of the procedures of several drug enforcement agencies, law enforcement seems to be perceived as a war, and consequently there are only practical limits placed on repressive action. Ends are claimed to justify the means, and negotiation becomes biased from the outset.

In the United States, however, the public realm is ideally the place of negotiated order, of contention and respect for the interests of distinct individuals, who have equal rights to their different individual identities. Thus, the public realm is not the place for the externalization of individual emotions. The system emphasizes dyadic relationships and networks as opposed to the emphasis on structured social frameworks in Brazil. In the United States, the "community" is the result of a voluntary association of individuals, as opposed to Brazilian groups (*grupos*), which are permanent and independent from the individuals. This is probably one of the reasons why Brazilian voluntary associations begin with statutes that will express this preexisting order, whereas voluntary associations in the United States will gather around practical issues that will be responsible for the building of a desired consensual order, only then made explicit in a set of rules.

It is not difficult to understand why patterns for conflict resolution will differ. In Brazil, the public realm will be the place where different orders—or different interpretations of a supposedly preexisting order—will meet, with previous hierarchical positions defining the outcomes of conflicts. The only place where the individual is free from disputing hierarchy is at home, in one's own house (*casa*), which ideally should extend its limits to the outside world, to the public realm of the street (*rua*, see DaMatta 1987). The extension of this private realm is intended to provide predictable outcomes to public conflicts. The public realm is thus a suspicious and indefinite area, where substantially different parties may engage in disputes, the settlement of which will rely on power sources located external to the disputing arena. Each party will try to impose its particular interest, with the use of external authority resources, in the name of reestablishing the always assumed preexisting harmony. The one who is able to present the best version of what would be the preexisting order, grounded on expertise and public authority, will win the feud.

As a consequence, for instance, in Brazil the police justify their use of deadly force as a fair proceeding to apply the law even when potentially violent situations are under control. In the United States, the police use deadly force in violent situations in order to bring them under control. In Brazil, police violence is a part of a collective negotiation unofficially conducted by the police. In the United States, it is the result of the failure of this negotiation. When the police kill in Brazil in a situation that is under control, they think that they are applying the general law of their society to a particular case, according to the general implicit principles for applying the law. When American police kill in a similar situation, they may be enforcing the law, but they do it in their own way, consequently in violation of the legal principles of universal application of the law that they are supposed to obey.

In the United States, public conflict is supposed to be solved by the universalistic, not particularistic, application of general rules. The state is the guarantor of this universal form of applying the law, which should allow the fair establishment of the facts. After that, each of the parties must argue on these grounds, until the best settlement is achieved for their interests. Public order is thus always negotiated, and there is not necessarily a winner of the conflict. Only when negotiation is impossible is judgment required, and mandatory adjudication will then solve the conflict.

Brazilian Decision-Making Processes in Comparative Perspective

These differences are responsible for distinct concepts of public life and public behavior. In Brazil, on the one hand, hierarchical and consequently holistic arguments are compatible with inquisitorial proceedings, in order to maintain the previously established hierarchy. However, Brazilian constitutional dispositions, connected with the Western legal and democratic political tradition, emphasize adversarial proceedings associated with egalitarianism and individualism. Explicitly different official mechanisms for conflict resolution, oriented according to different legal principles, are put together in the same society. The consequence is that the context for conflict resolution becomes ambiguous and the accusatory principles, linked to literality and explicit opposition, lose their power and credibility. The judiciary slowness traditionally functions as a forum for solving conflicts extrajudicially under the excuse of lack of resources and case overload. However, it turns against the institution in a modern cultural framework, where the judiciary must be an efficient and speedy alternative for resolving conflicts.

As a consequence, concepts and categories such as obedience/*obediência*, public/*público*, equality/*igualdade*, and their opposites cannot be translated literally, as is also the case for the judicial categories of the distinct procedures discussed above. In the American system, "obedience" would mean compliance to a consensual decision; "public" would mean a realm of contention and necessary respect for other individuals' spaces in order to avoid conflict; and the right to "equality" would be the right that individuals have to be themselves, to be different, and not to conform to anyone else.

In the Brazilian system, *obediência* means submission to the imposition of another individual's perspective or rule over oneself, something always undesirable, if unavoidable; *público* means a realm where one preferably would remain silent, accepting the shield of an externally given identity, which ensures mutual recognition, under a previously existing public order (and conflict arises from either ignorance of hierarchy or from disputes of status and hierarchical authority among "peers"); and *igualdade*, therefore, will mean similarity of status, leading to an assumed similarity of perspective on the established order, given not by individual opinion but by the mandatory perspective resulting from the same social position in hierarchy.

These features are not restricted to the criminal justice system. In Brazil, hierarchy associated with inquisitoriality has led to the privatization of information as a legitimate method for the distribution and control of power resources: if bureaucrats do so, most of the people who use public services feel that this is an uncomfortable, but acceptable, behavior. This is even the case of the National Security Information Services, the information of which could be used to produce legal effects against individuals with records on their files.

Here again, the borderline between the public and the private realm has not been clearly and previously defined: on the one hand, this lack of definition gives way to the so-called practice of *casuismo*, an exceptional decision-making process always suspected of favoring one party against the other; on the other hand, as the model inhibits negotiation and makes discretion suspect, it becomes actually impossible to investigate, to try, and to make any given public officer responsible for anything. If everything is a question of degree, nobody should start accusing anyone, because "quem tem telhado de vidro não joga pedra no telhado do vizinho" (those who have a glass roof don't throw stones on their neighbor's roof), or better, as a well-known gambler (*bicheiro*) said in an interview with the national press, we are all guilty of misdemeanors ("somos todos contraventores").

Academic relationships also are a privileged locus for observing these paradoxes at work. The patterns for using public libraries, very similar to the description of the abbey library in Umberto Eco's *The Name of the Rose*; the scholastic argumentative rhetoric, much more fond of arguments by authority than of the authority of arguments; the patterns for disputing in public and for editing and publishing; the principles underlying the production, circulation, and reproduction of cultural and intellectual goods—these are all clearly compatible with the Brazilian legal and political cultural model for truth-finding methods and conflict resolution (Kant de Lima 1992a).

Finally, the domestic realm is quite rich in examples related to the adaptation of this general model: in any authority relationship, the patterns which organize the relationships among the parties—whether they are housewives/domestic servants, parents/children, whites/blacks, men/women, etc.—may legitimately follow hierarchical and inquisitorial principles, despite any explicit contrary arguments made by the involved social agents.

In Brazil, police officers publicly encourage citizens not to stop at red lights when driving, apparently to preserve their safety while driving (from being robbed); as a consequence, nobody stops at red lights in any circumstance when they think that it is safe to cross, and they do not expect to be punished for this transgression. However, illegal gambling such as the *jogo do bicho* is well known for being the only context in which explicit rules are obeyed, always meaning literally what is written on the bets (*vale o que está escrito*). Peculiar relationships between the explicit and the implicit, the public and the private, certainly make of the Brazilian cultural context a quite unique and frequently not fully comprehended version of Western culture.

Solutions for the paradox of individual freedom in a state-controlled society never being the same, it is my point here that fact-finding procedures of Portuguese secular criminal procedure law with an ecclesiastical origin, namely the *inquirição-devassa*, were linked to particular representations of hierarchical principles in the organization of society. This association, although it is thought of as merely historical and currently completely overcome in Brazilian society, can still be identified in contemporary Brazilian criminal procedures and practices.

Of course, this is critically relevant to the understanding of the relationships between the legal and political systems in Brazilian society, including the definition of the current meaning of citizenship and democracy. Hierarchical and inquisitorial practices, easily identifiable in many everyday occasions—as in the "Você sabe com quem está falando?" ("Do you know who you're talking to?"), a traditional Brazilian ritual for conflict resolution studied by DaMatta (1991)—must not be understood or explained as undesirable distortions of an egalitarian, individualistic, or modern political system, but as the core of another legal and political culture, which is complementary to the first, in a well-known mechanism of Brazilian perverse syncretism.

Despite these differences it is important to notice that Brazil is a representative of the New World, of America, and as such it is a country made of voluntary and forced immigrants, who also killed almost all the native inhabitants in order to build a new version of European society. If its cultural roots are peculiar and different from other versions of America, it is critical to understand how that is so if one is to predict accurately any possible developments of Brazilian society.[23] The better people understand the options for decision-making processes, the better their political systems will operate.

As emerging structural tensions in modern society—between the units and the whole, the subjects and the sovereign, the citizens and the state— have had distinct solutions, proposed by different legal-political traditions, it is my belief that making explicit these contrasts, which are a part of the legal cultures' myths and traditions, will lead us to a better understanding of the relationships between the citizens and the state, the individuals and society, the public and the private realms. I also hope that this discussion may also shed light upon the different meanings of the apparently univocal social behavior in Brazil and in the United States today.

Acknowledgments

Data on the Brazilian criminal justice system were collected with the institutional support of CAPES, CPNq, and the Universidade Federal Fluminense (UFF). Research on the American criminal justice system was conducted from February to June 1990, in Birmingham, Alabama, and San Francisco, California; it was supported by USIS, the Fulbright Commission, UFF, CAPES, and the University of Alabama at Birmingham. Preliminary versions of this text were presented at the Kellogg Institute for International Research, University of Notre Dame; the School of Social Sciences, University of California at Irvine; and the UCLA Latin American Center. I am indebted to all the participants, as well as those who provided emotional and financial support and/or helped me to clarify my ideas on the subject: Roberto DaMatta, Belinda MacCarthy, Eric Monkkonnen, Jack Katz, George Bisharat, James Ferguson, Liisa (sic) Malkki, Charles Lindholm, Nelson and Edméa Jobim, Laura Nader, Glaucia Maria Pontes Mouzinho, Marco Antônio da Rocha, and Raymundo Romêo, as well as to all my American friends and/or informants on the Anglo-American criminal justice system who always provided very insightful remarks on my work. I am also indebted to David Hess for the accurate and generous editing, revisions, and notes, and to him and Roberto DaMatta for publishing the text.

Endnotes

1. Ed. note: The term "truth-finding" or "fact-finding" is a technical term in the English language that refers to any legal procedures that lead to conflict resolution in a so-called "rational" judicial system.

2. Ed. note: Brazilians tend to use the words "North American" (*norte americano*) or "United Stateser" (*estados unidense*) for a resident of the United States, and they reserve the term "American" (*americano*) for the residents of the entire Western Hemisphere. They are insistent on this point, and they find the "American" use of the term "American" imperialistic. However, this essay will follow the standard English-language usage, because the term "North American" for a resident of the United States might be offensive to Canadian and Mexican readers, and there is no other English-language word available at this time.

3. Constitutions in Brazil are also codified; that is, they are written in a sequential order of titles, chapters, and articles that ideally should formulate and make explicit legal and political theories and trends. Consequently, from time to time they become old and must be totally changed.

4. For a more extended discussion of this subject, see Kant de Lima (1990).

5. Recent debate in Brazil involved members of the intelligence agencies and right-wing politicians who wished to keep secret some of the intelligence records. Members of the agencies argued that in the entire democratic world this was a common procedure that was justified "by reasons of state." What they did not mention was that in Brazil this secret information may initiate a police investigation (*inquérito policial*) against citizens and consequently contribute effectively to their judicial conviction. For more information and a discussion of the institutional process for conflict resolution in Brazil in the criminal justice system as well as in the academy, from a comparative point of view, see Roberto Kant de Lima (1986, 1989, 1990, 1992a, 1992b).

6. See Código de Processo Penal, Article 295.

7. For example, such codes were evident in the treatment of the accused in incidents involving the family of Brazilian President Fernando Collor de Mello. In an honor dispute involving allegations that the President's wife mismanaged funds during her term as the director of a public welfare agency, the mayor of their hometown challenged them, and the President's wife's brother is said to have attempted to murder him. At the time, her brother received preferential treatment in both the police and the judiciary proceedings.

8. Here, I follow Pierre Bourdieu's methodological procedure of identifying "dominant conditioning questions" which are the subjects that all the legal authors agree to discuss, even when they disagree on the substance of the matter. Among his works that clarify and discuss this methodological option, see especially Bourdieu (1967, 1969, 1973, 1975, and 1982).

9. For discussions of the Anglo-American legal tradition, see Berman (1983), Bloomstein (1968), Dawson (1960), Devlin (1966), Kalven (1976), McCart (1964), Moschzisker (1930), Murphy and Pritchett (1979), Parry (1975), Simon (1975), and Spooner (1971).

10. Private prosecution, of course, is quite the structural opposite of the Portuguese state tradition of "proceeding on its own accord" (ex-officio). In the American legal tradition, prosecution could only be continued if provoked and sustained by the interested parties.

11. Here, I am referring to Foucault's discussion of Western models for social control. See, for instance, Foucault (1977, 1979, 1983).

12. Usually, comparisons between the American and British legal traditions, as well as between the civil law and Anglo-American common law traditions, are made in order to demonstrate the superiority of one over the other. Of course that is not the purpose here, because the methodological approach is one

of contrasting to compare (as in current developments in the anthropological tradition), and not to compare in order to make judgements. On these different comparative perspectives, see on the one hand the essay "Local Knowledge: Fact and Law in Comparative Perspective," by the anthropologist Geertz (1983), and on the other hand the work of legal experts (Hughes 1985 and Merryman 1969).

13. For a comparison of the American and French judicial systems, especially in respect to the role of the judges, see Tocqueville (1945); for a discussion of the Brazilian case, see Arruda Jr. (1991).

14. See, for example, the description of the legal proceedings of the ecclesiastic *inquisitio on canonic codes in Código de Derecho Canónico y Legislación Complementaria* (Madrid: Biblioteca de Autores Cristianos, 4th ed., 1951: Canon 1939-53), and *Código de Direito Canônico* (São Paulo: Edições Loyola, 1983: Canon 1717-1719).

The Portuguese ecclesiastic system never restricted spontaneous confessions, that is, accusations that were not obtained by coercion. They were called self-accusations (*auto-acusações*) and they actually constituted a form of plea-bargaining in which the defendant admitted a minor infraction to escape from a major accusation, which in turn could lead in some cases to the Portuguese metropolitan Courts of Inquisition (Boschi 1987). Today this form of negotiation is considered a crime similar to perjury, and both are prohibited in the Brazilian criminal code (articles 341–342). This contrasts with the defendant's right to lie on his/her own behalf in Brazilian criminal proceedings.

15. For a discussion of this subject and this period, see the excellent work by Flory (1981).

16. One of these resolutions was the *Aviso* dated April 30, 1855. For a detailed description of these facts, see Mendes de Almeida Júnior (1920, vol. 2: 76-77).

17. *Delegados,* unlike representatives, act on their own behalf, without consulting their original base of power.

18. See articles 4–23 (Decreto-Lei No. 3689, October 3, 1941) in *Código de Processo Penal* (São Paulo: Sugestões Literárias, 1981).

19. In this sense, the jurors must be "persons," not anonymous citizens, as in the Anglo-American system. Actually, many judges try to call as jurors important people, but usually only public civil servants have availability to perform the required duties, because they must be available not only for one trial, but for the whole month.

20. The Brazilian legal rhetoric used in these debates is quite different from that of the United States. The Brazilian style is scholastic; in other words, it opposes distinct and successive theses that are defended until the debating time runs out. No notes are taken on these debates, which use argument by authority most of the time, in contrast with the American style of argument by the

facts. Interrogation of the defendant and, when it occurs, of witnesses, is performed in inquisitorial style of asking leading questions, in contrast with the examination and cross-examination that is characteristic of American jury trials. In fact, Brazilian jury trials are not really trials by jury, but instead a scholastic oral confrontation between the counsel for the defense and the district attorney.

21. For a discussion of the American constitutional rights as guaranteed in the American Constitution, see Corwin (1978).

22. For more information on the historical traditions of the Brazilian judiciary, see Schwartz (1970, 1973).

23. Recent political facts in Brazil may exemplify this point. President Fernando Collor's strategy of modernization of the Brazilian economy and society seems to be implemented by very inquisitorial strategies, which include blocking checking and savings accounts for the whole population without any previous discussion or warning. Rules for the Brazilian Internal Revenue Service have also been changed many times in the same fiscal year, with the result being that the government was unable to collect taxes at the proper time in 1991. This style of modernization seems to conform to some Latin American examples of the *caudillos*, or charismatic leaders who have promoted transformations in their societies, despite their traditional background, and considered to be populist but inadequate to the role of modern democratic leadership.

References

Ana Miranda
  1989 *Boca no Inferno*. Rio de Janeiro: Companhia das Letras.
Arruda Jr., Edmundo Lima de
  1991 *Lições de Direito Alternativo*. São Paulo: Editora Acadêmica.
Barandier, Antonio Carlos
  1985 "Confissão: Supremo Objetivo da Investigação." In Julita Lemgruber (ed.), *A Instituição Policial*. Special issue of *Revista da OAB/RJ* 22(July): 113–28.
Berman, Harold J.
  1983 *Law and Revolution: The Formation of the Western Legal Tradition*. Cambridge: Harvard University Press.
Bloomstein, Morris J.
  1968 *Verdict: The Jury System*. New York: Dodd, Mead.
Boschi, Caio C.
  1987 "Inquisição na Colônia." In *Revista Brasileira de História* (São Paulo) 7(14).
Bourdieu, Pierre
  1967 "Systems of Education and Systems of Thought." *International Social Science Journal* 19(3): 338–58.

1969 "Intellectual Field and Creative Project." *Social Science Information* 8(2): 89–119.

1973 "Le marché de biens symboliques." *L'Année Sociologique* 22: 49–126.

1975 "The Specificity of the Scientific Field and the Social Conditions of the Progress of Reason." *Social Science Information* 14(6): 19-47.

1982 *Ce que parler veut dire. L'Économie des échanges linguistiques.* Paris: Fayard.

Corwin, Edward S.

1978 *The Constitution and What it Means Today.* Princeton: Princeton University Press.

DaMatta, Roberto

1987 *A Casa e a Rua.* Rio de Janeiro: Guanabara.

1991 *Carnivals, Rogues, and Heroes.* Notre Dame, Ind.: University of Notre Dame Press.

Dawson, John P.

1960 *A History of Lay Judges.* Cambridge: Harvard University Press.

Devlin, Sir Patrick

1966 *Trial By Jury.* London: Stevens.

Dumont, Louis

1977 *From Mandeville to Marx: The Genesis of Economic Ideology.* Chicago: University of Chicago Press.

1980 *Homo Hierarchicus.* Chicago: University of Chicago Press.

1983 *Essais sur l'individualisme: Une perspective anthropologique sur l'ideologie.* Paris: Collection Esprit/Seuil.

Flory, Thomas

1981 *Judge and Jury in Imperial Brazil, 1808-1871: Social Control and Political Stability in the New State.* Austin: University of Texas Press.

Foucault, Michel

1977 *Discipline and Punish: The Birth of the Prison.* New York: Pantheon.

1979 *The History of Sexuality.* Vol. 1. London: Allen Lane.

1983 "Afterword." In Hubert Dreyfus and Paul Rabinow (eds.), *Michel Foucault: Beyond Structuralism and Hermeneutics.* Chicago: University of Chicago Press.

Geertz, Clifford

1983 *Local Knowledge: Further Essays in Interpretive Anthropology.* New York: Basic Books.

Hughes, Graham

1983 "We Try Harder." *New York Review of Books* March: 17-18.

Kalven, Jr., Harry, and Hans Zeisel

1976 *The American Jury.* Chicago: University of Chicago Press.

Kant de Lima, Roberto

1986 *Legal Theory and Judicial Practice: Paradoxes of Police Work in Rio de Janeiro City.* Ph.D. dissertation, Harvard University. Ann Arbor: Mich.: University

Microfilms. (Portuguese edition: *A Polícia da Cidade do Rio de Janeiro: Seus Dilemas e Paradoxas*. Rio de Janeiro: Biblioteca da Polícia Militar do Estado do Rio de Janeiro, 1994.)

1989 "Cultura Jurídica e Práticas Policiais: A Tradição Inquisitorial." *Revista Brasileira de Ciências Sociais* (ANPOCS/Rio de Janeiro) 10(4, June): 65–84.

1990 "Constituição, Direitos Humanos e Processo Penal Inquisitorial: Quem Cala, Consente?" *DADOS, Revista de Ciências Sociais*. 33(3): 471–88.

1992a "The Anthropology of the Academy: When We Are the Indians." In David Hess and Linda Layne, eds., *Knowledge and Society*. Vol. 9: *The Anthropology of Science and Technology*. Greenwich, Conn.: JAI Press. (Translation of *A Antropologia da Academia: Quando os Indios Somos Nós*. Niterói: UFF; Petrópolis: Vozes.)

1992b "Tradição Inquisitorial no Brasil, da Colônia à República: Da Devassa ao Inquérito Policial." *Religião e Sociedade* (ISER/RJ) 16(1/2).

Malatesta, Nicola Framarino Dei
1971 *A Lógica das Provas em Matéria Penal*. Vol. 1. São Paulo: Editora Saraiva.

McCart, Samuel W.
1964 *Trial by Jury*. New York: Chilton Books.

Mendes de Almeida Júnior, João
1920 *O Processo Criminal Brazileiro*. 3d ed. 2 vols. Rio de Janeiro: Typographia Baptista de Souza.

Mendes de Almeida, Joaquim Canuto
1973 *Princípios Fundamentais de Processo Penal*. São Paulo: Editora Revista dos Tribunais.

Merryman, John Henry
1969 *The Civil Law Tradition*. Stanford: Stanford University Press.

Moschzisker, Roberto von
1930 *Trial by Jury: A Brief Review of its Origin, Development, and Merits and Practical Discussions on Actual Conduct of Jury Trials, Together with Consideration of Constitutional Provisions and Other Cognate Subjects of Importance*. Philadelphia: Geo. T. Bisel.

Murphy, Walter and Herman C. Pritchett
1979 *Courts, Judges, and Politics: An Introduction to the Judicial Process*. New York: Random House.

Parry, L. A.
1975 *The History of Torture in England*. Montclair, N.J.: Patterson Smith.

Peristiany, J. G.
1965 *Honour and Shame: The Values of Mediterranean Society*. London: Weidenfeld and Nicholson.

Rae, Douglas et al.
1981 *Equalities*. Cambridge: Harvard University Press.

Schwartz, Stuart B.

1970 "Magistracy and Society in Colonial Brazil." *Hispanic American Historical Review* 50 (Nov.): 715–30.

1973 *Sovereignty and Society in Colonial Brazil: The High Court of Bahia and Its Judges, 1609-1751.* Berkeley: University of California Press.

Simon, Rita James (ed.)

1975 *The Jury System in America: A Critical Overview.* Beverly Hills: Sage.

Spooner, Lysander

1971 *An Essay on the Trial by Jury.* New York: Da Capo Press.

Steinberg, Allen

1984 "From Private Prosecution to Plea Bargaining: Criminal Prosecution, the District Attorney, and American Legal History." *Crime and Delinquency* 30(4): 568-92.

1989 *The Transformation of Criminal Justice.* Chapel Hill, N.C.: University of North Carolina Press.

Tocqueville, Alexis de

1945 *Democracy in America.* New York: Knopf.

Chapter Eleven

For an Anthropology of the Brazilian Tradition or *"A Virtude está no Meio"*

⊠

Roberto DaMatta

For generations, Latin America has had its share of observers who like to prove that the continent is a true logical disaster. More precisely, it's a sociological disaster![1] The problem is that these observers rarely question their own starting point. They assume their position to be logical and precise to the extent that they are part of a system capable of defining itself with a word (capitalism, modernity, progress), two or three well-known concepts (usually made up by the observers, and on their own terms), and only one sort of logic—the excluded middle (the *tertium non datur* of the ancient philosophers)—that does not allow apples and oranges to mix. But none of this works for the so-called "Latin American reality."[2]

To define this region politically (and sociologically), one must use at least five concepts and two sets of logic, because south of the Rio Grande and below the equator we run on samba, *pisco*, *caudillismo*, Carnival, and a kind of historical belly laugh that echoes through a "living museum."[3] Or, as Howard Wiarda (1974) has said, Latin America is an extraordinary place, where "virtually all the systems of society that have ever governed [human] affairs continue to exist." In listing its characteristics, he creates an image that makes Jorge Amado's magical Bahia, Guimarães Rosa's fantastic *sertão* (backlands), Mario de Andrade's hallucinated São Paulo, Jorge Luis Borges' cities of the absurd, and Gabriel García Márquez's renowned Macondo—look like the most well-behaved places on earth.[4] Wiarda attributes this image to the

"A virtude está no meio"—"the virtue lies in between." The essay is dedicated to Richard Morse.

absence of any genuine social revolution, which has permitted the continuing coexistence of Thomism, divine-right monarchy, feudalism, autocracy, republicanism, liberalism, and all the rest (1974: 214).[5]

Brazilian specialists are not far behind and today can easily declare that in Brazil and Latin America we have a "class society" oddly coupled with clientelism, syndicalism, corporatism, and strong-arm bossism—all of it filtered through bureaucratic enclaves. This leads to the conclusion that we are not simply a living museum but a surgical room for conceptual and symbolic operations where everything is "out of place" but enjoys a theoretical free voucher. In other words, what one discovers in the Brazilian or Latin American "reality" is isomorphic to those fashionable studies that trace every twist and turn of every theoretical current of the political and social sciences. Just as Latin America was considered in the late nineteenth century a living museum of races mixed in strange and troubling ways, so today it horrifies observers as a political, juridical, and social kaleidoscope—especially (and this is always camouflaged in the analysis) because one speaks here of *another* "American" reality, one without social "linearity," where time seems to have passed without generating "history." What in fact this traditional vision hooks onto is a mysterious "blend" of institutional forms that apparently has no grammar.[6] Thus we jump from exaggeration to exaggeration, finding everything imaginable in Brazil, and, fascinated by theoretically and ideologically impossible permutations, we end up more interested in listing theoretically implausible amalgams than in exploring their deeper logic. In short, we sidestep fundamental issues.

One issue arises with the concept of tradition, the use of which has blocked any understanding of Latin American societies. When one speaks of tradition, care should be taken to avoid turning it into a mystery. To do this is to fall into a relativism that social anthropology has consistently avoided. Human societies are certainly diverse, but once differences are discovered, one must show how one difference can be turned into another; that is, one must go back over the road, retracing it inversely. Otherwise, all that is left is a catalogue of mutually inaccessible human experiences. Traditions reveal not only differences but similarities as well. Richard Morse was one of the first in the field of Latin American studies to show that traditions should be studied as "choices" or "options"—that is, as alternatives, made up of relatively integrated and dynamic groups of decisions about what to be, to do, to think; in a word, about what to value.[7] But there is only one road to get there: the contrast among various levels of different traditions.

If the concept of tradition is not seen as dynamic, it merely serves to legitimate domination, freezing differences and screening out an understanding of reality. So if there is, in fact, an "Ibero-American tradition," one must take a different route than do most scholars to reach it. We cannot allow ourselves to be content with the identification of the components of our tradition. The mere classification of butterflies—as Sir Edmund Leach said in 1961—is one thing, but it reveals little about the nature of these creatures. To break out of the routine of Latin American studies, it is necessary to give more weight to the less eloquent words of traditional descriptions. That is, we should be less taken with the fact that we might have Thomism, autocracy, and republicanism in Latin America and more concerned with words such as "mixture," "confusion," "combination," and others that designate what should really be understood: interstices and simultaneity or, simply, relations (DaMatta 1985, 1986a, 1986b, 1991).

Most authors who focus on the "Latin American" tradition address its constituent characteristics rather than relational ties among them and their underlying logic. Without recognizing such ties I do not think that an understanding of what constitutes tradition is possible. Every tradition implies a choice, a compromise (Morse 1982) and, obviously, a legitimacy (or explicit recognition of its elements, logic, and message). In this sense every tradition is a fact of conscience (or a "moral fact," in Durkheim's term) and a selection. It is a fact of conscience because every tradition tells us what should be remembered (and almost with what intensity and when) and what should be forgotten. It is a selection because a tradition implies distinctions within a sphere of infinite social possibilities and historical experiences. For example, a process of selection is involved in the Brazilian concept of race relations. The "fable of the three races" was a Brazilian cultural invention that had little to do with an "empirical" history of our racial differentiations (DaMatta 1981: 58ff.). But in order to situate this fundamental point of "Brazilian national ideology," it is necessary to contrast the way in which relations are conceived in Brazil and the United States.

In both countries, blacks, whites, and Indians played important roles in territorial conquest, colonization, and creation of a national conscience; but in the United States social identity was not constructed upon a fable of the three races that shows blacks, whites, and Indians to be symbolically complementary. In fact, America was founded on the ideology of the white element. Thus, in order to be an American one must be encompassed by the values and institutions of the "Anglo" world, which retains hegemony and operates in terms of a bipolar logic founded on exclusion.[8] In Brazil, the experience of slavery and of the diverse Indian tribes that occupied the territory colonized by the Portuguese generated a radically different mode of perception. This view is based on the notion of an "encounter" among the three races that occupy differentiated but equivalent positions in an ideological triangle. In Brazil, therefore, "Indians," "whites," and "blacks" relate via a logic of inclusion that is articulated on planes of complementary opposition. In this fashion, Brazil can be read as being "white," "black," or "Indian," depending on the aspects of Brazilian culture and society one might wish to accentuate (or negate). Brazilians can say that on the plane of happiness and rhythm, Brazil is "black"; it is "Indian" with respect to tenacity and synchronization with nature; and all of these elements are articulated by a language and social institutions of the "white" element (the Portuguese) that, within this ideological conception, acts as the catalyst that combines them into a coherent and harmonious mixture. It should not be forgotten that the *mestiço* (as a valued cultural category) is a fundamental aspect of Brazilian national ideology in contrast to the United States, where mixture and ambiguity are still highly negative elements. These ideologies come to the fore once again in the notion that the United States was produced historically; that is, it was founded on a gradual and linear implementation of Puritan values in a territory that was expanding. In Brazil, on the other hand, one speaks of discovery, a chance discovery in fact, which allows for the articulation—on a richly symbolic plane—of the idea of luck, encounter, miracle, mixture, hierarchy, and complementary relationships among different elements.[9]

In short, the same empirical elements that permeate the entire history of the Americas are combined and experienced in different ways in each society in the process of constituting their respective social identities. The United States's identity emphasizes the Puritan tradition, founded on a logic of exclusion that considers undesirable anyone who is not a member of the parish: one is a "member of the community" or one is outside of it, and all members are equal in accordance with the constitutional laws that govern it. In Brazil, although these elements are recognized and, in fact, adopted as part of its legal and "constitutional" framework, the values of complementarity, inclusion, and hierarchy are emphasized.[10] Racial ideology follows the same logic as other social institutions, in which an ideological pact hides or disguises differences, thereby making the ideology complementary. In the United States, the difference is undisguisable and produces a real dilemma, as Gunnar Myrdal taught us in his studies of American race relations (1962). In other words, in the society with an egalitarian credo, race relations reintroduce hierarchy by way of a natural ("racial") code, but in a society whose daily life is founded on inequality, the experience of different ethnicities does not spill out of the personal and quotidian sphere and thus allows for the creation of a fable that treats the three races as complementary and, at this level, equivalent. The result is the "equal but different" principle that Otávio Velho (1985) suggests might be the touchstone of an individualistic socio-logic. Relational logic would be founded on the opposite principle and would go something like this: "together and differentiated in a complementary fashion." In the American case, mediations are obviously impossible: one is black or white or Indian. In the Brazilian case, mediations are not only possible but fundamental.

As Louis Dumont says, contrast among traditions allows us to perceive their values, or their encompassing elements. To state that the Ibero-Latin tradition is a scandalous combination of feudalism, Thomism, capitalism, liberalism, hierarchy, favors, corporatism, class domination, bureaucratic insulation, dualistic reason, and whatever else one wants to throw into the stew (*feijoada*) is of little use—unless the respective weight and significance of each element within the tradition are analyzed.[11]

To say that in Brazil the deep-seated combination of slavery (and of "favor" as a system) with liberal ideas is a social and political scandal, a symptom of "impropriety," and obviously inconsistent morphologically, as Roberto Schwarz did, brilliantly and precisely, is to give up too soon. Everyone knows that in Brazil (as throughout Latin America) everything is "out of place." But why wouldn't it be?[12] And what logic presides over this apparently prelogical untidiness? This is precisely the question that nobody asks! And for this reason the Brazilian tradition and the institutional framework that it legitimates becomes such a tremendous mystery. Nonetheless, the puzzle begins to make sense when one reflects about the place of favor, of patronage, and of personal relations in the Brazilian social system, contrasting their importance with their role in liberalism. One then discovers what was tacitly known, that the personal relations and impersonal rules on which liberalism is based exist side by side in mutually exclusive, although complementary, social spheres.

In Brazil, liberalism is a matter for government and the world of economics—metaphorically, the universe of the street—while the ideology and values of favor and patronage in general function in the universe represented by the metaphor of the home. Not only does each set of values carry a different weight, but they move in very different spheres. Thus, the following type of circular logic may arise: precisely because I am a liberal in Congress (i.e., as recognized in national public life), I have the "right" to be a slave-holder or a paternalist at home! To use the very example of Machado de Assis, it is precisely because Machado is "a combative journalist and an enthusiast of the proletarian intelligence, of the classes," that he may also be (within the system that separates the streets and the home) the "author of chronicles and commemorative pieces on the occasion of the marriage of imperial princesses . . . a knight and eventually an Official of the Order of the Rose" (Schwarz 1977: 21). His behavior in the street seemed to confer the right to be opposite at home. Would this be a personal inconsistency or a deeply rooted manifestation of a system that does not operate in linear terms and is not, in fact, governed by a single set of rules?

In my opinion, the analysts have contented themselves too easily with identifying the duality and taking it as something simply incoherent and "out of place." But why can it not be a self-referential duality, founded in "hierarchical opposition"? In this case, it would be important to examine how the behavior of certain people changes in accordance with where they are. This changing behavior could reveal a logic to the cynicism or apparent confusion that in turn might be more than a mere symptom of the tragi-comedy that history seems to have reserved for Brazil.

When we investigate Brazilian reality, we are rarely able to do so from within the framework of Brazilian social logic; nor are we able to break out of the logical straitjackets we accept along with the grand intellectual designs of the West. From them we learned that ideological contradictions lead to conflict and profound social transformations. In the United States, however, the presence of two contradictory ideas presupposes a homogeneous setting wherein conflictive coexistence is its own "natural" resolution. But in Brazil and in the rest of Latin America contradiction merely engenders inflamed speeches in public and lively sessions of anecdotes at home.[13]

In a discontinuous medium, contradictory ideas can be hierarchically arranged on different planes, such that for some things I am a liberal and for others I am paternalist or patronal. The system allows me to use my right hand or my left hand to do different things and to give different meanings to the experiences of life. Certain anthropologists have shown that the right hand dominates for official purposes, while for others, such as washing one-self or having sexual relations, the left hand is key.[14] It is precisely for this rea-son that Carnival, a rite of inversion that was used as a form of social protest and transformation in certain European countries (see Davis 1975), has a secure place in Brazilian society alongside the solemn civil rites of the state and the relatively neutral celebrations of the Catholic church.

The study of our reality from this perspective has revealed not open conflict (which brings about transformative action) but growing political radicalism as well as "word-proof" enthusiasm and political creativity (the "pactism" of Schmitter 1971) that defy coherence in their cumulative adoption of all forms. The system is effectively cannibalistic (as Oswald de Andrade splendidly discovered) and has an incredible capacity to perform as did Dona Flor's second husband, Dr. Teodoro Madureira, whose motto was "a place for everything and everything in its place."[15] Here is a social principle capable of reconciling everything as long as the context from which one speaks of or asks for something is mentioned. So it is not at all scandalous for us to hear (or to say): "I am only a liberal in Congress . . . after all, nobody is made of steel!" Or, as I have heard, "Brazilian men are feminist only with other men's wives!" Almost all of Wanderly Guilherme dos Santos's *Kantianas Brasileiras* fits within this model of contradictory visions. It is too bad, however, that their author discusses them only in terms of a supposed "dual reason"—or to be more faithful to him, as a "dual ethic of national political reason"—when he could have done so in an "Amadian" fashion as a complementary, hierarchical opposition that has the tragic capacity to compensate the injustice of the system.[16] What is startling in the Brazilian case is not the existence of contradictions and cynicism, but the enormous tolerance of the system. To understand this tolerance would create the capacity to break through the duality and its web of compensations.

We must then investigate the dialectic of the Brazilian tradition more closely, paying more attention to anecdotes we recount at home with our friends and servants (*criados*) as well as to other cultural phenomena, which would move us to the complex grammar of encompassment and passages between "this world" and the "other world."[17] The Marquis of Paraná de Nunes Machado's favorite phrase, according to Oliveira Vianna, is known to every Brazilian: "I am capable of any sort of courageous act except saying no to my friends!" Revealing sociological intuition that is not always characteristic of his work, Oliveira Vianna (1923) explains that our "civic disposition" and our most intimate tendencies relative to our "conduct in power" are revealed in this phrase. We will not advance toward significant understanding of Brazilian and Latin American reality if we do not discover the deep relations between the impersonal commands of law (conceived as a function of "individuals") and "friends" (a universe governed by the implicit and personalized rules of *parentela*).[18] Thus, the Marquis' statement is but a variation on the old theme, "everything for my friends; for my enemies, the law." Such expressions of loyalty are the web that still envelops personal relations in Brazil, setting the stage for such little rituals as "Do you know who you're talking to?" and the *jeitinho*, which are Brazilian methods of corrupting, skewing, and—this is the point usually overlooked—relating the harsh impersonal hand of the law to the gradations and hierarchically differentiated positions that everyone occupies in a web of socially determined relations.[19]

What I am saying, then, is that *personal relations tend to encompass the law* when the context is not serious or solemn, as it is in a public forum. In public the acclaimed Marquis of Paraná would never have said things that made the relations created in the sphere of the home sound so definitive. But at home, amidst their friends, such persons could "let off steam" and express an occult social truth by way of a *boutade*, which is a Brazilian way of getting around a problem, turning a sociological dilemma into an anecdote. And this is a profoundly original and sociologically relevant way to divide the world and relate two fundamental elements of life in modern societies: the universe of personal relations on the one hand and, on the other, the impersonal rules that, constitutionally speaking, ought to determine our behavior in a hegemonic fashion.

It was in the context of personal intimacy that the great Brazilian abolitionist Joaquim Nabuco, with his proverbial honesty, wrote in his memoirs that he missed the slaves (1949: 231). Is this a manifestation of some sort of national perversion, or might it simply be the perfect recognition of a modality of "social navigation," a way of living Brazilian reality in which the economic and institutional world, the universe of the street, heads in one direction while the dominion of the home takes off in another?

What Nabuco said, to make it quite clear, is that while he helped to combat the institution of slavery, he missed the affective, personal relations that he had with certain slaves. We can condemn him as having a dualist, cynical, and irrational conscience, where everything is misplaced, in which case we are obliged to see the dilemma as a contradiction. Or we could observe that Nabuco is simply expressing what is a daily operation in the Latin American social universe: dividing the street and the home into two separate spheres so that he can relate one to the other in a deeper manner, by way of a personal comprehension that always allows him to *return, reconcile, reconsider*, and, above all, *start again*.[20]

Such observations point toward a question that is critical to the study of societies in general and to national societies in particular. To say that a slave society cannot adopt liberal ideas is to forget that ideologies marry without asking sociologists for permission. This gives salt to life; otherwise, the sense of social change and dynamism disappears. In the real world of societies it is the hope for change that creates alliances between the "most backward" and "most advanced." In fact, this relationship is in and of itself an innovation, although elites might see it as a disease or symptom. The problem is that this is an original innovation that we have brought about. In Europe it was the coupling of asceticism and work in the religious sphere that allowed for the liberation of the enormous energy that appeared with the advent of capitalism. According to Stanley Tambiah (1973), Weber's thesis—often cited but seldom read—revolves around the notion of an inverted, surprising, and "indirect relationship" between an ethic based on asceticism, control, modesty in food and behavior, continence, and radical equality and capitalist accumulation (Weber 1958). The discipline that liberates the individual from the collectivity to put him in God's service generates a religion of "this" world and makes it possible to unify "this" world and the "other"—the state and civil society; or, to use Brazilian sociological categories, the church, the home, the street, and the government.

As long as this context goes unperceived, nothing will change, and we will witness increasing contradictions on the strictly formal, institutional plane. Thus, we will continue to interpret Latin America as merely a battlefield for the forces of right and left, liberalism and statism, nationalism and cosmopolitanism (and imperialism), capitalism and communism. But the critical fact is that, alongside these formal and institutional battles—which are no doubt important and are, in any event, branded on our political factions and interest groups—another, more profound and clandestine battle is taking place.

What battle is this? It occurs between the formal or "constitutional" level of the system and the group of unwritten personal codes of conduct that are considered "natural" by members of the system. The question is to know whether these formal rules—which were born with the bourgeois state, these "national and constitutional laws" that are conscious, written down, and designed for the "individual" as a responsible political and juridical subject and that are at the base of the so-called "nation state"—encompass the rules that effectively order society. My thesis is that there is a deep relationship between these two dimensions of the social life of countries like Brazil, where a system of personal relations and a national order founded on this code perpetuated itself and later came into profound conflict with a liberal set of ideas invented in Europe and the United States on the basis of radically different historical experiences. This is especially true in the Brazilian case, which had an atypical, even unique colonial history, marked by the presence of the royal family in Rio de Janeiro from 1808 to 1832.[21]

At this point a cultural or symbolic analysis can be of help. I used it in studying Carnival as a national ritual. The question was not to analyze Carnival in and of itself but to show how the Brazilian social world and its consequent identity are constituted and celebrated by way of Carnival along with two other cycles of celebrations: civic rites that legitimate the transmission, recuperation, and even loss of power—such as graduation ceremonies, political rallies, and inauguration rituals (DaMatta 1983a, 1986b)— and the ceremonies of the Roman Catholic church, which serve as the paradigm and reference point for ties between this and the other world.[22] The social system, in other words, has institutionalized three modes of self-celebration that appear to be rigorously incompatible and even contradictory, as many foreigners have noted. In 1986 Briant Gumble, of NBC's "Today Show," after seeing the whole formidable and paradoxical parade of Rio's samba schools, asked me: "Why this celebration, with so much luxury and waste, when there are so many poor people here?" Clearly for Mr. Gumble the celebrations were out of place. How could a poor country ritualize a luxurious, sensual, and complete utopia that is, aside from all else, so joyful? This could never happen following the deepest Western logic: if a society is poor, it can celebrate only its own misery. This would be not only functional but also linear and coherent. Yet, in spite of the bourgeois logic that confines our imagination, there is a profound link between everyday suffering and the subversive drama that Carnival presents.

We may understand the problem if we avoid a linear answer. We might say that there is a luxurious Carnival precisely because there is social misery and little political space for the exercise of citizenship. Relations are then not linear or transitive but circular or dialectical. Only when there is hierarchy, attended by social and economic misery, is a ritual of disorder like Carnival celebrated, whose symbolism allows people to inquire into the possibilities of changing social places, even if briefly. Joãozinho Trinta, the immensely creative stylist of the Beija-Flor Samba School of Nilópolis, Rio de Janeiro, said it better than anyone else: "Intellectuals are the ones who like misery; the poor prefer luxury." This phrase describes not only the spontaneity and authenticity of *Carnivalization* (the ritual of trading social places) but also the more profound perception that things do not always "go together." On the contrary, they may follow complementary and apparently contradictory paths. In truth, Joãozinho Trinta is also saying that during Carnival the social world is not encompassed by the values of linear and practical reason that ties ideas in a Calvinist fashion to words and behavior. A Carnival cannot be confused with a jeremiad—"a ritual designed to join social criticism to spiritual renewal, public and private identity," as Bercovitch tells us.[23] In Carnival, existence is momentarily encompassed by the poor disguised as the wealthy; dominators and oppressed express a difficult and profound relationship.

To complicate matters further, a few months after Carnival a military parade engulfs this same reality in the values of nationalism—the "beloved country"—in all their symbolic and emblematic richness. Here we have another idea of *order*, where the system navigates under the hand of its "constituted authorities," geometrically grouped and packaged by the national anthem in commemoration of "Dia de Pátria," creating a community around the concept of "nation."[24] But when we celebrate our nationality within the realm of modern symbols of citizenship and informed by the idea of the nation state, we enact a drama that is the exact opposite of Carnival. Here we dramatize hierarchy and not Carnivalesque equality. In the military parade, and even in progressive rallies, we emphasize hierarchy, presenting an aesthetic space based on carefully demarcated positions, with each character in its proper place.[25]

This type of civic ritual, however, is not inclusive or dominant as it is in the American case where civic culture—or a true "civil religion," to borrow Robert Bellah's (1975) use of Rousseau's expression—permeates not only the values of daily life but also the logic of large-scale social dramatizations like Independence Day, Thanksgiving Day, and Veterans Day (splendidly analyzed by Lloyd Warner [1959] as a rite that celebrates war and empire).[26] But if Americans have days of celebration, we have weeks. After Fatherland week we find ourselves involved in "Holy Week," where we can celebrate the social unity encompassed by the values of the "other world" as propounded by the Roman Catholic church in its rites and ideology. Here, we know, there is a clear division of social positions but also an undifferentiated "Carnival" of pleas and supplications from all social levels and statuses, unified under the mantle of a saint or the Virgin.

I have emphasized the circularity and the various complementary and hierarchized modes of national celebration instead of claiming that this ritual behavior shows irrationality. Is it possible that Brazil is caught among one perspective that is truly Catholic, another that is authentically civic and modern, and still another that is fully popular and Carnivalesque? Or does society behave exactly like Dona Flor—Jorge Amado's character and also a metaphor for Brazil (DaMatta 1982, 1985)—who chose all three and accepted each at similar and complementary levels of seriousness? This interpretation is the key to a sociological understanding of Brazil and, by extension, Latin America and our so-called "Ibero-Latin tradition."

This sketch of Brazilian rituals reflects on the larger social sphere of elements that compose our tradition. But from the perspective I suggest everything changes. We are not dealing merely with contradiction, cynicism, or out-of-place ideas but with a social logic that interrelates the system and exploits the ambiguities of its intermediate ranges. This said, we must think of Brazilian society as a process of mediation between poles and not, as has been the practice, construe our reality as having but a "dualistic rationale." We have been using an individualized epistemology to study a reality that functions relationally.

We may speak of Brazil as a system of oppositions between blacks and whites with Indians mediating between the two; or between people and the government with the church mediating. Mediatorial figures are neglected in Brazilian sociology (excepting the classic works of Gilberto Freyre and Sérgio Buarque de Holanda). This has led analysts to see our social logic as contradictory when it is also triadic, complementary, and hierarchical. From a formal academic position the mulatto can be reduced to black or white, and this has been presented as an "advance" over other explanations.[27] From a societal perspective, however, the "mulatto" is not simply the empirical result of a physical and sexual relation between "races" but also the crystallization of the possibility for encompassing opposition. Using comparative historical analysis, Carl Degler (1986) understood the mulatto within the Brazilian racial system as an "escape hatch"—a valve that liberates social tensions and allows for compensations. I similarly interpret the Brazilian system as *substantively functional* and exhibiting original sequences of *social compensation*.

There are profound epistemological consequences when a society is halfway between liberal individualism and hierarchical holism. In such systems we may observe the *institutionalization of the intermediary*: of the mulatto, the *cafuso* (a mixture of black and Indian), and the *mameluco* (white and Indian) in the racial classifications;[28] of the *despachante* (a paralegal professional who sees paperwork through a bureaucracy) in the bureaucratic system; of the cousin, lover, and boy/girlfriend in the amorous system; of the saints and purgatory in the religious system; of prayers, popular music, serenades, and the empty talk and looks that appear in the mediation that permeates everyday life; of the *jeitinho*, the "Do you know who you're talking to?" and well-placed connections (*pistolões*) in confronting impersonal laws; of *feijoada* (black bean and pork stew), *peixada* (fish stew), and *cozido* (stew in general), food that is squarely between the solid and liquid in the culinary system; of *sacanagem* (a form of erotica, infused with pornographic elements) as a mode of sexual manifestation—all these are fundamental modes of sociability.[29] Here the intermediate and ambiguous cannot be reduced to a purely negative position, nor can its existence be denied. In Brazil's case, there is an obvious relation between liberalism and socialism, some sort of sociological "Dona Flor" that has yet to be discovered. It might well be found in the web of personal relations between liberals and socialists in spite of their divergent ideological options, half Carnivalesque and half skeptical, given to privilege and personalism (and bureaucracy for its enemies), which goes to the beach and above all is not made of steel. Brazilian liberalism reveals the same inconsistencies: it favors market forces only when profits are assured, is absolutely negligent with respect to the rights of the consumer, and uses the governmental apparatus as an ally in the search for profits but denies its role as a representative of the consuming public. From a strictly Aristotelian and rational point of view we are Kantians who divide the world into pure and practical reason—and are left without reason. That is, we see everything as hopelessly out of place. At the same time, in examining the relationship between these outlooks, we find hidden ties of friendship and interest that are certainly more powerful than futile ideologies.

From this angle the mystery of Dona Flor is certainly relevant, for it points toward the positive role of relations and their institutionalization. Of course, one might perform a "rational" or "dualist" reading of Jorge Amado's narrative, which would emphasize the dilemma of a woman forced to choose between two men and two ways of marital life, representing the classic poles of the bourgeois world. Vadinho would represent the traditional side, Teodoro the modern. From this point of view the resolution of the narrative, which allows her to choose both, would be interpreted as conservative. But if we read it in a relational mode, as I propose, then everything changes. Dona Flor can be seen as a character who refuses the Puritan (and bourgeois) contest that leads to a hegemony of logics and desires. She can thus emerge as the incarnation not of conflict (which would force her to choose individualistically between one or the other) but of the relation itself. As in our examples of the mulatto, *jeitinho*, "Do you know who you're talking to?" and reasons of friendship and family, Dona Flor says that the relation among different formal systems is possible, revealing mysteries unknown to Western sociology. The myth, thus, presented without masks, without the theoretical fetishism that characterizes the way we think about ourselves, allows for the possibility of encompassment by the relation and not by the forces in conflict. And would this not be the deepest logic of our social reality?

If this is indeed the case, we will have to change many logical signals. Instead of viewing the ambiguous, the transitory, the intermediary, and that which coexists or is mixed as necessarily negative characteristics, we will need to invert our analytical assumptions so as to become more aware of their positive elements. Dona Flor, like the novels of so-called fantastic realism, points to something paradoxical within the social logic of the West. She proposes to remain with both of her options, choosing not to choose. This opens the possibility of a still more absurd démarche in terms of the sociology that we have studied and, God willing, learned: she tempts us with the possibility of legitimizing ambiguity. Dona Flor recuperates everything that the history of the West since Luther (and long before him) has rejected with force, energy, and brutality. She wants to keep both of her husbands. She wants Vadinho and the street spirit, the disorder that emanates from him, the uncertainty born of his gestures, and the certainty of his complete fidelity to his friends and the universe of informalities and ambiguities characteristic of personal relations. Yet Vadinho is not enough, as Dona Flor discovers. This love of the uncertain and informal must be complemented by formal marriage to a character for whom everything is norms, rules, regularity, and impersonal institutions. Life emerges as if from a telephone book: clear, correct, and explicit. But it should not be forgotten that if Teodoro is visible like our constitutions and laws, which should apply to all, Vadinho is quite invisible for those who do not know him or do not want to see him. Thus the only person capable of dealing with him is Dona Flor. Or ourselves, if we are inclined to accept Jorge Amado's lesson and restore to sociology its former subject: social relations, which are the salt of life and also the pivot for a real sociology of Brazil.

We must be alert not only to the conflict seen as dividing two political parties, social categories, or interest groups but to the hidden motive of the relation between them. Such a motive certainly has to do with the historical fact that elites in Brazil are small and highly concentrated. But it expresses something deeper. The personal relations that exist among entities in conflict present a field of sociological motives largely unrelated to the rational and ideological objectives being discussed in the political and constitutional arenas. Such arenas—the universe of the "street"—permit the emergence of a third party or actor that can, if not encompass the other two, at least postpone conflicts and their resolution or make ideological disputes secondary. This is particularly so when such actors are confronted with the ties of loyalty that effectively and affectively bind the characters that make up the Brazilian elite.

Finally, and as I said in the beginning, I want to believe that in the case of Latin America the characteristics that make up our tradition are less important than the relations among them. In order to use this notion in such a way as to understand the system as a whole, however, we need to comprehend these relations themselves as actors and encompassers of situations. Otherwise, we will continue to practice a sociology of interests and individuals when in fact we live in societies where they coexist with friends, relatives, *compadres*, and *jeitinhos*.

Acknowledgment

"For an Anthropology of the Brazilian Tradition" originally appeared as Working Paper No. 182 of the Woodrow Wilson Institute and is reprinted here with permission.

Endnotes

1. I am referring particularly to the studies on Brazil's "impossible" racial grammar that run from Gobineau, Agassiz, Nina Rodrigues, and Sílvio Romero to the present day.

2. For an analysis of this perspective and its effects on Latin American studies, see Morse (1964) and Wiarda (1974).

3. Anderson (1964). And, as Oliveira Vianna (1974: 90) said, anticipating modern scholars: "Brazil is a kind of museum of retrospective sociology or social history."

4. Ed. note: These are some of the most well-known twentieth-century Latin American authors who are associated with the literary tradition known as magical or fantastic realism, which combines supernatural and fantastic episodes with realistic narrative in a way that is similar to Latin American society.

5. The similarity to Oliveira Vianna is noteworthy: "Every kind of social structure . . . all economic phases . . . all of the cycles of social economy—from

'hunting and gathering' to a 'plough economy' to the 'industrial' and 'metro-politan economy' . . . we find all of these types, phases, and cycles within Brazil, subsisting and coexisting out in its obscure backlands or blossoming on the plains or the coast: it's like the showcase of an ethnographic museum" (1974: 91-92).

6. Such an attitude reveals a predominantly "linear" vision and practice of history that assimilates all histories to those of Western Europe and the United States. All of them would reveal a process of "accumulation" by which certain institutions would substitute others seen as older, archaic, or "weaker." On this model no transformation would occur according to a logic for combining or mixing, allowing mixture to be understood in a positive fashion. And finally, this perspective does not allow for a distinction that I consider crucial: that between "nation" and "society." Ambiguous social forms can be adopted by a "nation," but excluded by a "society." This important problem has been over-looked by a wide variety of scholars.

7. It is not by chance that Morse characterizes his book *El Espejo de Próspero* as a study of the "dialectics of the New World" and throughout explicitly con-trasts the Anglo-American universe with its "variant" and alternative in the Americas, the "Ibero-Catholic" universe.

8. I use the expression "Anglo" as a synthesis of certain crucial aspects of the North American experience, such as individualism, egalitarianism, capitalism (and the resulting commodification of social life), and the institutionalization of universalist criteria as central points in the rules of social life. See Parsons (1958).

9. I cannot refrain from pointing out that the first chapter in Brazilian history books always addresses the question of "discovery," and that there is a classic debate among Luso-Brazilian historians about whether the "discovery" was accidental or intentional. The thesis of intentionality would undermine much of the mythology that presents the Portuguese colonizer as innocent. It was Lívia Neves de Holanda Barbosa of the Anthropology Department of the Fed-eral Fluminense University who called my attention to the question of the dis-covery of Brazil as opposed to the founding of the United States and how this was consistent with the contrast between societies articulated in terms of indi-vidualism and those based on individualism combined with holism. For the question of holism and individualism see Dumont (1970a, 1970b, 1986) and Tcherkézoff (1987). For studies of Brazil as a system divided between individu-alism and holism, equality and hierarchy, see DaMatta (1985, 1986a, 1986b, 1991).

10. Ed. note: "Complementarity" means that opposing systems (such as the modern, Western, legal form of government and the traditional, personalistic form) may coexist; "inclusion" refers to the principle of Catholicism by which everyone is included in the community, in contrast to the Protestant principle by which society is organized into mutually exclusive sects; and "hierarchy" is

the principle by which different levels of society are related (rather than by relations of equality that tie together individuals).

11. *Feijoada*—a stew of black beans and every conceivable cut of pork.

12. The question is hardly rhetorical. If we take a sharp, unbiased look at the United States, we will see pockets of hierarchy, patronage, and "favors" in university fraternities, in clubs and voluntary associations, and in rituals such as Mardi Gras in New Orleans (DaMatta 1991: ch. 3). One needs only to examine university life, where personal ties open doors and provide scholarships or where antipathies generate sour reviews and limit hopes for tenure. Here we have Thomism, bureaucratic insulation, and all the rest; but in this case, as in France and England (to stay within this admired trilogy), ideas are rigorously in place. It appears so precisely because the empirical variety of social reality (which is by nature variegated) is orchestrated and encompassed by a single credo or system of values—that of liberal individualistic egalitarianism, which is effectively hegemonic. The distinct impression of order and coherence produced by these societies, then, is closely tied to a heavy ideological framework that makes other forms illegitimate. The problem therefore is not that of discovering that things are "out of place" but that of understanding how articulations are undertaken by the society itself.

13. One astute observer of Brazilian life, Ernest Hambloch (1981), who was consul of England in Brazil, used to say that "Brazilians are wordproof" because there was absolutely no consistency between what they said and what they did. He authored other observations, such as, "Politics in Brazil has nothing to do with political phrases," and: "Personal questions are a part of political life in all countries. But since the establishment of the Republic, they have become the quintessence of what is called Brazilian politics. There are no political plans, and even the question 'What plan should we adopt in order to convince the country to put us in power?' is not suggested. The question is but one: 'With what political elements should we reconcile in order to stay in power, or alternatively, to get there?'"

14. See Needham (1973) and Beidelman (1961). In this case, however, I take Dumont's (1986) perspective, from which he criticizes the static nature of these studies and their ability to see hierarchical encompassments in the dualism of hands and consequently their inability to register the importance of the "left" in certain contexts that are defined by a logic of inversion. See also Tcherkézoff's broad critical study on the subject (1987).

15. Oswald de Andrade was the Brazilian modernist writer who issued an "Anthropophagic Manifesto" in 1928. (Ed. note: see Carvalho, this volume.) The reference to Dr. Teodoro Madureira is to Jorge Amado's novel *Dona Flor and Her Two Husbands*.

16. My reference to *Dona Flor* is not intended as a literary judgment. I use it simply as a revealing example (for reasons I have developed elsewhere [1982, 1985] and repeat here) of "Brazilian ideology."

17. The enormous disenchantment with the so-called redemocratization process after the fall of the military regime in 1985 has made some intellectuals pick up on the intolerant, authoritarian, cynical, and group-oriented side of the Brazilian system. As far as I am concerned, these characteristics are not the consequences of a static or immutable tradition, nor of "preceding institutional structures and behavioral dispositions," to use the unimaginative and sophisticated phrase of the otherwise perceptive Philippe Schmitter (1971: 182). I think rather that they arise from a dilemma in the social forces that govern Brazilian society and the Brazilian nation. At the risk of repeating myself, I refer to the modern forces of equality (which are involved in and put pressure on the constitutional side of Brazil) as well as to the traditional forces of hierarchy that operate on the personal and familiar side. The street and the home continue to be incompatible in Brazil, as they are in many other Latin American societies.

18. An extended family structure on which social influence is based.

19. The Brazilian *jeitinho* is situated in harmony with the "favor." There are two aspects to the *jeito*: (1) the humanization by which the unequal (those who have power in a particular situation and those who do not) are equated by means of an irresistible appeal to the fact that we are all human and, in principle, ought all to have pity on one another; and (2) to get the "other" to trade places with the person who needs the *jeito*, thereby making the "other" see things from the person's viewpoint. For studies of the *jeito* see DaMatta (1991) and Barbosa (this volume, 1986). Roberto Campos and, following his lead, Philippe Schmitter speak of the *jeito*, but they do so from a moralistic point of view informed by the practicality they assume to be ever present in social life. From this perspective the *jeito* is nothing more than a flaw and an epiphenomenal result of dysfunctional laws and antimodern Catholicism, not a profound expression of social values. For a critique of "practicality," see Sahlins (1979).

20. Certain students of Brazilian society have called attention to the "hybridism" and the notable ability for these values to survive, without—to my mind—understanding their deeper logic. Schmitter (1971), for example, in the course of an extremely keen and important argument with respect to what I am discussing, speaks of a system (sic; p. 376), mentioning the logical difficulties of a researcher who is attempting to describe it. In his words: "I needed a model stressing certain unique, relatively stable, and interrelated characteristics of an intermediary system that was neither pluralist nor mobilizational, yet has some features of both" (377). He then goes on to make a series of formal observations, contending that Brazil is a weakly integrated society. Yet, he reveals exactly the opposite. In fact, we are speaking of a highly functional system that, operating on the basis of three codes, is capable of confronting all of its problems without, however, opting for any hegemonic or definitive solution.

21. Brazilian studies seem to have a case of sociological amnesia with respect to this fact for which, as far as I know, there exists no good symbolic, political, or ideological evaluation.

22. No one has studied the symbols associated with the peaceful transmission of power in Brazil and Latin America, such as the "presidential sash" which is "penetrated" by the president-elect, the man who encompasses the entire system (see DaMatta 1986a, 1986b). Nor has anyone studied the symbols associated with violent takeovers in which "putting the tanks on the street" and/or "closing the Congress" literally signify the use of the armed forces in favor of the political interests of a certain group.

23. Bercovitch (1978: 11) then speaks as follows of the American jeremiad: "The question in these latter-day jeremiads, as in their seventeenth-century precursors, was never 'who are we?' but, almost in deliberate evasion of that question, the old prophetic refrain: 'When is our errand to be fulfilled? How long, O Lord, how long?' All the answers, again as in the Puritan jeremiads, invariably joined lament and celebration in reaffirming America's mission." Again, the contrast with Brazil is flagrant. Among us the big question is "Who are we?" a question that leads not to voyage but to a metaphysics of "races" and political and social doctrines.

24. "Fatherland Day," although overly Teutonic, is the closest translation of "Dia de Pátria." It commemorates Brazil's independence (September 7) from Portugal.

25. All Brazilian political rallies follow a standardized pattern that combines elements from processions, Carnival, and military parades. The quasireligious and charismatic nature of certain themes and personalities is characteristic of processions. The climate of political change, the possibility of changing regimes, the times, and the people by trading places is carnivalesque. And military parades lend a hierarchical element to political rallies, visible in the emphasis on the speakers' platform and consequently in the division between candidates and politicians on the one hand and the people on the other. There is also a rigid hierarchy in the order of speeches. It is important "to get the last laugh," and whoever speaks last dominates the entire event. There are frequent incidents—as in the charismatic campaign for free elections in 1984—caused by people attempting to climb up onto the platform and be near those who organize and address the event. But pictures of these rallies demonstrate their kinship with military parades, with the "superiors" affirming their position in the spatial and temporal organization of the event.

26. Parodying Almond and Verba (1963), one could say that America does not have a "civic culture" but a "culture" encompassed by civic values, which seems to be a very different matter.

27. I particularly have in mind "Marxist" interpretations that reduce racial prejudice to a mere reflex of the economic structure that is interpreted as "class structure." Crasser forms of this model forget two crucial points. The first is that

"class structure" in the case of Brazil and Latin America should be discussed in terms of patronage and favors; the second is that the "Brazilian racial system," with all of its mythology and fables, creates its own etiquette and symbolism, and it manifests itself in a style that should be investigated. The "Brazilian racial system" certainly does not exist in a sociological vacuum, but this does not mean that it should be seen as a reflex of a "class structure," which ultimately is also symbolic (and conventional). Once invented and implemented in a credo, a system of ideas comes to make up part of the picture and is confused with social reality.

28. In this context it is worth remembering what Antonil, the Jesuit Giovanni Antonio Andreoni who wrote a treatise on Brazil's society and economy, wrote in 1711: "Brazil is Hell for Blacks, Purgatory for Whites, and *Paradise for Mulattoes.*"

29. As far as I know, I am the only author to have analyzed *sacanagem* as a sociological category.

References

Almond, Gabriel A. and Sidney Verba
  1963 *The Civic Culture: Political Attitudes and Democracy in Five Nations.* Boston: Little, Brown.
Anderson, Charles W.
  1964 "Toward a Theory of Latin American Politics." Occasional Paper No. 2, Graduate Center for Latin American Studies, Vanderbilt University.
Barbosa, Lívia de Holanda
  1986 *O Jeitinho Brasileiro: Um Estudo de Identidade Social.* Rio de Janeiro: Museu Nacional.
Beidelman, Thomas
  1961 "Right and Left Among the Kaguru: A Note on Symbolic Classification." *Africa* 31(3): 250-57.
Bellah, Robert
  1975 *The Broken Covenant: American Civil Religion in Time of Trial.* New York: Seabury Press.
Bercovitch, Sacvan
  1978 *The American Jeremiad.* Madison: University of Wisconsin Press.
DaMatta, Roberto
  1981 *Relativizando: Uma Introdução à Antropologia Social.* Rio de Janeiro: Editora Rocco.
  1982 "*Dona Flor e Seus Dois Maridos*: A Relational Novel." *Social Science Information* 21(1): 19–46.
  1983a "A Questão da Posse." *Humanidades* 1(2).
  1983b "Para uma Teoria da Sacanagem." In *A Arte Sacana de Carlos Zéfiro.* Rio de Janeiro: Editora Marco Zero.

1985 *A Casa e a Rua: Espaço, Cidadania, Mulher, e Morte no Brasil.* São Paulo: Brasiliense.

1986a *O Que Faz o brasil, Brasil?* Rio de Janeiro: Rocco.

1986b *Exploraçes: Ensaios da Sociologia Interpretativa.* Rio de Janeiro: Rocco.

1991 *Carnivals, Rogues, and Heroes: An Interpretation of the Brazilian Dilemma.* Notre Dame, Ind.: University of Notre Dame Press.

Davis, Natalie

1975 *Society and Culture in Early Modern France.* Stanford: Stanford University Press.

Degler, Carl,

1986 *Neither Black nor White: Slavery and Race Relations in Brazil and the United States.* Madison: University of Wisconsin Press.

Dumont, Louis

1970a *Homo Hierarchicus.* Chicago: University of Chicago Press.

1970b *Religion, Politics, and History in India.* The Hague: Mouton and Co.

1986 *Essays on Individualism: Modern Ideology in Anthropological Perspective.* Chicago: University of Chicago Press.

Hambloch, Ernest

1981 *Sua Majestade o President do Brasil: Um Estudo do Brasil Constitucional (1889-1934).* Brasília: Editora Universidade de Brasília.

Leach, Edmund

1961 *Rethinking Anthropology.* London: Athlone Press, University of London.

Morse, Richard M.

1964 "The Strange Career of Latin American Studies." *Annals of the American Academy of Political and Social Studies.* CCCLVI (November).

1982 *El Espejo de Próspero.* Mexico City: Siglo XXI.

Myrdal, Gunnar

1962 *An American Dilemma: The Negro Problem and Modern Democracy.* New York: Pantheon Books.

Nabuco, Joaquim

1949 *Minha Formação.* Rio de Janeiro, São Paulo, Porto Alegre: W. M. Jackson.

Needham, Rodney (ed.)

1973 *Right and Left: Essays in Symbolic Classification.* Chicago: University of Chicago Press.

Oliveira Vianna, Francisco José

1923 *Pequenos Estudos de Psicologia Social.* São Paulo: Monteiro Lobato.

1974 *Instituições Políticas Brasileiras.* Rio de Janeiro, São Paulo: Record/Fundação Oliveira Vianna, Government of the State of Rio de Janeiro.

Parsons, Talcott

1958 "The Pattern of Religious Organization in the United States." *Daedalus* 85: 82–92.

Sahlins, Marshall
1979 *Culture and Practical Reason.* Chicago: University of Chicago Press.
Schmitter, Philippe
1971 *Interest Conflict and Political Change in Brazil.* Stanford: Stanford University Press.
Schwarz, Roberto
1977 *Ao Vencedor as Batatas: Forma Literária e Processo Social nos Inícios do Romance Brasileiro.* São Paulo: Duas Cidades.
Tambiah, Stanley
1973 "Buddhism and This-Worldly Activity." *Modern Asian Studies* 7(1): 1-20.
Tcherkézoff, Serge
1987 *Dual Classification Reconsidered.* Cambridge: Cambridge University Press/Editions de la Maison des Sciences de l'Homme.
Velho, Otávio
1985 "As Bruxas soltas e o Fantasma do Funcionalismo." *Dados* 28(3).
Warner, Lloyd
1959 *The Living and the Dead: A Study of the Symbolic Life of Americans.* New Haven and London: Yale University Press.
Weber, Max
1958 *The Protestant Ethic and the Spirit of Capitalism.* New York: Scribner's (1904-1905).
Wiarda, Howard (ed.)
1974 *Politics and Social Change in Latin America: The Distinct Tradition.* Amherst: University of Massachusetts Press.

The Distorted Mirror:
Brazil and the United States

⊠

Many of the authors in this volume have used the United States as a touchstone against which they make their observations and analyses of Brazil. As
a result, a book about Brazil may be of special interest to American readers
because we get an opportunity to learn how Brazilians represent the United
States. Brazilians sometimes include Canada, Australia, and Western Europe
as points of comparison, but I have limited the discussion here to the United
States. The use of the United States as a point of comparison has a long history in Brazilian studies, in part because there are some obvious similarities—regional variations, demographic diversity, and a history of slavery—
that invite comparison. For Brazilians the comparison is often more than an
intellectual exercise, for many see the United States and other developed,
Western countries as models of economic success and political stability that
they hope their own country will achieve.

What are the uses and dangers of such comparisons? The most obvious
danger is, of course, cultural stereotyping. I frequently met Brazilians who
idealized the United States, especially if they had not lived abroad. Sometimes the United States represents the elusive status of being a "developed"
country, which Brazilians hope their own country will someday achieve.
The comparative project is therefore laden with all sorts of evolutionary
ideas and notions of progress, and Brazil comes out in the minds of many
Brazilians as backward and undeveloped. I remember once walking through
the Museum of Natural History in New York and pausing at an exhibit
when some Brazilian teenagers came waltzing through. They stopped for a
minute, then one of them said in Carioca Portuguese, "Look, the North

American Indians have more clothing than ours. Even our Indians are less developed!"

Carvalho probably does the best job of exploring the fetishism of the foreign in her discussion of Brazilian musical tastes. I was always surprised at the way Brazilian radio stations played American and British rock at the expense of their own beautiful music. Urban and middle-class Brazilians tend to adore everything that is from the "exterior," especially when it comes from the developed world. The logic is hierarchical in the sense that Brazilians from the hinterlands and the poorer classes tend to look upward at the fashions and movie stars of Rio and São Paulo. Recall, for example, Prado's description of how the people of Cunha long to leave Cunha for Brazil's larger towns and cities or for travel to the "exterior." Furthermore, the "exterior" is also constructed hierarchically, and the United States is often below Europe in the hierarchy. For example, Brazilian intellectuals tend to identify so much with French thought that they look down on American philosophy, arts, and social theory.

Thus, while Brazilians often look to the United States as an example of a successful New World society, they are conscious of the limitations of the developed country to the north. As Barbosa pointed out, and as I have frequently heard from middle-class Brazilians, they may admire the economic and political successes of the United States, but at the same they think of the United States as an efficient land of cold, inflexible, and relatively unemotional people. Thus, as Jarrad shows, Brazilians are likely to adapt American institutions such as Alcoholics Anonymous to make them more flexible and personal. As a Protestant-based organization, Alcoholics Anonymous is an example of what DaMatta describes as the rigidity and inflexibility of the American moral system, which after nearly four hundred years still bears the rather provincial imprint of seventeenth-century Puritanism. In this sense, Brazilians sometimes think of Americans as self-righteous, inflexible, judgmental, and incapable of seeing beyond polar oppositions. The great example that Brazilians always raise is race relations, which they usually describe as relatively more relaxed, less tense, and less violent in Brazil than in the United States. Although some middle-class, white Brazilians wrongly believe that Brazil is a racial utopia, they nevertheless are realistic when they point to American race relations as one way in which the United States is far from a utopian society. As Kottak noticed with acuity, he rarely saw any people of African descent among the American swim teams, but African-Brazilian swimmers were common in Rio.

The flip side of the argument that Brazilians do not construct the United States (and other rich Western countries) as complete utopias is the argument that Brazilians are also quite realistic about the complexities of their own country. For example, Barbosa finds a double-edged quality in her discussion of the *jeitinho* and national identity: the *jeitinho* represents Brazilian warmth and flexibility even as it exerts a corrupting force on Brazil's "modern" institutions. Likewise, Sarti points to the double-edged sword of kin ties in Brazil: they are necessary as sources of identity and financial security but they also pose restraints on social mobility. Finally, in the wonderful phrase "heaven and hell of personalism," Prado sums up this double-edged quality of Brazilian culture quite clearly, noting that in Cunha everyone knows everyone else but everyone also controls everyone else. No wonder people fetishize the exterior, where their outsider status affords them release from the web of personalism and patronage. Of course, as soon as they get there, they are likely to miss (have *saudades* for) the interwoven hierarchy by which they are defined and constrained.

Thus, when one goes beyond utopian/dystopian polarities, the Brazil/U.S. comparison is a complicated one in which both countries oscillate back-and-forth between desirable and undesirable characteristics. In other words, both take on a Januslike quality. That mixture of desirable and undesirable traits is a logical one in which one side implies the other. In other words, wherever modern institutions appear—either in Brazil or in the United States—their emphasis on individualism and equality requires that personalistic and hierarchical considerations be excluded in order for the institutions to function properly, and as a result those institutions take on a cold and inflexible flavor. Likewise, warmth and flexibility as it is played out in personalistic ties—either in Brazil or in the United States—tends to undermine individualistic and egalitarian institutions. In other words, it may not be possible to have one's cake and eat it, too: that is, to live in a utopia characterized by warmth, personalism, and flexibility and at the same time by smoothly functioning modern institutions.

Instead, what one finds in Brazil—and this is DaMatta's central argument—is an ongoing negotiation of the two, mutually contradictory systems. A less-developed but nonetheless provocative corollary to this argument is that the more deeply one thinks about the Brazil/U.S. comparison, the more likely one is to find a "Brazilian" side to American culture. For example, once I understood and learned to use the *jeitinho*, I became more aware of, and adept at manipulating, the art of "schmoozing" and maintaining connections in the United States. Many of the professions, particularly academic disciplines, have strong streaks of personalism and hierarchy that Americans' conscious ideology obscures. Likewise, it has long been recognized that in the United States large bureaucracies of all sorts—especially political institutions—operate according to old-boy networks, family and ethnic ties, school ties, and so on. However, as DaMatta has pointed out, there are still some crucial differences even within these points of similarity: in the United States nepotism is considered a scandal, but Brazilian leaders frequently hire their relatives because they are the only people who can be trusted. In other words, even where one finds similar institutions of personalism, they are likely to be constructed and valued differently: similarity yes, but difference as well.

I also lived for several years in a small American town, and I found points in common between that town and Cunha. There are clearly ways in which Brazilian and American small towns are like each other. Likewise, large cities everywhere share similar characteristics of anonymity and individualism. Prado is well aware of such complexities, and she is now completing a comparative study of Cunha and a small town in Michigan. This next step of her research will sort out the ways in which the two small towns are both similar and different. For example, I know that in the American small town where I lived my friends and I felt a similar desire to escape from the gossipy, personalistic, "fishbowl" confines of the small town to the anonymity of the cities. In general, as I read about Cunha I found much that would apply to my experience in small-town U.S.A. However, at the same time there were many differences between Cunha and the small town where I lived, among them Cunha's political and festival systems.

Another example of how the United States may be more like Brazil than first appears involves race and gender relations. Some white Brazilians still believe that Brazil has harmonious race relations, but social scientists have now documented that "Brazilian racial democracy" is a myth. It is more accurate to say that both countries have a long-standing history of racism, just as they do of sexism. Likewise, in both countries there has been an increasing tendency in recent years to talk about racism and sexism, and with this talk to move from hierarchical toward more egalitarian relationships. Notwithstanding such similarities, there are also differences. For example, it would be hard to imagine the ceremony that Silverstein describes as occurring in the United States. The southern United States, while in many ways like Brazil, was mainly Protestant and as a result African religious practices generally did not survive in such intact, institutionalized forms as they did in Brazil (with French Catholic Louisiana the main exception).

Kant de Lima's essay also suggests ways in which the United States is more Brazilian than Americans may think. The system of privileges that operates in the Brazilian legal system has parallels with the ways in which the very rich and very poor in the United States also participate in *de facto* parallel legal systems. Of course, in the United States African Americans, women, gays, lesbians, the poor, and other historically excluded or underrepresented groups have claimed for a long time that they do not have access to the same law as middle- and upper-class, heterosexual, white men. In addition to the question of hierarchy as it is legally encoded as privilege, Kant points to the increasing use of secrecy and inquisitorial procedures as means for obtaining evidence in the United States (such as in drug enforcement projects). After studying the Brazilian legal and judicial system, the American system now appears to have "Brazilian" features.

In this sense, as so many of the essayists have emphasized, but especially Kant de Lima and DaMatta, the Brazilian puzzle is solved by seeing Brazil not in evolutionary terms as a developing counterpart of the developed West, but instead as a different mix of general characteristics shared by each country in different ways and to different degrees. This view would recognize the fundamental differences between Brazil and the United States without failing to miss some of the similarities. Furthermore, by seeing both societies as complex and dynamic mixes of modernizing and traditionalizing tendencies, this view can also recognize the ways in which the societies are changing. For example, the fact that Brazil was able to resolve the corruption of President Collor through impeachment rather than another coup provides hope that Brazilian political institutions are modernizing. Coelho's essay on the importance of media scandals also flags a crucial site for the development of modernizing discourses and practices.

Furthermore, while there are ways in which Brazil is modernizing and in a sense becoming more "Westernized," it is also possible to examine how the United States is becoming "Brazilianized." As I think about frightening features in my own country such as its huge underclass, sprouting shantytowns, increasing crime, staggering national debt, and growing gap between rich and poor, Brazil is a useful point of reference. I also think about Brazil as I puzzle through discourses on multiculturalism in the United States and our transition from a relatively bipolar system of black/white race relations to a system with multiple and mediating categories.

In short, I see the comparison of Brazil and the United States not as an academic game but as a useful resource. When used well, sharp differences at one level are rendered complex by similarities at another level, only to be made further complex by more differences, more similarities, and so on. The utility of this exercise for the study of Brazil is that it helps Brazilians and foreigners alike to construct alternative visions of their societies in terms of democracy and social justice. Most frequently, social scientists concerned with that issue focus on electoral politics, the economy, or differential access to resources. The essays in this volume complement those studies by focusing more on the informal aspects of Brazilian culture and society. By doing so, it may be possible to make discussions of democratization and social justice in Brazil—as in any national society—more wide-ranging, more sensitive, and more effective.

Notes on Contributors

Lívia Neves de H. Barbosa is an associate professor in the Department of Anthropology of the Instituto de Ciências Humanas e Filosofia (ICHF) at the Universidade Federal Fluminense in Niterói. She has an M.A. in social science from the University of Chicago and a Ph.D. from the Graduate Program in Social Anthropology (PPGAS) of the Universidade Federal do Rio de Janeiro. She is the author of *Jeitinho Brasileiro ou a Arte de Ser Mais Igual que os Outros* and *Garimpo, Meio Ambiente, e Sociedades Indigenas*, and she is a coeditor of *Na Corda Bamba: Ensaios Sobre a Cultura da Inflação*. She is also the author of several articles and is now engaged in an extensive comparative study of Brazilian and North American ideas about nature and their links with national identity.

Martha de Ulhôa Carvalho is an ethnomusicologist and adjunct professor at the Universidade Federal de Uberlândia, Uberlândia, Minas Gerais. She has an M.F.A. degree in piano performance from the University of Florida and a Ph.D. in musicology from Cornell University. Her articles include "Canção da América—Style and Emotion in Brazilian Popular Song" in *Popular Music* (1990) and "Musical Style, Migration, and Urbanization: Some Considerations on Brazilian *Música Sertaneja*" in *Studies in Latin American Popular Culture* (in press).

Maria Claudia Pereira Coelho is an assistant professor in the Department of Communication Theory of the Universidade do Estado do Rio de Janeiro and an adjunct professor in the Department of Social Communication of the Pontifícia Universidade Católica (PUC) of Rio de Janeiro. She has a master's degree in anthropology from the Museu Nacional of the Universidade Federal do Rio de Janeiro, and she received her Ph.D. in sociology at the Instituto Universitário de Pesquisa do Rio de Janeiro (IUPERJ). In addition to the research presented here, she has studied Catholic youth organizations, soccer scandals, and the theater community in Rio de Janeiro. Her articles have appeared in *Comunicações do Museu Nacional, Ciência Hoje, Jornal do Brasil*, and other publications.

Roberto DaMatta is the Reverend Edmund P. Joyce, C.S.C., Professor of Anthropology and Senior Faculty Fellow at the Kellogg Institute of the University of Notre Dame. One of the few anthropologists to have made important contributions to the anthropology of indigenous and national societies as well as anthropological theory, his books include *Divided World: Apinaye Social Structure; Carnivals, Rogues, and Heroes: An Interpretation of the Brazilian Dilemma; A Casa e a Rua: Espaço, Cidadania, Mulher, e Morte no Brasil; Ensaios da Antropologia Social; Explorações: Ensaios de Sociologia Interpretativa; O que faz brasil, Brasil?; Relativizando: uma Introdução à Antropologia Social*, and *Conta de Mentiroso: Ensaios de Antropologia Brasileira.*

David J. Hess is an anthropologist and an associate professor in the Science and Technology Studies Department at Rensselaer Polytechnic Institute. He is coeditor with Linda Layne of *Knowledge and Society*, vol. 9, *The Anthropology of Science and Technology*; and he is the author of *Spirits and Scientists: Ideology, Spiritism, and Brazilian Culture; Science in the New Age: The Paranormal, Its Defenders and Debunkers, and American Culture; Samba in the Night: Spiritism in Brazil*, and *Science and Technology in a Multicultural World: The Cultural Politics of Facts and Artifacts*, as well as of various articles on social and cultural aspects of religion, psychology, medicine, science, and technology.

Jeffrey Jarrad is a lecturer at Trinity College in Burlington, Vermont. He received his Ph.D. from the Anthropology Department of the New School for Social Research; his dissertation research focused on Alcoholics Anonymous in Brazil and the United States.

Roberto Kant de Lima is an associate professor in the Department of Anthropology of the Instituto de Ciências Humanas e Filosofia (ICHF) at the Universidade Federal Fluminense in Niterói. He has been a consultant for the Rio de Janeiro State Research Foundation and the Brazilian National

Research Council (CNPq); a visiting researcher at the Office of the Public Defender in San Francisco, California; a recipient of USIS and Fulbright fellowships; a visiting professor in the Department of Criminal Justice at the University of Alabama, Birmingham; and a visiting professor in the Graduate Program in Law of the Universidade Federal de Santa Catarina. Author of *A Antropologia da Academia: Quando os Indios Somos Nós* (translated in *Knowledge and Society*, vol. 9 , JAI Press), and numerous articles on the anthropology of law, Dr. Kant is currently engaged in an extensive comparative study of the Brazilian and American police and judicial systems.

Conrad Kottak is a professor in the Department of Anthropology at the University of Michigan. He is the author of numerous books in anthropology and Brazilian studies, including *Anthropology: the Exploration of Human Diversity*; *Assault on Paradise: Social Change in a Brazilian Village*; *Cultural Anthropology*; *Madagascar: Society and History*; *The Past in the Present: History, Ecology, and Cultural Variation in Highland Madagascar*; and *Prime-Time Society: An Anthropological Analysis of Television and Culture.*

Rosane Prado is a visiting professor in the Department of Social Sciences at the Universidade Estadual do Rio de Janeiro. Her dissertation research was based on fieldwork in the American small town of Dundee, Michigan, and it took as a point of reference her master's thesis based on fieldwork in Cunha, São Paulo. Her research interests also include the anthropology of women and mass culture and the study of ecology and risk perception; her publications include "Um Ideal de Mulher: Estudo dos Romances de M. Delly" in *Perspectivas Antropológicas da Mulher* (vol. 1), and "Beauty Betrayed: Risk Perception at a Nuclear Site in Brazil," which was based on fieldwork in Angra dos Reis, R.J., and is forthcoming in a special issue of *Environmental Professionals.*

Cynthia A. Sarti is an anthropologist who received her M.A. in social sciences at the University of São Paulo, where she is currently a Ph.D. candidate. She worked at the *Fundação Carlos Chagas* (São Paulo) and was a Residential Fellow of the Kellogg Institute for International Studies (University of Notre Dame) during the fall semester of 1991.

Leni Silverstein is a Program Officer in the Population Program of the John D. and Catherine T. MacArthur Foundation. Previously she taught in the Integrative Studies Progam at Michigan State University. She completed her Ph.D. dissertation, titled *Candomblé Authenticity Struggles and the Brazilian National Project: Gender, Race, Religion, and Power in Bahia, Brazil*, at the Anthropology Department of the New School for Social Research. She offered the first anthropology of gender course at the Museu Nacional of the Universidade Federal do Rio de Janeiro, and she continues to research questions of gender, race, nationalism, and power.

Index